The Book of Swamp and Bog

0 11557 02518 7

The Book of Swamp and Bog

Trees, Shrubs, and Wildflowers of Eastern Freshwater Wetlands

John Eastman

Illustrated by Amelia Hansen

STACKPOLE
BOOKS

Published by
STACKPOLE BOOKS
5067 Ritter Road
Mechanicsburg, PA 17055
www.stackpolebooks.com

Printed in the United States of America

10 9 8 7

First edition

Cover design by Mark Olszewski

Library of Congress Cataloging-in-Publication Data

Eastman, John (John Andrew)
    The book of swamp and bog : trees, shrubs, and wildflowers of the
    eastern freshwater wetlands / John Eastman ; illustrated by Amelia
    Hansen. — 1st ed.
        p.   cm.
    ISBN 0-8117-2518-9
    1. Swamp plants—East (U.S.)   2. Bog plants—East (U.S.)   3. Swamp
ecology—East (U.S.)   4. Bog ecology—East (U.S.)   I. Title.
QK115.E285   1994
582.13'0974—dc20   94-33396
                                                                                    CIP

ISBN 978-0-8117-2518-7

To all bog trotters, fen gazers, ditch probers, pond watchers, river rats, and swamp things; the marsh-mellowed, hip-booted, and cold-toed lovers and preservers of our North American wetlands.
Look closely, tread lightly.

Nothing exists for itself alone, but only in relation to other forms of life.
—Charles Darwin

I enter a swamp as a sacred place.
—Henry D. Thoreau

Contents

Acknowledgments

I could not have accomplished a work of this scope alone. My gratitude extends to many friends and associates who granted me their valuable time, expertise, and advice in important quantities large and small.

I thank Dr. Richard Brewer, professor of biology at Western Michigan University, for reading the manuscript and for offering useful suggestions. Much of what I know about ecology I have learned, both formally and informally, from this renowned educator, writer, researcher, and environmentalist. I also owe foremost thanks to noted Michigan entomologist William P. Westrate, who often interrupted his busy schedule to help identify many insect species associated with certain plants. Chances of small error escaping detection in a work of this magnitude are fairly large despite one's best efforts. I claim solely as my own any such errors of fact or interpretation that may occur.

The drawings of illustrator Amelia Hansen, whose brilliant portrayals of natural history subjects exemplify only one facet of her wide–ranging artistic accomplishments, provide a vital part of this book's aim and utility. Countless times her intelligent eyes have helped me focus my own. I am grateful for her collaboration.

I treasure the friendship of Jacqueline Ladwein, teacher, naturalist, and steadfast field collaborator, who helped photograph, collect, and observe all sorts of life-forms in many wetland environments.

I owe special thanks to editor Sally Atwater of Stackpole Books for immense patience and help; to William J. Mills for his constant friendship and for lending his north-woods cabin as a working refuge; and to Dr. Edward G. Voss, curator of the University of Michigan Herbarium, for providing helpful references. Jane Davis drew the detailed illustration of the dragonfly nymph.

Others who made important contributions to this effort include Raymond J. Adams, Jr., Stephan Allen, Joy Andrews, Jennifer Byrne, Richard Johnson, Emma B. Pitcher, Sarah Reding, Lois Richmond, and Chris Thommen.

This book, like my previous ones, could never have been realized without the constant support and uncomplaining labors of my beloved and caring companion, Susan Woolley Stoddard. It is she who makes it happen.

Introduction

This book follows the pattern of its predecessor volume, *The Book of Forest and Thicket.* The focus, rather than duplicating that of typical field guides used for plant identification, is ecological. Both volumes view plants in their roles as habitat and community dwellers.

Since plants provide the ultimate power base for all the food and energy chains and webs that hold our natural world together, they also form the hubs of community structure and thus the centers of our focus. Sometimes the effort to make biological knowledge systematic and comprehensible (that is, classifying organisms into neat, individual slots based on group similarities) results in an obscuring of the broader picture—the way things really are in the natural world. The natural world, to be seen truly, must be seen whole, even as a mosaic can only be perceived when its multiple fragments are joined. Each organism depends upon and provides support to others, which in some cases may be absolutely vital to its own existence.

Thus the questions become these: Once you have identified a plant, what other organisms, plant and animal, might you expect to find on or near that plant? What patterns of the mosaic reveal themselves? Answering these questions, at least in part, is the purpose of this book.

It is no longer news that American wetlands are endangered. In the past two hundred years, more than half of the wetlands in the contiguous forty-eight states have been lost—drained, paved, or filled—mainly to agriculture. Many of those that remained became wastewater sinks, hazardous repositories of toxic metals and polychlorinated biphenyls (PCBs), among other substances. Runoff from both urban and agricultural lands has resulted in overfertilized lakes and ponds, aging them prematurely with overgrowth of dense vegetation. Atmospheric pollution has given us acid rain, which has completely changed the chemical identities of many lakes in certain areas unfortunate enough to be found downwind of the sources.

In economic terms, wetland loss and degeneration have been expensive. Not only have wildlife and fish habitats drastically declined as a consequence, but many wetland benefits that more directly impinge upon our health and well-being—flood control, safety of aquifers, tourism, and commerce—are also adversely affected.

Even more vital than these factors are the implications for the big picture. Destroying wetlands means destroying habitats. Destroying habitats means destroying species. Destroying species means destroying the gene pools of biodiversity. Biodiversity means having potential genetic options in the bank—for the benefit of ourselves no less than for other organisms. Ultimately, of course, biodiversity represents the fount of survival on Earth.

And the fount of biodiversity is wilderness. Today American forest wilderness exists, when at all, in patches, "museum cases" of public lands, which give only pallid ideas of the large biodiversity our ancestors blithely relinquished. Wetland wilderness, however, has fallen not quite so far. Considerable areas of it remain, despite studious efforts to "improve" all of it that lax laws will allow. Although many surviving wetlands have indeed suffered irreversible changes (including invasions of aggressive alien plants such as purple loosestrife and Eurasian water-milfoil), it is remarkable how many of them still remain relatively pristine. Most American wetlands have existed as such since the retreat of Pleistocene glaciers. Some of their plant populations may, in many cases, be directly descended from the original wetland species of their locales. The pleasure and adventure of experiencing a bog or marsh of native vegetation may bring us as close to encountering true American wilderness as most of us may ever come. For that reason alone, our surviving wetlands are worth preserving.

Like its predecessor volume, this book emerges from a twofold effort of library and fieldwork (one hour of the latter requiring some three to six hours of the former). What has previously been learned about these plants and their ecology? And what is directly observable in the field? With practice, these simultaneous efforts become mutually reinforcing (I recommend the procedure to all outdoor observers). I have personally inspected all the plants mentioned in this book, as well as a large majority of the other organisms. The illustrations were drawn from field specimens I collected or photographed.

The "Swamp and Bog" of the title is intended as a generic designation for all freshwater wetlands of northeastern and north-central North America and their marginal edges. The plants covered here include most of the common and typical residents of these habitats.

Certain plants presented in the aforementioned *Book of Forest and Thicket* may also reside in lowland or wetland habitats. Accounts for a few of those species have been refocused for this book, but species accounts not included may be consulted in the previous volume. These nonexclusive wetland dwellers include the following:

Balsam Fir	Elm, American
Birch, White	Ginger, Wild
Birch, Yellow	Hackberry, Northern
Box Elder	Hornbeam, American
Buckthorn, Common	Leek, Wild
Bunchberry	Mayflower, Canada
Butternut	Poison Ivy
Cleavers	Spicebush, Common
Clubmosses	Sycamore
Dogwood, Gray	

So what are wetlands? The U.S. Fish and Wildlife Service defines them as "lands where saturation with water is the dominant factor determining the nature of soil development and the types of plant and animal communities living in the soil and on its surface. Wetlands are lands transitional between terrestrial and aquatic systems where the water table is usually at or near the surface or the land is covered by shallow water."

Various wetland classifications exist. The most useful one for this book encompasses five major categories:

Bog: An acidic wetland dominated by sphagnum mosses and shrub heaths, characterized by the accumulation of plant materials as peat, and with rain or snow as its only water source. Some authors use the term *bog* for any peatland, whether it consists of sphagnum or sedge peats; but in this book the term always refers to nutrient-poor *acid* environments.

Fen: In contrast to bogs, a *mineral-rich* wetland (alkaline bog) usually dominated by sedges and calcium-loving herbs and shrubs, characterized by the accumulation of peat. Two fen extremes enclose many transitional forms: *Rich* fens constantly receive nutrients by means of surface and ground waters flowing into and through them. *Poor* fens are transitional to bogs. They are characterized by waters that are increasingly sealed off from surface and ground inflow, thus leading to acidic conditions. Fens often develop into swamps or bogs.

Marsh: A mineral-rich wetland dominated by emergent grasslike herbs, such as grasses, cattails, rushes, and others. Marshes often develop into swamps.

Swamp: In contrast to marshes, a wooded wetland that includes either or both conifers and hardwood shrubs or trees. Swamps often develop into swamp forests. Flooding or raised water tables, however, may kill woody vegetation, and the swamp may revert to a marsh.

Shrub-carr: A wetland thicket dominated by shrubs such as alders, willows, buttonbush, and red-osier dogwood. Often shrub-carr borders bogs and fens as transitional zones between wetland vegetation and upland forest. Shrub-carr may also invade marshes, fens, and bogs as islands of woody thicket;

and it may become the dominant form of vegetation in swamps.

Some wetlands exist as such only seasonally and thus may host a particular complex of plants adapted to such alternations of wet and dry conditions (*hydroperiods*).

A few more repeatedly encountered terms: *Herb, shrub,* and *tree* are general and ultimate size designations (though such shrubs as many bog heaths are very low in stature). The main distinction is that shrubs and trees are woody; herbs are not. An *aquatic* is an herb that grows wholly or partially submersed in the water. *Emergent* herbs are those that germinate in shallow water but show stems, leaves, or flowers rising above the surface. In most wetland herbs, sexual or seed reproduction is often a low second to vegetative reproduction (that is, by fragmentation or cloning from rhizomes) as a means of survival.

Technical biological terms, though kept to a minimum, are usually defined at the places they occur in the text. A list of recurring terms appears in the Glossary. With rare exceptions, Latin names are given only for plant and invertebrate animal species, since common or popular names (when they exist) for these organisms often lead to confusion. The common names of many water plants are hyphenated, a style adopted by many botanists to indicate taxonomic nonrelationships; cotton-grasses and nut-grasses, for example, are not actually grasses but sedges.

Wetlands, if you would know them, require a bit more effort to explore than forests and meadows. Not as accommodating to the land mammal that is man or woman, they often demand proper footgear, insect repellent, and suitable degrees of caution where footing is unstable. They force slow travel, deep breathing, and constant attentiveness to one's steps and surroundings. If your life has become too fast and distracted, get thee to a bog or marsh. See how the water borderland exists. Watch how wetland things are done. Take this book along, and enjoy some of America's last wilderness.

Experiencing the richness and complexity of wetlands cannot fail to revive and nourish one's own sense of wholeness to a degree beyond common expectation.

Alder, Speckled *(Alnus rugosa)*. Birch family. Shrub or small tree in wet thickets. Its egg-shaped leaves with prominent veins on the underside, drooping catkins, and white-speckled bark identify it. Similar, less-common species include European black alder *(A. glutinosa)*, smooth alder *(A. serrulata)*, and mountain alder *(A. crispa)*.

Other names: Tag alder, hoary alder, hazel alder, black alder (the latter usually designating *A. glutinosa,* European black alder).

Close relatives: American hornbeam *(Carpinus caroliniana)*; hop hornbeam *(Ostrya virginiana)*; birches *(Betula)*.

Lifestyle: Named for the speckled appearance of white, warty lenticels on its bark, speckled alder forms dense, cloning thickets along streams, in mineral-rich swamps, and on lakeshores. It is a characteristic species of rich fens.

Each shoot of the clone contains both male and female catkins (female catkins usually directly above the male), which appear before the leaves in spring. Catkins are wind pollinated. The pollen matures slowly, accumulating in cuplike sections of the flower, from which it is blown. The conelike female catkin produces tiny winged nuts, then turns woody, often remaining on the plant into the following year. This is the only common eastern shrub that shows catkins of both sexes on the winter twigs. The seeds germinate quickly.

Alder is intolerant of shade. There may be twenty or more of the typically arching, contorted stems in a clone. They are often curved at the base because snow weight flattens the young stems, which later bend upward toward the light.

Besides cloning, alder also reproduces by *layering*—a horizontal stem or side branch buried in mud and debris may sprout new stems along its length. Fluctuating water levels often result in the growth of *adventitious roots* along the lower stems, a means by which alder and other wetland shrubs sprout roots along the length of flooded or buried stems (see illustration for Willows, Shrub).

Like legumes, alders are soil enrichers, hosting nitrogen-fixing bacteria in root nodules. Up to five grams of nitrogen per square meter of topsoil may be added each year. The roots themselves, which may graft with those of other alder clones, form a mesh of shallow mats, anchoring the soil and preventing streambank erosion. Alder leaves are also rich in nitrogen.

This plant needs at least some flowage of oxygenated water and will not grow in stagnant swamps or poorly drained wetlands.

Associates: Alder belongs to the shrub-carr community of wetland thicket species. Shrub associates include willows, dogwoods, and buttonbush. Northern white cedar is a frequent associate in swamp thickets. You may also observe alders invading tussock sedge communities on pond edges.

Spring, summer. Among wildflowers typical of rich fen habitats, the wild calla is a frequent alder associate. Sensitive fern is also common here, as is a sphagnum moss *(Sphagnum teres).*

A black, lumpy, gelatinous fungus on dead alder branches becomes especially conspicuous after rains; in dry weather, it shrinks to a paintlike crust. This is warty jelly fungus, also called black alder jelly *(Exidia glandulosa),* a club fungus.

Alder branches overhanging lakeshores or streambanks are often the first perches of winged subimago mayflies (Plectoptera) as they emerge in hordes from their aquatic nymphal forms. Here they molt again into their adult forms. The adult insect does not eat, lives only to mate on the wing, drops eggs into the water, then dies—all in the span of only a few hours. Look for the cast-off subimago "skins" that tell of a prolific mayfly hatch.

Other emerging long-winged insects include alderflies *(Sialis),* so named from their frequent perching site. Look for their flat, brown egg masses on alder leaves hanging over the water. Other distinctive egg masses on leaves, from which hatched larvae drop into the water, include those of dobsonflies *(Corydalus)* and fishflies *(Chauliodes).*

Leaf feeders—especially moth caterpillars—are numerous on alder. Several species of dagger moth *(Acronicta)* feed in groups on the leaves; you can recognize them by their resting "fishhook" posture. On alder branches you'll sometimes find dead caterpillars of this genus killed by a fungous growth that entirely fills the body cavity.

Arches *(Polia, Lacanobia)* are another group of noctuid moth caterpillars that feed on alder. The adult dark-spotted palthis moth *(Palthis angulalis)* is grayish brown and immediately recognizable by its large, tufted mouth parts; its larvae also feed on alder leaves. Caterpillars of arched and two-lined hooktip moths *(Drepana arcuata, D. bilineata)* lack rear legs; the adult moths are yellowish white. Hübner's pero *(Pero hubneraria)* is an inchworm caterpillar, as is the renounced hydriomena *(Hydriomena renunciata).*

On leaf undersides, look for the rounded blotch mines of *Cameraria auronitens,* a leaf-mining moth caterpillar.

Pimplelike pocket galls on the leaves generally indicate *Eriophyes* mites at work.

Several spittlebugs (Cercopidae) produce their spittlelike froth on alder. These are the sap-sucking nymphal forms of adult jumping insects called froghoppers. The alder spittlebug *(Clastoptera obtusa)* is probably the most common species.

Alder flea beetles *(Altica ambiens)*, oval-shaped and shiny blue, appear in cyclic irruptions, defoliating many alders. Densely clustered perforations in the leaves signal its presence.

A rolled-up leaf may contain the gelechiid moth caterpillar *Telphusa belangerella.* The leaf-rolling weevil *Attelabus rhois* makes a thimble-shaped roll containing an egg or larva.

Swollen, distorted buds with a whitish bloom indicate larval feeding of the alder bud gall midge *(Dasyneura serrulatae).* Oozing wounds (slime fluxes) in alder stems are good places to look for *Nosodendron unicolor,* the wounded-tree beetle, oval-shaped and black.

Mating swarms of midges and other flies often occur above *swarm markers—* the top point of an alder shrub, beneath a branch tip, or some other distinctive spot in the localized environment. Swarm sites often remain constant, and times of day for swarming also tend to be consistent

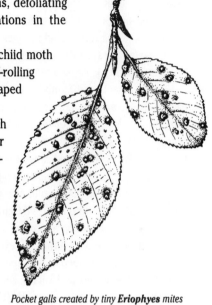

Pocket galls created by tiny **Eriophyes** *mites are common on alder and many other leaves. Note this leaf's prominent veins and characteristic shape.*

for a given midge species. Watch too at dusk for dancing swarms of male silver-spotted ghost moths *(Sthenopis argenteomaculatus)*; female moths enter the swarms to mate. These moths have a two-year life cycle. The larvae are borers in submerged alder roots.

Many insect feeders on willow foliage may also be found on alder (see Willows, Shrub).

White-tailed deer and moose browse foliage and twigs; for deer, however, alder is "stuffing" or "starvation" food, not preferred browse. Beavers crop the stems, consume the bark, and use the wood for lodge and dam material; such cropping instigates more alder clonal sprouting. Ruffed and sharp-tailed grouse feed on alder catkins. Muddy alder thickets are also frequent feeding places for American woodcock, which stabs for earthworms with its long bill. Round holes in the soil indicate its presence.

Common birds nesting in alder thickets include yellow-bellied and alder fly-catchers, yellow warblers, common yellowthroats, Wilson's warblers, red-winged blackbirds, swamp and white-throated sparrows, and American goldfinches. The high density of alder clones along shorelines or in swamp thickets provides excellent cover for both land and aquatic wildlife.

Late summer, fall. On alder cones, look for green or reddish tonguelike extrusions resembling sprouts, sometimes causing distorted enlargement of the cones. This abnormality is caused by *Taphrina,* a parasitic sac fungus.

Three insects commonly associate on alder in late summer and fall as well as earlier. These are the alder blight aphid *(Prociphilus tessellatus),* which feeds on red maple leaves earlier in summer; the harvester or wanderer butterfly *(Feniseca tarquinius)*; and various ant species. Both the butterfly caterpillar and the ants rely on the aphid, a white-woolly insect, for food. Other aphid genera may include *Schizoneura* and *Pemphigus. Feniseca,* one of the few butterfly larvae that are carnivorous, is a small orange and brown caterpillar that feeds on the aphids; you'll often find it buried beneath a mass of them. Its mollusklike, spiral-shaped pupa, resembling a monkey's face, may also be found on the leaves. The adult butterfly feeds on aphid honeydew and lays its eggs on the aphid masses. The ants, which also feed on the aphid honeydew, aggressively guard the aphids and sometimes attack and kill the caterpillar.

The wandering brocade moth *(Oligia illocata),* a noctuid, also feeds on the leaves at this time.

I have often noted large numbers of stink bug nymphs (Pentatomidae) on alder cones. At least some of them overwinter in this subadult stage.

Alder stems are frequent rubbing posts for white-tailed bucks; scarred and shredded stems indicate where deer have rubbed the velvet from their new antlers. Although alder is not a preferred food of beavers, these animals often cut the shrubs for their winter food stores when aspen trees are in short supply.

Among the most frequent songbird seed feeders in alder thickets are black-capped chickadees, hoary and common redpolls, pine siskins, and American goldfinches.

Winter. Alder "seems to dread the winter less than other plants," wrote Thoreau. "With those dangling clusters of red catkins which it switches in the face of winter, it brags for all vegetation."

A common greenish-yellow foliose lichen on alder branches is easily seen now. This is *Cetraria pinastri,* which also appears on other wetland shrubs.

Stem galls—usually irregular, oval swellings—show up best after alder has dropped its foliage. These are usually produced by the alder stem borer *(Saperda obliqua)*, a long-horned beetle, and *Eupristocerus cogitans,* a buprestid beetle.

Bunches of withered, silken-tied leaves remaining on alder branches in winter are often the work of pyralid moth caterpillars called leaf crumplers *(Acrobasis rubrifasciella).* Look for cone-shaped silken tubes of the pupae inside the leaf mass.

In addition to the aforementioned seed feeders in alder thickets—plus budfeeding grouse and bark-gnawing cottontail rabbits and snowshoe hares—vacated nests of spring and summer birds are most easily seen now.

Lore: Alders are good for controlling erosion and flood and for stabilizing streambanks. Alder plantings for erosion control remain relatively infrequent, however, at least in the United States; in England, hedges of European black alder are often established to "fence in" a stream's natural tendency to meander. Alders also provide protective cover for wetland wildlife, a function that probably outweighs their value as a food resource.

Like many tree and shrub barks, speckled alder bark found medicinal usage among Native Americans. Astringent bark teas were given in various strengths and quantities for diarrhea and toothache, and as an emetic and purgative. Bark solutions were also used externally to treat rashes, swellings, the eyes, and hemorrhoids.

Plant-insect associations extended to the medicine bag: The Chippewa mixed alder root scrapings with ground-up bumblebees *(Bombus)* for treating difficult childbirth—two tablespoons taken internally were said to be sufficient. They also used the inner bark of alder as an ingredient for black and red dyes.

Algae, Blue-green. Division Cyanophyta. Simple submersed, floating, and terrestrial plants. Large mats of blue-green algae species become especially prevalent during late summer and fall in *eutrophic* (oxygen-poor) lakes and ponds. Blue-green color, though frequent, is not a reliable identification guide; greenish-yellow, brown, and reddish blooms may characterize different species in various light and chemical conditions. Some of the most common genera include *Oscillatoria, Nostoc, Anabaena,* and *Rivularia.*

Other names: Water bloom, blanket algae, pond scum, frogspit.

Close relatives: None. Blue-green algae constitute a plant division by themselves, but they structurally resemble many of the bacteria.

Lifestyle: The blue pigment phycocyanin in combination with green chlorophyll gives this group of algae—about 1,400 species worldwide—its name. Where it grows the water often appears red or purplish.

Blue-green algae are simple, one-celled plants. They are the most primitive plants on earth because these cells have no well-defined nuclei (their nuclear material is scattered throughout the cell) and no sexual reproduction. Cells are often coated with a slippery, gelatinous sheath. Most species of the eight blue-green algae families found in North America grow in long, filamentous chains or strings of cells, though some display round colony shapes. As is the case with most algae, species identification requires you to see the distinctive cell or colony characteristics—something accomplished only with the aid of a microscope.

Asexual reproduction occurs by simple cell division *(fission)*, fragmentation, or in some cases, by bacterialike spores. A massive increase in growth (water bloom) indicates a period of accelerated fragmentation. These plants, along with green and yellow-green algae, constitute most of the *phytoplankton,* the myriad, free-floating microscopic plants that inhabit most bodies of water.

Surface mats of blue-green algae often have a fishy or "pigpen" odor caused, at least in part, by rapid decomposition; exposed to surface sunlight, the mat may die quickly. Optimal light conditions for most species occur in the subsurface. Daytime photosynthesis produces gas bubbles, which cause portions of the mass to become buoyant, rise, and form the surface mats or rafts. New strands of algae may descend from the underside of such rafts and form new colonies on the pond bottom. The raft itself may sink at night; *Oscillatoria* and *Lyngbya* colonies frequently display this vertical movement.

Like the bacteria in root nodules of alders and legumes, some sixty species of blue-green algae fix atmospheric nitrogen, thus making it available to the ecosystem in usable form. Nitrogen-fixing algae require the element boron, concentrating it in quantities many times higher than environmental levels. Many blue-green algae also precipitate calcium carbonate in the form of *marl,* a chemical by-product of the plant's extraction of carbon dioxide from calcium bicarbonate during photosynthesis.

Abundant blue-green algae generally indicate oxygen-poor or polluted waters containing high nitrate and phosphate levels. These algae also help maintain such oxygen-poor conditions: Algal mats may shut out light for subsurface plants, thus preventing or slowing those plants' photosynthesis and oxygen production. Their decomposition plus ongoing decomposition of the algal mat also deplete oxygen from the water.

Associates: Though water-blooming mats of *Anabaena* and other pond genera are often the most conspicuous examples, blue-green algae range throughout damp and wetland habitats in both colonial and solitary forms. They occur in soil, greenhouses, and flower pots, and on moist rocks and other pond vegetation. Around hot springs, some species precipitate calcium and magnesium salts to form the chalky rock called travertine. *Oscillatoria* species and others inhabit mammal digestive tracts, while *Gleocapsa* and *Nostoc* provide algal partners in such crustose lichen species as dog lichen *(Peltigera canina)*, *Leptogium,* and *Collema.*

In ponds, blue-green algae are usually found in association with green and yellow-green algae species and with such free-floating plants as duckweeds.

Summer, fall. Reddish-green mats of water fern also float on pond surfaces, and colonies of *Anabaena* often reside in cavities of their scalelike leaf lobes. This is an example of *commensalism,* a coaction in which the guest organism derives benefit (shelter) while doing the host no harm. Another example is the presence of *Nostoc* in liverworts.

Look for gelatinous brown clumps of *Rivularia* coating subsurface pond vegetation such as stoneworts, water-milfoils, and pondweeds, and also on dead, water-soaked cattail leaves. The nitrogen-fixing *Nostoc, Gleotrichia,* and *Anabaena* often attach to *Lemna* and *Spirodela* duckweeds.

Algal mats provide food and shelter for a host of minute creatures including protozoans, worms, mollusks, crustaceans, and aquatic insect larvae (see Algae, Green). Tadpoles, minnows, and turtles also consume filamentous algae. But abundant blue-green algae may also inhibit the growth of other organisms by shading out sunlight and depleting oxygen or by the effects of certain toxins they produce *(allelopathy),* resulting in "summer kills." Some blue-green algae (such as *Anacystis*) are known to poison animals that may drink water containing these colonies.

The carp—a bottom-feeding fish with low oxygen requirements— often associates with blue-green algal blooms.

Lore: These primitive plants exist very near the indefinite border separating plants from animals at their simplest levels. Not so large an evolutionary gap, one may argue, divides them from simple one-celled animals as from the more complex green algae they superficially resemble. Many scientists believe we owe the earliest accumulation of oxygen in Earth's atmosphere to blue-green algae. The oldest fossils on Earth are Precambrian stromatolites—layered, concentric mounds of limestone deposits from reef-forming *Cryptozoön* blue-green algae (see them on display at Petrified Gardens in Saratoga Springs, New York).

Today we most often see the effects of blue-green (as well as certain green) algae in their precipitates—the limy marl sediments that form the mud bottoms of many lakes. Marl is a commercially valuable fertilizer and is mined from lakes and former lake deposits for this purpose.

Blue-green algae are also useful as water-quality indicators. Lakes or ponds receiving septic tank seepage or runoff from fertilized fields and lawns show a vastly speeded-up process of eutrophication. These sources of phosphate and nitrogen overfertilize the water, producing dense water blooms that smell unpleasant and tend to choke out the basin with weedy as well as algal growth. Sewage pollution often fosters the growth of *Anabaena* and *Lyngbya*; combined with the presence of green algae *Chlorella, Euglena,* and *Spirogyra,* these plants tell environmental inspectors where problems exist. *Anabaena, Rivularia,* and *Microcystis* sometimes give reservoir water a bad taste and odor and may also clog sand filters, so blue-green algae bring mixed blessings to water technology.

Beyond these aspects, the realm of the blue-greens holds much interest. A marine species, *Trichodesmium erythraeum,* gives the reddish color to water in the Red Sea. And dried, preserved specimens of *Nostoc* have survived more than eighty years, becoming green again when placed in water.

Algae, Green. Division Chlorophyta. Simple submersed, floating, and terrestrial plants, mostly grass-green in color. They appear most conspicuously as surface or subsurface water blooms in summer, and also in spring as bright green clumps or streamers in pools and brooks. Common genera include *Chlorella, Spirogyra, Cladophora, Euglena* (sometimes classified as a protozoan), and desmids.

Other names: Pond silk, grass-green algae. See Algae, Blue-green.

Close relatives: See Stoneworts.

Lifestyle: In a typical pond, a seasonal progression of various algae species occurs, each with its own period of maximum growth and reproduction. These include winter, spring, summer, and autumn annuals plus perennials and ephemerals. The successional patterns are closely related to changing water temperatures. By far most of these plants are green algae, which outnumber all other algal groups combined—some 5,500 green algae species worldwide.

Green algae are more complex in structure than the blue-greens. Their green chlorophyll is localized into *chloroplasts,* as in the leaves of higher plants, and their cells have definite nuclei. Plants may be one-celled, colonial, or multicelled, depending upon species. Green algae species appear in many cell and colony shapes: spheres, filaments, spirals, rectangles, swimming blobs, even netlike sheets. Some cells or colonies and algal gametes swim by means of whiplike flagella, resembling protozoa in their motility. Much reproductive variation occurs. Some species reproduce by the same asexual means as the blue-greens; others unite sexually by means of conjugation and gametes (sex cells), producing zygotes from which new plants develop. All of these features require a microscope to see. Likewise, most species can be precisely identified only under high magnification.

Muskrat trails wind through the algae mat, a familiar sight in ponds where surface algal growth is dense. Such mats provide food and shelter for many small organisms, but their density may also shade out and chemically inhibit the growth of subsurface plankton.

Sitting beside a pond or pool, however, your view of green algae will probably be restricted to one or both of the following: (1) a green, cottony fuzz (pond silk) suspended in "clouds" just beneath the water surface; or (2) a cottony mat on the surface, which rapidly turns brown and unpleasant looking. Both may be termed *water blooms,* but the latter manifests the plants' rapid reproduction, death, and decomposition. Those plopping sounds are gas bubbles being released as the mat decomposes in hot sunlight (see Algae, Blue-green). As with blue-greens, green algal growth is generally most abundant in nutrient-rich waters high in nitrogen and phosphates—often the result of human abuse of wetland environments. *Cladophora* and *Spirogyra* are two common mat-formers.

Green and yellow-green or golden algae (diatoms) together make up most of the *phytoplankton,* the base of the food chain for freshwater and marine organisms. The *zooplankton* (microscopic animals) and larger creatures that feed on the phytoplankton begin the energy transfer up the chain. Evidence exists, however, that dense phytoplankton populations can also slow or prevent the growth of zooplankton. Abundance of the green alga *Chlorella,* for example, can inhibit populations of the water flea *Daphnia,* a minute crustacean that feeds on algae; the inhibitory substance produced by the alga is apparently the antibiotic chlorellin.

Such toxic effects of algae on plankton exemplify *allelopathy,* a common, if not well understood, chemical interference that reduces competition among many higher plants as well.

Associates: Most foliose and fruticose lichens contain solitary cells of green algae as a component of the alga-fungus symbiosis characteristic of these plants.

Spring, summer. Although various green algae species can be found in water year-round, their most conspicuous growth appears during the warmer seasons. Several species often occur together, intermixed or scattered, also with blue-green and yellow-green algae. Desmids and *Zygnema,* for example, may interlace in mats of *Spirogyra* or *Chlorella.* Water from pools in sphagnum bogs frequently appears green with cells of the desmid *Closterium* (see Mosses, Sphagnum). Green algae also color other organisms such as protozoa, freshwater sponges and jellyfishes, and lichens. Most such symbiotic green algae are species of *Chlorella.*

As biotic communities, algal mats feed and shelter diverse zooplankton and larger animals as well. Various species of rotifers, those strange microscopic wheel animalcules, often eat out the cells of filamentous algae. They are often abundant in *Spirogyra* mats, as is the turbellarian flatworm *Stenostomum.* Bristle-worms (Oligochaeta), related to earthworms, are tiny, transparent-bodied feeders on decayed organic matter. They are largely responsible, it is said, for the quick cleanup of dying algal mats; *Nais* is a common genus. Among crustaceans, copepods (Copepoda) such as the water flea *Cyclops,* the clamlike ostracods or seed shrimps (Ostracoda), and scuds or amphipods (Amphipoda) are also common scavengers. *Hyalella* and *Gammarus* are two common amphipods that feed on dead algal filaments in early spring.

Insect larvae in the algal mat may include mayflies, crawling water beetles *(Haliplus, Peltodytes),* and especially midges such as *Chironomus* (a staple fish food), which feed entirely upon algae and decayed vegetation. The green alga *Mougeotia* is particularly favored by insect larvae.

Adult insects also feed in the mat: water boatmen (Corixidae), omnivorous diving bugs, "tap" into algal filaments, sucking the cells empty; and tiny preda-ceous diving beetles *(Bidessus flavicollis)* are common. Both larvae and adults of *Berosus,* a water scavenger beetle, feed on green algae, but only the adults of *Hydrophilus* and *Tropisternus,* two other water scavenger genera, are algae feeders, having "graduated" from meat-eating larval forms.

Algal mats also receive countless eggs. Watch for violet-colored damselflies, called violet tails or violet dancers *(Argia violacea);* the darker female, flying in tandem attachment with the colorful male, dips her abdomen into the mat and deposits her eggs.

Among mollusks, the tiny wheel snail *Trivolvis parvus* is common in algal mats, as is the quarter-inch shell of pill clams *(Pisidium)*. The fingernail-sized zebra mussel *(Dreissena polymorpha)* is a recent accidental European introduction to the Great Lakes. A colonial phytoplankton feeder, it clogs water intake pipes and encrusts piers and boat hulls. Where numerous, it also produces abnormally clear water conditions, a result of its voracious planktonic feeding. Although their appetite for algae can sweeten the taste of drinking water, zebra mussels may consume algae to the point where little is left to support other animal life. (As with most irruptive introductions, natural predators will probably, in time, bring this pest species into better balance.)

*Freshwater sponges (**Spongilla**) resemble coatings of bright green felt on submersed sticks and vegetation, but green is not the sponge's own color. Cells of the green alga **Chlorella** live in and on the tissue, making these sponges conspicuous in their submersed habitats.*

Many small fishes (such as the northern fathead minnow) and most frog and toad tadpoles are also algae consumers. Turtles, especially painted turtles, also eat algae, but algae and turtles associate in another way, too. In summer, you may sometimes see a "mossback" turtle—that is, a painted, musk, or snapping turtle showing green algal growth on its carapace (upper shell). This alga is *Basicladia*; only two species exist, and both grow only on turtle shells. Whether the relationship is mutualistic (providing a surface for the alga and camouflage for the turtle) remains unknown. Painted turtles shed their scutes (carapace plates) in the fall, and with them, the algal growth.

Many waterfowl consume filamentous algae, though, as one wildlife food expert remarked, "one suspects that the animal life resident in the algal mass is as much a food inducement as the alga itself." Among the most prevalent feeders are mute swans, brant, American black ducks, common pintails, American wigeons, blue-winged teal, buffleheads, and American coots.

Spirogyra and *Vaucheria* are sometimes eaten by white-tailed deer.

Lore: Most paleobotanists believe that single-celled green algae were the probable ancestors of green plants as we know them in all their multicelled complexity and variety. These were probably also the first sexually reproducing organisms, introducers of sex to the world. (Dwell on this when next you visit "pond scum.")

As with blue-green algae, too much of a good thing can occur when eutrophic conditions overnourish a body of water and redolent water blooms appear. Thus the green algae *Spirogyra* and *Cladophora glomerata* have become major nuisances around Great Lakes cities, indicating high phosphate levels. (When found in combination with *Rhizoclonium* and *Merismopedia* algae, however, *Cladophora* can also be an indicator of clean, unpolluted water.)

Green algae has also found a niche in space-age technology, with researchers trying to devise ways to "farm" it in quantity for processed human and domestic animal food. Some scientists believe its food potential is enormous. Growing it aboard spaceships to provide oxygen and food for star trekkers is one of the more visionary aims. *Chlorella* algae are the main subjects of such efforts.

Arrow-arum. *(Peltandra virginica).* Arum family. Herb in swamps, fens, shallow water, along pond margins. Its large, arrow-shaped leaves; its erect, pointed sheath *(spathe)* enfolding the green, tapering flower spike *(spadix)*; and its cluster of greenish-brown berries in the fall identify arrow-arum.

Other names: Green arrow-arum, tuckahoe, poison-arum, Virginia wake-robin.

Close relatives: Skunk-cabbage *(Symplocarpus foetidus)*; wild calla *(Calla palustris)*; Jack-in-the-pulpit *(Arisaema triphyllum)*.

Lifestyle: Arrow-arum leaves are easily confused in size and shape with those of broad-leaved arrowhead. Note, however, that arrow-arum leaves are feather-veined, while arrowhead leaves have parallel veins.

Both male and female flowers occur on the largely enclosed spadix, which may be seen through a vertical gap in the spathe. Male flowers occupy most of the spadix; the female flowers occupy the lower fourth or fifth of it. They are insect pollinated.

The fleshy base of the spathe swells as the berry cluster grows inside it, and the seed stalk bends toward the ground. Usually the top part of the pointed spathe dries and falls off, leaving a roundish green pod full of seeds enmeshed in a jellylike mass. Sometimes, however, the now-inverted spathe point remains and serves as a kind of drill or auger into the soft mud, thus "planting" the seed packet. Released seeds also float, dispersing the plant. Cloning from the thick, fibrous roots, however, probably accounts for most plant colonies.

Like arrowheads, this plant is often a shoreline emergent, growing in several inches of water. It also thrives on muddy banks.

Associates: *Spring, summer.* Shallow emergent vegetation including arrowheads, wild calla, bur-reeds, and pickerel-weed are frequent arrow-arum associates.

A common insect feeder on the leaves in early spring is the smut beetle *(Phalacrus politus)*, oval and shiny black.

The major pollinators are probably flies.

Like most arums, this plant's chemical defenses make insect feeders relatively uncommon (see Jack-in-the-pulpit).

Late summer, fall. Arrow-arum berries are especially relished by wood ducks. Other consumers include mallards and king rails. Muskrats also occasionally eat the berries.

Arrow-arum seedpods bend toward the mud as they mature. The upright pod on the right shows the crowded black berries, which are relished by some water birds.

Lore: Raphides, acrid, needlelike calcium oxalate crystals, are found in all parts of most arums. They are intensely burning and irritating if eaten and will actually create numerous tiny wounds in mouth membranes. Only thorough drying renders the rhizomes harmless and edible. American natives collected them for making a flour.

Arrowhead, Broad-leaved *(Sagittaria latifolia).* Water-plantain family. Emergent aquatic herb on pond edges, in marshes and shallow water. This is the commonest of ten or more species in eastern North America. Its broad, arrow-shaped leaves and white flowers, usually in whorls of three, are distinctive. It can grow four feet tall but usually stands less than a foot.

Other names: Duck potato, swamp potato, tule, wapato.

Close relative: Water-plantain *(Alisma plantago-aquatica).*

Lifestyle: Arrowhead is a true amphibian among plants, thriving equally well submerged in water or stranded on a mud bank. The leaves adapt their shapes to either mode: Submersed plants develop narrow, ribbonlike leaves; broader, arrow-shaped leaves characterize emergent plants. Most typically, a plant stands with its "feet" in water. But where water levels fluctuate, arrowheads may show both kinds of leaves plus broad, leafless stems called *phyllodia.*

Flowers and leaves occupy separate stems. Usually the three-petaled flowers, each lasting about a day, are unisexual on the same plant. Bisexual flowers or unisexual ones on separate plants, however, are not uncommon. Female flowers are lowest on the stem, while the more conspicuous male flowers circle the upper stem at intervals. Flowers are insect pollinated, developing into stemmed, ball-like fruits, again in the radiating pattern of three.

This perennial plant also produces cloning stems from potatolike tubers that form at the ends of long runners extending from the rhizome.

Associates: Arrowhead occupies the emergent vegetation zone of the shoreline. Typical associates of this zone include arrow-arum, cattails, reeds, rushes, pickerel-weeds, bur-reeds, and wild-rice.

Spring, summer. Leaf mines or wilted stems may indicate larval feeding of the cattail borer moth (see Cattails). Other noctuid caterpillar feeders include the golden looper moth *(Argyrogramma verruca)* and other loopers *(Plusia).*

Weevil genera commonly associated with arrowhead and other aquatic plants are *Anchodemus, Listronotus,* and *Hyperodes,* all called underwater weevils. They feed as both larvae and adults on the basal parts of the plant, including the rhizome. More conspicuously, *Listronotus* also feeds on upper parts of the plant. Small circular holes in the leaves probably indicate *L. echinodori,* which also feeds in the flowers and deposits egg masses resembling mud spatters on leaf and flower stalks. *L. appendiculatus* often damages young flowers and seed heads by its feeding. *L. caudatus* is another common species.

On emergent leaves, common insects include

Three-ranked seedpods of arrowheads are distinctive in late summer and fall. This stem's top portion, which held the male flowers, has fallen off.

leafhoppers *(Draeculacephala)*, ladybird beetles *(Coleomegilla maculata)*, and long-horned leaf beetles *(Donacia;* see Bur-reeds). Submersed leaves and stems host larval tube-making caddisflies *(Neureclipsis, Polycentropus)*, northern caddisflies *(Pycnopsyche)*, and long-horned caddisflies (*Leptocerus americanus, Leptocella,* and *Triaenodes*).

Insect pollinators include bees and flies but also dragonflies and damselflies. Although the latter two insects are strictly carnivores, they often alight on the flowers, where their movements result in much cross-pollination. Water snails, which sometimes feed on the flower petals, may also carry and deposit pollen.

Arrowhead tubers (duck potatoes) have long been lauded as a prime waterfowl food. They are, but unless they occur in very soft mud, their large size and deep burial often make them too difficult for most ducks to retrieve. Waterfowl consumers include tundra (and probably mute) swans, American black ducks, mallards, common pintails, American wigeons, wood ducks, northern shovelers, blue-winged and green-winged teals, canvasbacks, redheads, ring-necked ducks, scaups, and ruddy ducks.

Beavers and muskrats consume the tubers and other parts of the plant, often storing them in caches; the Ojibwa would obtain their winter's supply of the tubers by raiding these animal caches. Porcupines also venture into wetlands to relish arrowhead leaves and stems.

Fall. Arrowhead seeds are consumed by ducks and herons plus king, sora, and Virginia rails at this season.

Look for thick clusters of tiny leaping insects on emergent leaf undersides in the fall. These may be nymphs of a fulgorid planthopper (Delphacidae), which feed on the plant sap. Though not exclusive to arrowhead, they seem to favor broad-leaved aquatic plants.

Lore: Wherever arrowheads grow, superbly efficient water-to-air movement is occurring. Each plant lifts a veritable fountain of water vapor, in quantities greater than most other green plants of its size. Because of this extensive transpiration through their leaves, arrowhead plants are often eliminated from reservoir areas. Large beds of arrowhead can draw down water levels to some significant extent. This plant gets most of the credit for drying up seasonal and temporary pools or water holes in summer.

The starchy tubers make nourishing food for humans as well as wildlife. Native American women collected them in the fall by feeling them out in the mud with their toes, then detaching them with sticks; when loosened from their runners, the tubers float (a hoe or rake does the job better). The tubers can be cooked like potatoes. Indians also made a tuber tea to relieve indigestion, and they applied poultices of tubers and leaves to treat wounds and sores.

Skin contact with some arrowheads may cause a rash in allergic individuals.

Ash, Black *(Fraxinus nigra)*. Olive family. Tree in deciduous and conifer swamps, floodplains. Opposite feather-compound leaves, broad shield-shaped leaf scars, and winged "canoe-paddle" fruits called samaras mark the ashes. Black ash differs from other ashes in its unstalked leaflets (seven to eleven per compound leaf), bluish-black buds, blunt-ended samaras, and wetland habitat.

Other names: Hoop ash, basket ash, swamp ash, water ash, brown ash, pumpkin ash.

Close relatives: White ash *(F. americana)*; forsythias *(Forsythia)*; privets *(Ligustrum)*; lilacs *(Syringa)*.

Lifestyle: Most ash species bear unisexual flowers on separate trees, but black ash has both unisexual and bisexual flowers. The wind-pollinated flowers open on twigs of the previous year before the leaves appear in early spring. The winged samaras, which mature in summer, sometimes hang on the tree through winter; often the gauzy wing is slightly twisted, giving it an aerodynamic spin when it falls. Seeds, dispersed by air and water, usually lie dormant for two years before they germinate, though they may remain viable for eight or more years.

The leaves appear relatively late in spring and drop early in the fall, adding a mineral-rich blend of calcium, magnesium, nitrogen, and potassium to the soil. To Thoreau, they had "an elderlike odor."

Black ash grows slowly, is quite short-lived, and is only moderately shade tolerant. Cutting or fire encourages vigorous sprouting. It is often a leaning, crooked tree, with shallow, fibrous roots. The soft, scaly bark (usually lighter in color than white ash bark) flakes off easily when rubbed.

Distinctive features of black ash are its almost rectangular winged samaras and its unstalked leaflets. Wetland plants with similar compound leaves include common elderberry and poison sumac.

Associates: Look for black ash in swampy or lowland sites in company with northern white cedar (which it may replace after fires), speckled alder, red-osier dogwood, red maple, black spruce, and tamarack.

Spring, summer. Although various insect defoliators may attack this tree, its usual growth in mixed rather than pure stands provides protection from serious outbreaks of insect pests. Probably its most consistent feeder is the oystershell scale insect *(Lepidosaphes ulmi)*, which infests many other plants as well. These shell-shaped insects coat entire twigs and branches in brownish masses; they are sap feeders.

Spring cankerworms *(Paleocrita vernata)* feed on the leaves; a small caterpillar dangling from a bough on a silken thread is probably this inchworm.

All ash species are subject to attacks of the lilac or ash borer moth *(Podosesia syringae)*; look for scars on the trunk where its caterpillars have burrowed. The adult moths mimic the paper wasp *(Polistes)* in appearance.

White-tailed deer sometimes extensively browse the foliage, especially of young trees. Beavers readily cut the tree for bark food.

Late summer, fall. The honey mushroom *(Armillaria mellea)*, a tan-capped saprophyte on dead wood, sometimes appears in clusters around the bases of black ash, as well as many other trees.

Winter. Evening grosbeaks relish the seeds of black ash, and cottontail rabbits gnaw the bark.

Lore: Along with northern white cedar, white birch, and sugar maple, black ash was one of the foremost resource trees for eastern North American natives. Its primary usefulness lay in the property of its wood to split, when pounded, along the annual growth rings, forming thin sheets. These were cut into strips and woven for basketry and other containers. Gladys Sands, a Michigan Potawatomi who was still weaving baskets from black ash in 1968, specified precise materials: a trunk section of unvarying diameter six feet long, producing seven or eight thin sheets. These are cut, smoothed, seasoned, and dyed. Today, most weaving of Indian basketry is done decoratively for tourists' money, not for workaday utility. The Chippewas also used large sheets of black ash bark to cover their dwellings.

Later, black ash wood strips were used for barrel hoops and caning for chairs. "No wood [is] equal to our black ash for oars, so pliant and elastic and strong," reported Thoreau. Large burls that sometimes develop on trunks are still used for making veneers and rustic furniture. Though usually sold commercially with white ash as simply "ash," some lumberyards label this softer, weaker wood brown or pumpkin ash. It burns well as a firewood.

American ashes are repeatedly cited in old literary sources as effective snake repellents and venom antidotes. "One never finds [serpents] in the swamps where this tree abounds," swore one French missionary in Quebec, probably repeating Indian tales of the tree's charmlike powers. How these tales achieved such durable credibility is the real mystery.

The astringent bark was often used in medicinal tonics.

Bladderwort, Common *(Utricularia vulgaris)*. Bladderwort family. Submersed herb in ponds, swamps, marshes. This species floats horizontally beneath the water surface, unattached to the bottom. Identify it by its finely branched vinelike form, threadlike leaves, yellow flowers projecting above the water surface, and small sacs ("bladders") attached in rows to leaf branches.

Other names: Greater bladderwort, hooded water-milfoil, pop-weed.

Close relative: Butterwort *(Pinguicula vulgaris)*.

Lifestyle: All of our insectivorous plants (see Pitcher-plant, Sundews) are wetland residents. Bladderworts, however, are not strictly insectivorous—a better term would be carnivorous. In contrast to the others, bladderworts probably trap fewer larval insects than smaller zooplankton, owing to the pinhead size of their *utricles,* the creature-capturing bladders. There are up to six hundred of these small, deflated, pear-shaped pouches on a plant. When triggered by sensitive hairs outside a "trapdoor" entry, they suddenly inflate with water. The quick suction into the bladder carries with it the creature that touched the outer hairs. Inside the bladder, digestive enzymes and bacteria go to

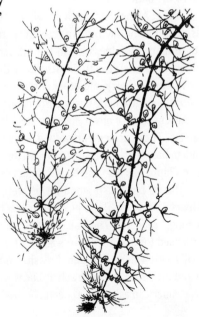

Three increasingly close-up views of bladderwort. At near right, a gross pendant aspect of the plant shows the arrangement of bladders. The middle view shows the large turions, which account for most of the plant's reproduction; attached along branches are the smaller bladders. At far right, a magnified view of the bladders shows several in various stages of inflation; the full ones are digesting their captures.

work on the trapped victim, reducing it to plant nutrients (in fifteen minutes to two hours, depending on its size and digestibility). Special cells then extract the nutrient water into the stem. This restores a partial vacuum and deflated concave shape to the bladder, thus resetting it to trap again.

Zooplankton are probably attracted to the bladders by a sugar secreted from special glands outside the trapdoor device. This almost microscopic portal, which opens and shuts in something like two-thousandths of a second, is one of the most intricate wonders of the plant kingdom. Some researchers suggest a triggering electrical stimulus from the hairs to the bladder. Whatever the precise mechanism, you can sometimes *hear* it operating by holding a plant close to your ear; removal of the plant from water may cause sufficient disturbance to trigger the bladders, which gulp air with slight popping sounds. (Unlike most plants lifted for inspection, bladderwort can be replaced in the water hardly the worse for wear, since it has neither roots nor anchorage.)

Before they understood the bladders' true function, many botanists believed they were simply flotation devices. But since the bladders never inflate unless the plant is "feeding," and since they inflate with water, not air, this theory was obviously not based on observation. One investigator estimated that all the inflated bladders on one large plant held a total of 150,000 organisms, based on counts of

captured animals in sample bladders. So the presence of these plants indicates tremendous abundance of life in their pond environments.

Though one of the most common submersed plants, bladderwort may be easily overlooked unless it is in flower—and most of the plants in a given area do not bloom. The bright yellow flowers, rising a few inches above the water, resemble the spurred, lipped flowers of butter-and-eggs *(Linaria vulgaris)*, a meadow snapdragon. Bladderworts are insect pollinated. Vegetative reproduction, however, is much more common. In late fall, look for bright green dwarf tips, densely compact masses of crowded leaves at branch ends. These are starch-filled winter buds (called *turions*), which fall off the dying plant, sink, remain dormant through winter, then elongate to produce new plants as the water warms in spring. Air spaces that develop in the leaves cause the new plant to become buoyant.

About fourteen bladderwort species exist in east-central North America. Quite common is horned bladderwort *(U. cornuta)*, which differs from common bladderwort in its long-spurred flower—naturalist John Burroughs called it "perhaps the most fragrant flower we have"—and muddy shoreline (rather than shallow-water) habitat. Some species are mud creepers *(U. cornuta)* or epiphytes in moss rather than free floaters. And some have violet-colored flowers.

Associates: *Spring, summer, fall.* Bladderworts often grow submersed beneath duckweeds. Coontail is also a frequent plant associate.

The presence of bladderwort indicates rich zooplankton populations. More than just plant carnivores, however, bladderworts provide thriving microhabitats for many small organisms that attach themselves to the plant as a "home base" for their own feeding. For example, more sessile rotifers (that is, rotifer species that attach to plants or animals rather than swim freely) attach to bladderwort than to any other aquatic plant. A few minute organisms, having evolved defenses against the digestive secretions (similar to organisms inhabiting pitcher-plants), even thrive and reproduce inside the enzyme-secreting bladders. These include species of the green flagellates *Euglena* and *Phacus* plus a few protozoan species.

Bladderwort prey include just about any creature small enough to get trapped, including protozoans such as paramecia, rotifers, nematode worms, and microscopic insect larvae. Most bladderwort prey, however, consist of minute crustaceans: fairy shrimps (Branchiopoda), water fleas (Cladocera), copepods (Copepoda, mainly *Cyclops*), and scuds (Amphipoda). The abundance of microscopic life, either captured or resident, inside a bladder can be astonishing. One observer reported an average of 215 *Euglena* per bladder in a study of several plants. Sometimes a larger organism gets caught half-in, half-out of a trap, and the half-in part is promptly digested. Observers have reported insect larvae, tiny tadpoles, and young fishes being caught in this way.

Certain narrow-winged damselflies *(Coenagrion)* lay eggs in the subsurface flowering stems.

Vertebrate species eat bladderworts, but the plants are not preferred foods. Although most ducks consume them occasionally, they are eaten quite sparingly by waterfowl and muskrats. Small tadpoles and fishes, however, sometimes lurk in the plants' dense growth for shelter and feed on smaller organisms swimming there. Once I lifted a mass of bladderwort to discover a live minnow enmeshed among the strands—the easiest fish I ever caught!

White-tailed deer and moose likewise eat the plant but not as a staple item.

Lore: In 1875 Charles Darwin, concurrently with two other biologists, established that the bladders were indeed animal traps; this discovery ended once and for all the presumption that they were flotation devices.

Only one other plant genus combines trapping with the floating aquatic habit—*Aldrovanda* of the Mediterranean and Orient, related to Venus fly-trap *(Dionaea muscipula)*, which is native only to North Carolina coastal areas.

Blueberries *(Vaccinium* spp.). Heath family. High or low shrubs in bogs, swamps, and upland areas. Blueberries show warty, zigzag twigs; dangle small, whitish, bell-shaped flowers; and bear sweet, purplish or blue-black fruits. The three most common wetland species are common highbush or swamp blueberry *(V. corymbosum)*; late lowbush or sweet blueberry *(V. angustifolium)*; and velvetleaf or sourtop blueberry *(V. myrtilloides)*.

Close relatives: Cranberries *(Vaccinium)*; Labrador-tea *(Ledum groenlandicum)*; laurels *(Kalmia)*; bog-rosemary *(Andromeda glaucophylla)*; leatherleaf *(Chamaedaphne calyculata)*; azaleas *(Rhododendron)*.

Lifestyle: An acid soil rather than amount of moisture seems to be the determining factor for blueberry growth, since many of the almost thirty species of east-central North America occupy both wetlands and dry upland habitats (see Blueberries in *The Book of Forest and Thicket*). These are cloning plants, forming dense, shrubby thickets of profusely branched stems.

Highbush, which may grow twelve feet tall, is probably the most consistent blueberry wetland dweller. It occupies both bog and fen borders, often where a mineral-nutrient flowage reduces localized soil acidity; this plant can colonize sites somewhat higher on the pH scale than the other two wetland species. It typically grows in compact clumps, often forming shrub-carr islands.

Lowbush blueberry flowers earlier in spring than the other two, usually before its leaves fully emerge. Lowbush requires high soil acidity (less than pH 5), and its seeds germinate best on bare, open ground following clearcutting or burning. Its extensive clonal colonies, usually established after a fire, can survive more than a century, especially when periodically "reinvigorated" by fire. This is the typical three-foot-high blueberry shrub of open, drier peatlands and tundra barrens, often growing so densely as to make walking virtually impossible. It is very cold-hardy. Sometimes, when fall daylength equals the plant's spring-flowering daylength, occasional plants can be seen blooming in October. Unlike highbush, lowbush blueberry has a long taproot, which may help account for its tolerance of drier soil.

Velvetleaf, another low blueberry, is also dependent on fire. Its velvety leaves and twigs are good identifying marks. Its fruit sometimes tastes quite sour. It is also a bit more tolerant of shade than the other two species.

Blueberry flowers are bisexual and pollinated by insects. Flowers and fruits are produced on one-year-old shoots; as summer progresses, tips of these shoots die suddenly. The plants also spread by rhizomes. Twigs and leaves of most blueberry species turn orange and red in the fall.

Blueberries often hybridize, sometimes producing combined characteristics that make species identification difficult.

Associates: Important to the healthy existence and survival of blueberries (as well as most heath family plants) are root-fungus symbiotic associations called *mycorrhizae*. Although these associations exist for the majority of land plants, mycorrhizae are relatively uncommon in wet, acid peatlands; heath plants are the exceptions in these environments. "Many functions that we regard as being done by roots," according to ecologist Richard Brewer, "are actually performed by the plant-fungus union and are done poorly or not at all if the fungus is absent." The fungal threads function as root hairs, increasing the uptake of nutrients, especially nitrogen, phosphorus, and potassium—the very nutrients that are most scarce in a bog. Having no means of generating their own food, the fungi derive food and energy from the green plants. "The result of this symbiosis," writes botanist Howard Crum, "is that both host and fungus can exploit habitats unsuited to either alone." Heath mycorrhizae consist mainly of cup fungi (Ascomycetes).

All three wetland blueberry species often associate together in bogs, a situation that results in hybridized forms. A common associate of low blueberry shrubs is leatherleaf, another low heath. The presence of blueberry and leatherleaf in a bog generally indicates a historic passage of fire. Fire enables blueberry to invade the dense leatherleaf thickets where it otherwise could not have germinated.

Other common bog plant associates include tamarack, black spruce, and sphagnum mosses. In less acidic wetlands, red maple, black ash, common elderberry, bog birch, and poison sumac are frequent blueberry associates.

Spring, summer. Blueberry pollinators include a large size range of insects. They are chiefly bees, including bumblebees *(Bombus)*, which occasionally bite holes through the flower base as a "shortcut" to the nectaries. Bees that enter the conventional way often vibrate their wings vigorously, dislodging the pollen. Other pollinators include blackflies *(Simulium)*, which also feed on the nectar and pollen.

Bees also transmit a fungous disease called *Monilinia* between plants. They lick the sweetish-tasting diseased leaves, which appear water-soaked and discolored along the midveins, and carry fungous spores into the flowers. The result is a hard, whitish, distorted fruit called mummy berry, filled with the ascomycete fungus. These berries drop off and produce small, mushroomlike cups beneath the plant in early spring.

Other leaf fungi common on blueberry include *Pucciniastrum goeppertianum*, which causes a bunchy "witch's broom" branching; and *P. vaccinii*, the hemlock or blueberry leaf rust, causing yellow pustules. Both are club fungi and have alternate tree hosts: firs for the former, hemlocks for the latter. Azalea leaf gall *(Exobasidium vaccinii)*, also a club fungus, causes bright red leaf blisters on blueberries and other heaths.

Blueberry leaf feeders include a host of caterpillars. Only a few of them can be mentioned here. Butterfly larvae include elfins *(Incisalia)*, which are green, sluglike caterpillars. A downy,

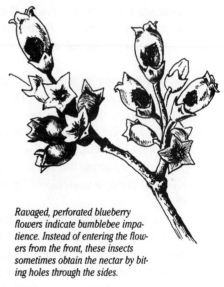

Ravaged, perforated blueberry flowers indicate bumblebee impatience. Instead of entering the flowers from the front, these insects sometimes obtain the nectar by biting holes through the sides.

yellowish caterpillar is probably a pink-edged sulphur *(Colias interior)*. Short-tailed swallowtails *(Papilio brevicauda)* and the aforementioned elfins also visit the flowers as adult butterflies.

Large, conspicuous, green caterpillars with projecting rear horns are sphinx moths; pawpaw sphinx *(Dolba hyloeus)* and huckleberry sphinx *(Paonias astylus)* commonly feed on blueberry. Smaller caterpillars may include several dart, arches, underwing, and other noctuid moths, as well as some inchworm (geometrid) species.

The heath spittlebug *(Clastoptera saintcyri)*, nymph of a froghopper (Cercopidae), creates frothy masses as it feeds on sap.

Blueberry fruit is an important wildlife food for wetland birds and mammals. It also attracts many that usually don't frequent bog or fen habitats. Ruffed and spruce grouse, tufted titmice, red-eyed vireos, gray catbirds, brown thrashers, American robins, Swainson's thrushes, veeries, scarlet tanagers, rufous-sided towhees, and orchard orioles are prominent berry foragers. One study estimated that up to 85 percent of summer bird foraging in blueberry plantations consisted of juvenile birds; the figure would probably be similar for wild blueberry crops.

Among mammals, white-footed mice, least chipmunks, striped skunks, and black bears are probably the foremost berry consumers.

Fall, winter. A coral mushroom called the blueberry club *(Clavaria argillacea)*, appearing in late fall, is the fruiting stage of a probable symbiotic mycorrhizal fungus, as previously described.

The aforementioned mummy berries are plainly seen now on diseased plants.

Very common on blueberry stems and branches are kidney-shaped galls, best seen after the leaves drop. These may distort branches, bending them at ninety-degree angles; more often, they kill the branches above the gall so that eventually the gall terminates the branch. These galls form in spring, created by larvae of the blueberry stemgall wasp *(Hemadas nubilipennis)*. During the winter, groups of wasp larvae live inside the blackened galls along with two species of tiny flies that reside as *inquilines* ("guest" organisms that inhabit abodes made by others).

Fall is the best season to observe the work of two spiders that often construct webs in the upper twigs and branches of blueberry. *Dictyna* weaves a chaotic mesh of strands in the topmost twigs and branch tips (see *Dictyna* illustration for Leatherleaf). Bowl-and-doily spiders *(Frontinella communis)* build bowl-shaped webs above a flat platform web where the spider waits.

Cottontail rabbits and white-tailed deer relish blueberry twigs in winter. You can identify which animal has nibbled by the appearance of the nipped ends: If clipped at a sharp, oblique angle, it was a cottontail; if the twig end is ragged, a deer has cropped (its lack of upper incisors prevents a clean bite).

Lore: Blueberry harvest in the bogs was an important season for American natives, who dried the berries and pounded them into strips of dried venison to make the staple winter food called pemmican. A recipe that French-Canadian pioneers labeled "savage cheese" consisted of blueberries boiled for hours into a paste, which was then dried and stored for mixture and consumption with other foods. Leaf and root teas were also used as tonics and medicinal relief for colic and labor pains. Burning the dried flowers and inhaling the smoke—a prescription of the Chippewa deity-prankster figure Winabojo—was said to remedy craziness.

Though various blueberry species grow all over the world, blueberry is not commercially raised outside North America. And not until 1912 did commercial cultivation begin here, using highbush clones from the New Jersey pine barrens.

Highbush blueberry is still the main species used to develop cultivated varieties (cultivars), of which more than forty exist. Cultivars are mainly grown on upland sites. Certain lowbush cultivars are also widely planted, but the fresh fruits (claimed by devotees to be much tastier than highbush berries) are seldom sold outside New England. "Bluecrop," the leading commercial cultivar, is a highbush-lowbush hybrid.

Bog-rosemary *(Andromeda glaucophylla)*. Heath family. Low shrub in bogs, poor fens. Narrow, leathery, evergreen leaves with a white "felt" on leaf undersides and inrolled leaf edges mark bog-rosemary. The foliage often has a bluish-gray color.

Close relatives: Wild-rosemary *(A. polifolia)*; leatherleaf *(Chamaedaphne calyculata)*; laurels *(Kalmia)*; Labrador-tea *(Ledum groenlandicum)*; blueberries and cranberries *(Vaccinium)*; azaleas *(Rhododendron)*. Though the leaves are similar, bog-rosemary is unrelated to the common garden rosemary *(Rosmarinus officinalis)*, a mint of European origin.

Lifestyle: Two other common bog plants have similar leaves: bog laurel and Labrador-tea. Bog-rosemary's blue-gray foliage, however, makes it impossible to mistake and gives it distinctive visibility across the bog. It usually grows in scattered clumps or islands, often indicating areas of slight mineral enrichment, where a small surface or groundwater inflow modifies the acidic habitat.

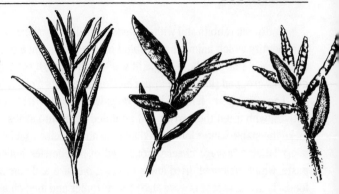

Bog-rosemary leaves (left) show features once widely believed to be desert adaptations. They share these characteristics with leaves of other acid wetland heaths such as bog laurel (center) and Labrador-tea (right).

The thick, leathery, inrolled leaves of several bog heaths also characterize many desert plants, which must conserve water and limit its loss from the leaves. The traditional view of "physiological drought" holds that bogs are actually waterlogged deserts because the water's acidity prevents its use by most plants. Water uptake is minimal, and leaf adaptations such as few and sunken *stomata* (respiratory pores) and "furry" undersides help reduce water loss. More recent research, however, reveals that physiological drought does not exist; water uptake and loss is no problem for these plants. Rather it is habitat nutrient deficiency (especially of phosphorus) and cold winters that account for the leaf adaptations. The evergreen habit conserves scarce nutrients in the leaves, and winter snow insulates them to a considerable degree.

Others dismiss the apparent water and nutrient conservative strategies entirely, saying these are mere taxonomic features of heath family plants; the low growth forms and tough, leathery leaves are mainly adaptations to snow and cold. Still another theory combines elements of all these views: The difference in temperature between root level (cold, often frozen) and leaf level (warm, unshaded from sun) plus water acidity favor plants that have evolved water-conservative strategies. The plain fact is that, despite plausible guesses about the questions posed by bog heaths, nobody *really* knows the answers.

Bog-rosemary produces small, white or pinkish flower clusters in early spring. Flowers are bell-shaped, bisexual, and insect pollinated. By fall, flower buds for the following year are well developed; I have seen them on the verge of blooming in October. This advanced timing gives them a head start in spring, especially vital if the roots are still frozen, as is often the case. The fruit capsule, maturing in late summer, contains numerous brown seeds. These plants mainly reproduce, however, by creeping rootstocks. They thrive only in open sun and are intolerant of shade.

Associates: Look for bog-rosemary growing from deep, wet sphagnum moss. Plant associates mostly consist of related low, shrubby heaths: leatherleaf, Labrador-tea, bog laurel, and lowbush blueberry.

Spring, summer. Pollination is mainly accomplished by early-foraging bumblebees *(Bombus)*, other bees, and small flies.

Relatively few fungi and insects attack or feed on bog-rosemary. *Exobasidium andromedae,* a club fungus, sometimes produces leaf galls that appear blackish and crustlike. The yellow-necked caterpillar *(Datana ministra),* a moth of the prominent family, sometimes feeds on the leaves.

Winter. Willow ptarmigan, one of the few recorded vertebrate consumers, will eat the leaves to some extent. Browsing mammals tend to avoid most evergreen bog heaths, apparently because of the toxin they produce.

Lore: This is not a plant for brewing tea, even though the Flambeau Ojibwas were said to do so. The leaves contain a poisonous compound called acetylandromedol, most potently in spring, which probably accounts for bog-rosemary's relative freedom from pests and browsers. Several sources cite instances of it killing sheep. In small doses, the toxin has proven useful in veterinary medicine for lowering blood pressure.

Boneset *(Eupatorium perfoliatum).* Composite family. Herb in wet ground, along marsh and pond edges. Identify boneset by its flat-topped clusters of dull white flowers that bloom all summer; and by its opposite, crinkly leaves united at their bases to enclose the hairy stem.

Other names: Thoroughwort, ague-weed, Indian-sage, crosswort, feverweed, sweating-plant.

Close relatives: Joe-Pye-weeds *(Eupatorium)*; ironweeds *(Vernonia)*; thistles *(Cirsium)*; asters *(Aster)*; goldenrods *(Solidago)*; bur-marigolds *(Bidens)*; sunflowers *(Helianthus)*; and all other composites.

Lifestyle: More than twenty *Eupatorium* species reside in various habitats of east-central North America, but boneset is the most common one. This plant is so frequent along open shorelines and marshy spots that its absence is more remarkable than its presence.

The flowers, as in most composites, consist of multiple bisexual florets that are insect pollinated. Flower heads usually contain fifteen to twenty florets, which secrete abundant nectar. Occasional purple-flowered and three-leaved forms occur. Like many plants in this family, the seeds come equipped with a hairy *pap-*

pus, or "parachute," a more efficient device for wind distribution than the seed wings seen in maple and ash trees.

This plant sometimes hybridizes with upland boneset *(E. sessilifolium),* a woods dweller.

Associates: *Summer.* Boneset frequently dwells among its close relatives, the Joe-Pye-weeds, and also with wetland sedges and grasses, jewelweeds, and other typical edge plants of swamps and fens.

Adult Baltimore checkerspot butterflies *(Euphydryas phaeton)* often alight on the flowers and feed on the nectar; look for a black butterfly with reddish marginal spots.

Usually, however, more beetles than butterflies favor the off-white flowers. Most of them are quite tiny and may also be found crawling among the florets of Joe-Pye-weeds. Dark brown *Olibrus semistriatus,* a shining mold beetle, is common, as is the handsome fungus beetle called *Rhanidea unicolor,* usually on late-season flowers. The redbud bruchid *(Gibbobruchus mimus),* a seed beetle, also feeds in the flower head.

Several gall midge species frequently reside as larvae on boneset. The boneset blossom midges *Contarinia perfoliata* and *Clinorhynca eupatoriflorae* feed in the flowers. Oval stem galls may indicate the presence of two other flies, the boneset stem midges *Neolasioptera perfoliata* and *Brachyneura eupatorii.*

Bees and flies are probably the foremost pollinators. Sometimes they become victims of an insect predator often seen on *Eupatorium* (and goldenrod) flowers. The ambush bug (Phymatidae) has swollen forelegs that are adapted for catching prey. You may often find dead flies or bees snagged on the flower head (usually the exoskeletons of insects thus consumed). One common ambush bug is *Phymata erosa,* greenish-yellow with a transverse black band.

Hairy caterpillars that feed on the leaves include several tiger moth species: clymene moths *(Haploa clymene)* and ruby and lined ruby tiger moths *(Phragmatobia fuliginosa, P. lineata).*

Whitish serpentine leaf mines or skeletonized leaves may indicate larval feeding of *Bucculatrix eupatoriella,* a leaf-mining moth.

Ants and other wingless insects rarely appear on boneset because the plant's hairy stem discourages crawlers.

Mallards sometimes eat *Eupatorium* seeds, and ruffed grouse consume both seeds and leaves.

Lore: The name boneset probably refers to this plant's historic usage as a tea treatment for breakbone fever (now identified as the viral disease dengue), characterized by severe pains in the joints. The plant's fused, opposite leaves may also have suggested it as a treatment for mending bone fractures; the antiquated doctrine of signatures theory of medicine held that the shape or appearance of a plant part indicated its intended curative use. Boneset tea was one of the most widely used folk remedies for general aches and malaise by American natives and pioneers alike. It reportedly became one of the most effective relief medicines during nineteenth- and early twentieth-century flu epidemics. Today boneset tea, a bitter brew indeed, remains a popular herbal drink to induce sweating, as a tonic for colds, and, still, as a medicine that supposedly promotes bone healing. Larger doses have emetic and laxative effects.

Modern medical research verifies some of boneset's reputed benefits; some of its compounds apparently stimulate the immune system. Its potential for producing anticancer chemotherapeutic drugs is also being explored.

Each tier of paired boneset leaves grows at a right angle to the tiers above and below, thus maximizing exposure to sunlight. Predatory ambush bugs (inset), with enlarged, grasping forelegs, are common residents in the flower heads.

Bulrushes (*Scirpus* spp.). Sedge family. Tall, emergent herbs in marshes, fens, along shorelines. Identify bulrushes by their smooth, dark green, spearlike stems and scaly brown flower clusters emerging from one side or the top of the stem. Almost thirty highly variable species exist in east-central North America. Many have triangular stems (but some are round); some resemble cotton-grasses (*Eriophorum*) and others are easily mistaken for rushes (*Juncus*).

The three general types of bulrush include triangular-stemmed, round-stemmed, and leafy-stemmed plants. The most common species include great or soft-stem bulrush (*S. validus*), with round, thick, but lax stems growing in dense

Some species of bulrushes and rushes look much alike. Wool-grass (top), one of the most common bulrushes, is not easily mistaken; but the one-sided flower clusters of soft rush *(Juncus effusus, bottom)* resemble the growth form of some bulrushes.

patches; hard-stem bulrush *(S. acutus),* with round, rigid, dark green stems in water up to five feet deep; the common three-square or chairmaker's rush *(S. americanus),* with triangular, bayonetlike stems and small, unstalked, tight-clustered spikelets; and wool-grass *(S. cyperinus),* tall with a slightly triangular stem, long, leafy bracts, and a large, drooping, fuzzy-brown flower cluster at the top.

Other name: Tule.

Close relatives: Spike-rushes *(Eleocharis);* nut-grasses *(Cyperus);* cotton-grasses *(Eriophorum);* beak-rushes *(Rhyncospora);* sedges *(Carex).*

Lifestyle: Along with cattails, sedges, and rushes, bulrushes rank among the most common plants of marshy, mineral-rich wetlands. But many plants of this complicated genus so closely resemble the nonrelated rushes *(Juncus)* in general form and appearance that precise identification becomes almost impossible if the plants lack flowers, as many do for much of the year. Without close inspection, even the one-sided flower clusters of each genus look alike. Here's how to tell the difference: *Scirpus* flowers show scales on their spikelets, and each scale encloses a minute flower; *Juncus* flowers are three-parted (three petals, three sepals), with fruit capsules also splitting into three sections (see illustration for Rushes). Another way to distinguish the two: *Scirpus* flowers easily crumble if you crush them in your fingers; *Juncus* flowers do not.

Most bulrushes grow in densely colonial, offshore patches. Their emergent, dark green spears form one of the most familiar aspects of lake and pond margins. In the fall, these plants turn yellow-brown, sometimes producing an interesting horizontal two-tone color effect when viewed from a distance. Flowers are bisexual and wind pollinated. Perennial rhizomes sprout new green stems in spring, and most reproduction is vegetative from the rhizome rather than from seed.

Bulrushes are important land-building, pioneer plants of hard-bottomed shoreline edges. Their growth (especially *S. acutus*) on windy, wave-buffeted margins provides breakwaters allowing other aquatic plants to gain footholds, anchoring soil and building land. Some species are not so hardy; soft-stem bulrush, for example, cannot withstand heavy wave action, and thus it more often colonizes sheltered coves.

A broken stem reveals light, pithy partitions enclosing numerous air spaces (as with many other emergent aquatics).

Associates: *Spring, summer.* Bulrushes frequently occur in pure stands, but two or more species may also be found together; "island" patches of soft-stem bulrush, for example, often accompany surrounding stands of hard-stem bulrush. Other associations, such as wool-grass with soft rush, may also occur. I have often found wool-grass and rattlesnake grass (a true grass) in close association.

Larvae of several borer species tunnel inside stems, causing them to turn brown and die. These may include the oblong sedge borer *(Archanera oblonga)* and the subflava sedge borer *(A. subflava).* Lost owlet moth caterpillars *(Ledaea perditalis)* feed on wool-grass. These are all noctuid moths. Another tiny moth larva *(Aphelosetia inaudita)* sometimes mines in the grasslike leaves of leafy bulrushes.

Bulrushes often provide the means for aquatic insect larvae to assume their winged, aerial lifestyle. Sooner or later amid the bulrushes you'll see the cast-off "skin" of a dragonfly nymph, still firmly attached to the vertical stem. These insects emerge from the water and crawl up the stems, often at dawn. Clinging to the stem, they split free from their nymphal bodies as winged, mature insects, deserting the aquatic life along with their shed exoskeletons. Other ready-to-transform aquatic larvae also climb the "bulrush path" to a higher existence.

Bulrush seeds and tubers are important wildlife foods, especially for water birds. Most goose and duck species relish the seeds, as do swans, rails, and many shorebirds. Ring-necked ducks, as well as geese and other diving ducks, consume the rhizomes as well. Finches such as snow buntings and song sparrows also feed on them.

Dense bulrush stands provide nesting and concealing cover for birds such as redheads, least bit-

The cast-off exoskeleton of a dragonfly nymph still clings to a bulrush stem, whence the insect first took wing. Note the broad underside of this aquatic predator's jaw.

Floating, raggedly bitten-off fragments of bulrush stems indicate muskrat activity. These aquatic mammals not only eat all parts of the plant but also use stem parts in lodge construction.

terns, marsh wrens, and red-winged blackbirds. Dead bulrush stems become material for waterfowl platform nests, and muskrats use them in building their lodges.

Muskrats are also the foremost mammal consumers of bulrush rhizomes, tubers, and stems.

Lore: Infant Moses was never hidden in these bulrushes; his cover would have been the papyrus sedge *Cyperus rostrata.* True bulrushes have, however, provided materials for basket making and chair caning, as well as for beehives. The Chippewa used basswood twine and frames for weaving bulrush floor mats.

Indians especially relished the small, bulblike tips of the rhizome, which they pulled up in summer. These portions are rich in starch and sugar and can be eaten raw, roasted, or dried and pounded into flour. Pollen and crushed seeds can also be made into flour, and early spring shoots are quite tasty raw or cooked.

Impromptu camp candles can be made by soaking bulrush stems in melted fat, which the pithy stems absorb like a wick. They will burn for an hour or more. Bound together in loglike bundles, bulrushes can also serve as an emergency raft or boat.

Bulrushes and cord-grasses *(Spartina)* have recently gained attention as aids of salt pollution cleanup near natural gas wells, where brine waste often accumulates. These plants' salt tolerance and ability to absorb targeted contaminants make them potentially valuable tools for toxic waste management.

Bur-reeds *(Sparganium* spp.). Bur-reed family. Floating and emergent herbs in shallow water, wet ground. Identify bur-reeds by their ribbonlike floating leaves, or in erect species, their cattail-like leaves bulging at the base of the flower stems. Both kinds have emergent stems bearing green burs of closely packed nutlets. The most common of our ten species are giant bur-reed *(S. eurycarpum),* which may grow six feet tall; branching bur-reed *(S. americanum),* which is much shorter and more slender with branching flower stems; and *S. angustifolium,* with long, narrow, floating leaves.

Other names: Bur-weed, bur-flag, ox-tongue.

Close relatives: None.

Lifestyle: The erect, straplike leaves of bur-reeds resemble those of cattail or iris, but *Sparganium* leaves are somewhat spongy and *keeled,* giving them a flattish, triangular shape. Leaves of the other two plants are simply flat. In floating-leaved bur-reeds, the leaves resemble the streaming-ribbon leaves of wild-celery. Close inspection, however, reveals a finely checkered pattern of veins on bur-reed, while wild-celery leaves are vertically three-zoned.

In summer, when bur-reeds flower, there is no mistaking them. The downy, brownish or whitish, unisexual flower clusters ascend the stem, with small male flowers at the top and the larger female ones lined below them. Later the male flowers wither away, while the burlike seed heads, their surfaces somewhat resembling tiny pineapples, swell with beaked nutlets *(achenes).* The flowers are mainly self-fertilizing, but insects sometimes assist the process.

Giant bur-reed seems to favor mineral-rich wetlands. *S. angustifolium* tolerates somewhat more acid conditions.

Associates: *Spring, summer.* Depending on the species, bur-reeds may occupy or overlap two aquatic habitats—the emergent plant zone and the floating-leaved zone—just as, taxonomically, they rank between the emergent cattails and the submersed and floating-leaved pondweeds. Both cattails and pondweeds are frequent bur-reed associates.

Various flies and other insects aid pollination.

Wilted stems may indicate the presence of boring moth caterpillars such as the red sedge borer *(Archanara laeta)* and the cattail borer *(Bellura obliqua),* both noctuids. Putnam's looper moth *(Plusia putnami),* a noctuid caterpillar that resembles an inchworm, feeds on the leaves.

Giant bur-reed displays its beaked nutlets in round seedheads. Many waterfowl, shorebirds, and muskrats relish them. The somewhat zigzagged stem is characteristic.

Common larvae found on the submersed stems and roots of many aquatic plants include species of *Donacia,* the long-horned leaf beetles. These larvae tap into the plant tissue for oxygen by means of two rear spines. Rows of their cocoons, attached to stems, may also be seen.

Fall. Bur-reeds are valuable food plants for many waterfowl and shorebirds. Mallards, American black ducks, blue-winged teal, American wigeons, wood ducks, redheads, ring-necked ducks, greater scaup, king and sora rails, and common snipe feed on bur-reed seeds.

Muskrats feed on the entire plant; wetlands containing cattails and bur-reeds are almost certain to host these animals. Bur-reeds also number among the preferred foods of white-tailed deer.

Lore: As with several emergent aquatics, the starchy tubers are edible to humans. Small and scattered, they are difficult to find when stems and leaves have died back.

Buttonbush *(Cephalanthus occidentalis).* Madder family. Shrub along pond and stream margins, in swamps. Buttonbush has whorled and opposite shiny-green, leathery leaves, often with red stalks; the densely clustered, white flowers in pincushionlike heads appear in summer.

Other names: Pond dogwood, pin-ball, little snowball, crane-willow, crouper, honey plant, honey-balls, globe-flower, button-ball shrub, river-bush, knuckle-brush.

Close relatives: Partridgeberry *(Mitchella repens)*; buttonweeds *(Diodia)*; bluets *(Houstonia)*; cleavers *(Galium)*; coffee *(Coffea arabica)*; cinchona *(Cinchona).*

Lifestyle: Buttonbush, one of the latest shrubs to leaf out in spring, often forms dense, cloning thickets on shorelines or in low areas where water stands for most of the year. It is intolerant of shade but tolerates flooding, often putting out side roots on the stem. These adventitious roots, when "stranded" above the surface, are always good indicators of shifting water levels (see illustration for Willows, Shrub). Buttonbush also tolerates varying soil pH (acidity) levels.

The cream-white, ball-shaped flower heads contain many individual insect-pollinated flowers. They are highly fragrant and loaded with nectar. Though bisexual, the flowers on any given head (some two hundred or more) pass through two stages of separate sexual identity. First the pollen develops and is shed by the anthers on the immature pistil. As the pistil elongates, the pollen brushes off on alighting insects. Then, after the pollen's removal, this same pistil matures and becomes sticky, receiving the pollen carried from other flowers. This timed "brush-pollination" mechanism is similar to that of willow flowers, in which the female organ first functions as pollen dispenser, then as receiver.

Ball-shaped seed heads containing small nutlets succeed the flower heads. They turn brown in fall and often remain on the shrub over winter, resembling the spherical seed heads of sycamore trees. The seeds often disperse by floating. Thoreau described a "mass transplantation" of buttonbush along the Sudbury River in 1859: Chunks of shoreline shrubbery torn loose by flood were deposited far-

Buttonbush shrubs provide spectacular flower displays along shoreline edges in late spring. These flowers are favorites of butterflies, like the black swallowtail shown here.

ther downriver, thus establishing a new river "fence."

Associates: Look for buttonbush among shoreline alders and willows, two of its most frequent shrub associates. Cattails and red-osier dogwood are other common companions. Water moss *(Dichelyma)* can often be found encircling the stem bases.

Spring, summer. Long-tongued insects—mainly bumblebees *(Bombus)* and butterflies—are the chief pollinators, for they can best reach the deep nectaries. Indeed, a flowering buttonbush is one of the best places to look for various butterfly species. Two skippers especially favor the flowers: the black dash *(Atrytone conspicua)* and the golden-banded skipper *(Autochton cellus)*, the latter more common in southern states.

Distinctive ball-shaped seed heads of buttonbush probably account for this plant's name. Strange alignments sometimes occur, as shown by this "satellite" seed head stemming from the base of a larger one.

Tiger swallowtail butterflies *(Papilio glaucus)* and black swallowtails *(P. polyxenes)* are also frequent visitors.

Many other insects, such as bees, flies, wasps, and beetles, also come to the fragrant flowers, and their movements among the flower heads likewise aid pollination. Most buttonbushes fruit heavily, mute testimony to summer's abundant insect activity.

Feeding on the foliage, a large, smooth-skinned caterpillar with a projecting rear horn may be a hydrangea sphinx moth *(Darapsa versicolor)*. The beautiful wood-nymph (the common name of *Eudryas grata*) is a noctuid moth; at rest the adult moths resemble bird droppings. Smartweed caterpillars *(Acronicta oblinita)*, also noctuids, feed on buttonbush as well as many other plants; the adult insects are known as smeared dagger moths. Promethea moth caterpillars *(Callosamia promethea)* also feed on the foliage.

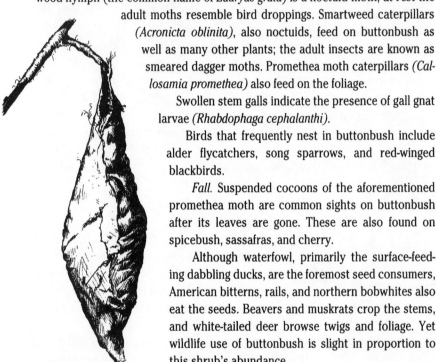

Swollen stem galls indicate the presence of gall gnat larvae *(Rhabdophaga cephalanthi)*.

Birds that frequently nest in buttonbush include alder flycatchers, song sparrows, and red-winged blackbirds.

Fall. Suspended cocoons of the aforementioned promethea moth are common sights on buttonbush after its leaves are gone. These are also found on spicebush, sassafras, and cherry.

Although waterfowl, primarily the surface-feeding dabbling ducks, are the foremost seed consumers, American bitterns, rails, and northern bobwhites also eat the seeds. Beavers and muskrats crop the stems, and white-tailed deer browse twigs and foliage. Yet wildlife use of buttonbush is slight in proportion to this shrub's abundance.

Promethea cocoons, often found attached to buttonbush branches in winter, release the large adult moths in spring. These cocoons are also commonly seen on cherries, spicebush, and several other shrubs and trees.

Lore: Roots and bark of buttonbush were well-known medicinal ingredients for various ailments among Native Americans and pioneers. The tannic properties provided bitter tonics, astringents, and washes for inflammation. Taken internally, the teas were said to promote sweating, relieve coughs and kidney stones, and check menstrual flow. Resembling in appearance its South American relative cinchona, the source of quinine, buttonbush likewise achieved a folk reputation for relieving fevers and malaria (a common disease that northeastern U.S. pioneers called "ague"). Self-dosage is, however, ill-advised. The plant contains powerful glucosides (cephalanthin and cephalin), and the foliage has been known to poison livestock.

Buttonbush is occasionally cultivated as a yard ornamental, especially for low, wet spots.

Calla, Wild *(Calla palustris)*. Arum family. Herb in shallow water, swamps, on pond and bog edges. Identify wild calla by its golden, club-shaped flower head *(spadix)* clasped by a white bract *(spathe)* and its broad, heart-shaped leaves.

Other names. Water-arum, bog-arum, arum lily, swamp robin, female dragon, water dragon, marsh calla.

Close relatives: Skunk-cabbage *(Symplocarpus foetidus)*; arrow-arum *(Peltandra virginica)*; Jack-in-the-pulpit *(Arisaema triphyllum)*; calla lily *(Zantedeschia aethiopica)*; philodendrons *(Philodendron)*.

Lifestyle: All of the arums have tiny flowers crowded on a blunt, vertical "club" sheathed or hooded by a modified leaf. This leaf in wild calla is petallike and white with somewhat rolled edges. Calla's yellow florets are mostly bisexual, but a cluster of exclusively male florets often crowns the spadix. The flowers are somewhat ill-scented. In late summer, the plant becomes more conspicuous with its terminal cluster of bright red berries replacing the spadix.

Wild calla often grows in small or large colonies, reproducing vegetatively from flattish green rhizomes as well as by seed.

Associates: A good place to look for wild calla is on margins of the mineral-rich *laggs* (moats), which often surround sphagnum bogs. The plants are also quite common in alder swamps.

Spring, summer. Pollination is mainly accomplished by midges and other small flies attracted

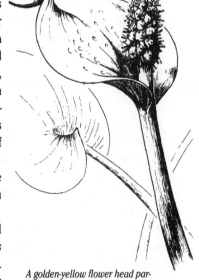

A golden-yellow flower head partially enclosed by a white spathe makes wild calla distinctive in spring and summer. Note the tiny male flowers crowding the top of the spadix.

to the plant by its white flag and fetid odor. (Such insects "lack esthetic taste," opined one early botanist.)

Pond snails *(Lymnaea)* and other aquatic snails also pick up, carry, and deposit pollen as they glide over the floret surfaces.

Little information exists on this plant's value as wildlife food, but it cannot be large. Muskrats eat the rhizomes sparingly.

A close European relative, the cuckoopint or lords-and-ladies *(Arum maculatum)*, was believed to poison birds that consumed the fruits, with the bird's decaying body providing a rich seedbed for the plant.

Lore: Most arum fruits will severely burn your mouth if you taste them. Wild calla's attractive berries—the entire plant, in fact— contain calcium oxalate crystals, which are extremely acrid and irritating to mucous membranes. Crushed berries will also burn and irritate the skin. Thorough drying removes this acrid property, and the dried seeds and rhizomes can be ground to make a nutritious, if not very tasty, flour. The Lapps in northern Europe, however, made a palatable bread (missebroed) of it.

The forest Potawatomi used the pounded root of wild calla as an effective poultice for swellings. Other tribes made a medicinal tea-tonic from the dried rhizome.

In England, the rhizomes of *A. maculatum* provided the source of white starch used to stiffen those huge ruffled collars seen in Elizabethan portraits. Cuckoopint, its common name, was a literal Anglo-Saxon expression for "lively penis," probably derived from the phallic shape of the spadix.

Cardinal-flower *(Lobelia cardinalis)*. Lobelia family. Herb in wet soil, along stream and pond margins. Its spike of large, brilliantly scarlet flowers in summer makes cardinal-flower impossible to misidentify.

Other names: Red lobelia, slinkweed.

Close relatives: Great lobelia *(Lobelia siphilitica)*; bellflowers *(Campanula)*.

Lifestyle: "It is not so much something colored as it is color itself," wrote naturalist John Burroughs. Cardinal-flower probably shows the reddest red of any American wildflower. Though not a rare plant, it is hardly abundant even in prime habitats.

Except for flower color, it closely resembles the great (blue) lobelia, which grows in similar habitats. The color difference between these close relatives probably stems from their very unalike pollinators, which may also explain the cardinal-flower's lack of a landing platform for insects.

Examining a cardinal-flower closely reveals its conspicuous sexual part: a red tube projecting above the brilliant petals. The petals are gaudy flags for attracting ruby-throated hummingbirds, the flower's chief pollinators. This sexual tube is at first "male," displaying pollen-bearing stamens at the tube tip. As the stamens decline, the sticky, Y-shaped pistils extend from the tube, which is now "female" and ready to receive pollen from a cardinal-flower still in the pollen stage. This type of sex-sequential flower development is called *protandry*. The sequencing proceeds from the bottom to the top of a flower spike. Thus a single plant may show flowers in both stages of development, plus new flower buds at the top and developing fruits below. The flowers grow somewhat one-sided on the spike.

Hummingbirds pollinate the plant by brushing their foreheads against the tube tip as they plunge their needlelike bills into the "flag tube" below, where the nectaries are located. They do all this on the wing, so the flower needs no landing platform for its pollinator partner.

The dry fruit capsules split open in the fall, spilling hundreds of small seeds, which are dispersed by wind and water. The plant dies back to clusters of green, basal rosettes of leaves lasting all winter. From these arise the single flower stalks in late spring.

Cardinal-flowers often occur in sparse, patchy colonies, frequently in light shade, which may partially account for their brilliance. An occasional plant with pink or white flowers also occurs.

Associates: *Summer.* I have often found cardinal-flowers in the company of boneset, though the latter is a much more common wildflower.

Without ruby-throated hummingbirds, their main pollinators, cardinal-flowers would surely be far fewer than they already are. Cardinal-flower abundance not only depends upon hummingbirds but also reflects, to some extent, their own abundance. These unique birds, no bigger than large moths, are attracted to red; cardinal-flower patches are excellent places to watch for them and to listen for their buzzing wings. A hummingbird usually begins foraging in the middle of a flower spike and works its way upward. The male flower stage always produces the most nectar, so the bird spends most time where the flowers are youngest—the top half of the spike. The ongoing loss of wetlands, which is probably indirectly responsible for the decreasing trend in hummingbird populations, gives a double whammy to the cardinal-flower.

Bumblebees *(Bombus)* occasionally pollinate the flowers, as do the pollen-collecting andrenid bees, such as *Augochlora pura,* and halictids, including *Halic-*

tus connexus. Cardinal-flower is imperfectly designed to prevent nectar robbery. Small bees, often unable to reach the nectar, find the slits in the upper corolla tube, enabling them to bypass the flower's regular entry.

Narrow, winding mines in the leaves are created by several *Agromyza* species, the larvae of tiny leaf-miner flies.

Cardinal-flower is not abundant enough to provide any significant food for birds or mammals.

Lore: "Thy sins shall be as scarlet. Is it my sins that I see?" pondered Thoreau as he viewed these flowers, which also reminded him of "red men, war, and bloodshed." But he could not resist plucking them; they grew by the thousands in the Concord ditches. Since his day, however, the wild plant has drastically declined in occurrence, owing to a century of industrious conversion of wetland habitats to "productivity." Today, cardinal-flower is a legally protected species and should never be picked or removed from the wild. It can be obtained from seed suppliers by those who want to attract hummingbirds to the garden.

Native Americans used root and leaf teas of cardinal-flower as remedies for stomachache, fever, headache, and colds. The teas were believed to expel worms, soothe the nerves, and cure syphilis and typhoid fever to boot. Some tribes used the dried, ground-up plant as a ceremonial powder to dispel storms, to strew into graves, and to mix into love potions. The plant, however, contains potentially toxic pyridine alkaloids similar to nicotine (lobeline is one). New England farmers believed that cows miscarried from eating the plant, and some people are allergic to the sap on their skin. If you're not a shaman (and even if you are), leave it alone.

The plant's common name refers to the flower's long corolla tube, which is peaked like a cardinal's miter, memorializing or ridiculing those red-hatted princes of the church. If French-Canadian explorers had not sent the plant back to Catholic France for inspection, we might now know it by another name. But another tale attributes the name to Henrietta Maria, queen of England's Protestant Charles I, who "laughed excessively" on first seeing the imported plant because it reminded her of a "cardinal's scarlet stockings."

Cattails *(Typha* spp.). Cattail family. Tall, emergent herbs in marshes, swamps, ditches. Long, erect, bladelike leaves and characteristic sausagelike flower heads identify the cattails.Two species are most common: common or broad-leaved cattail *(T. latifolia)* and narrow-leaved cattail *(T. angustifolia).* Common cattail usually lacks a gap between the topmost male flower head and the female section below; narrow-leaved cattail shows a bare-stemmed gap between the two. Differing width of leaves, as indicated by their names, also separates the species. *T. latifolia* has a fan-shaped plant base, and *T. angustifolia* often shows a round or cylindrical base.

Other names: Flag, cat-o-nine-tails, marsh beetle, bulrush (a misnomer; bulrushes are *Scirpus*), great reed-mace (England), candlewick, cossack asparagus.

Lifestyle: Cattails are among our foremost wetland plants, in terms of both their abundance and their ecological importance as the dominant vegetation in many marshes. Pure stands of cattail often form dense "forests" across marshland expanses. Cattail "islands" cover low, wet spots, and they typically rim the margins of ponds and streams. Constant requirements seem to be fairly mineral-rich waters, flowing surface or ground waters, and relatively stable water levels.

Both cattail species may grow together in wide zones of habitat overlap, sometimes producing hybrids *(T. x glauca)*, which can confuse identification. Each species has its own niche preference, however. *T. latifolia* is generally less tolerant of pollution and disturbance but has a wider tolerance of soil acidity; it thrives best in water depths of six inches to two feet. *T. angustifolia* better tolerates polluted or overfertilized waters but is not so colonially aggressive as the other; it favors highly alkaline soils and deeper water (up to three feet or more), though its growth often spans the entire depth gradient.

Cattails clone from creeping rhizomes. Tiny new shoots appear on rhizomes in the fall, remain dormant through winter, and then rise with the first warm days of spring. Colonies generally establish themselves inshore and migrate outward in the shallows (a growth pattern sometimes called a "phalanx strategy"). In pure stands, the clones become closely intermixed so that, without digging up the rhizomes, it is impossible to differentiate separate clones. Colonies grow and maintain themselves mainly by vegetative reproduction; the spread of a colony by this means measured seventeen feet in one year at Lake Erie. Colonial density actually inhibits cattail seedling germination and growth.

Yet these plants produce prolific seed (an estimated average of 220,000 seeds per spike), which mainly serves to disperse the plant to noncolonized areas. (A quick experiment, one that Thoreau delighted to perform, demonstrates how tightly the dry seeds are packed in the spike: Pull out a small tuft and watch it immediately expand to fill your hand with a downy mass.) In places where seeds can germinate, the first flowering generally occurs in the second year of a new rhizome's life. According to one researcher, growth from one seed in a single season may produce a rhizome system ten feet in diameter that sends up one hundred clonal shoots.

A cattail marsh in spring is a place of "yellow smokes," as the powdery, sulfurlike pollen sheds in clouds from the topmost (male) flower spikes. Although the lower (female) spike tends to mature and be pollen-receptive before pollen is produced on the same plant, in actual fact these timings overlap. Thus most cattails are partially or entirely self-fertilized as their own pollen sheds from above. (Experiments reveal that seed develops at a 50 percent success rate from completely "selfed" cattail flowers).

The male flower spike soon dies and drops off, leaving the brown "sausage" (the female seed spike) that gradually dries and falls apart, seed clumps scattering to the wind. Featherlike plumes of tiny brown hairs attached to each seed aid in this dispersal. On the seed spike, these outer hairs comprise the spike's brown, feltlike surface.

The long leaf's internal anatomy accounts for its firm yet flexible rigidity. A cross section reveals a framework of horizontal struts and partitions, not unlike the interior of an airplane wing. These prevent the vertical leaf from falling over.

Associates: *Spring, summer.* Some stands of cattail admit few plant associates, owing to their dense growth, shading of smaller plants, and possible allelopathic (toxic) secretions, which may inhibit other plant growth. Except for dominant cattail itself, cattail stands are mainly zoological communities, hosting and supporting many types of animal life. In botanical jargon, they remain "lacking in floristic complexity."

More open cattail stands, however, display a variety of undergrowth, such as marsh fern and sedges. One inconspicuous plant often found in cattail marshes is the ivy-leaved, or star, duckweed *(Lemna trisulca)*; it hangs suspended in zigzag chains just beneath the water surface.

Inspecting the cattail leaves, you may begin to gain some idea of this community's populace. One conspicuous resident is not a leaf feeder but a spider *(Clubiona riparia)* that uses the leaf tip for both nursery and coffin. This sac spider folds down the leaf tip to make an enclosure fastened and lined with silk, a small, triangular "box" at the very top of the leaf. Inside the enclosure it deposits its egg sac and simply remains there, dying inside its cage. The first meal of its young will be the mother's body (the ultimate in maternal sacrifice), after which the young escape through the deteriorating chamber.

Sap-sucking leaf feeders include about a dozen species of aphids, some of which have alternate plant hosts.

Larvae of several moth species mine the leaves. The cattail borer moth *(Bellura obliqua)* mines downward in the leaf, eating out the transverse partitions and finally exiting through a hole at the end of its mine. In a later stage, it bores into the stem. Other related species that do the same include the white-tailed diver *(B. gortynoides)*, the pickerelweed borer *(B. densa)*, and the oblong sedge borer *(Archanara oblonga)*. These are all noctuid moths, as is the smeared dagger moth, also called smartweed caterpillar *(Acronicta oblinita)*, which feeds on the leaves.

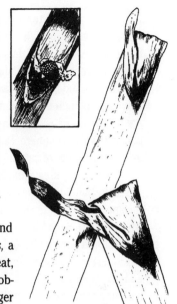

Some insects feed only on and in the flower and seed spikes. Larvae include *Dicymolomia julianalis,* a pyralid moth, which later bores into the stem. A neat, bite-sized chunk eaten from a brown seed spike probably indicates the presence of a white-veined dagger moth caterpillar, also called Henry's marsh moth *(Simyra henrici)*; later the tufted caterpillar makes a vertically aligned cocoon in a folded leaf. I have seen a species of syrphid fly *(Platycheirus)* clustering head downward on the male flower spike in early spring;

*Folded-over leaf tips of cattail tied down with silk are **Clubiona** spider nurseries. The female spider lays eggs, then dies in the enclosure (inset), providing food for the spiderlings.*

these are aphid eaters. In July and August, watch for small, brownish adult cattail moths *(Limnaecia phragmitella,* also called the shy cosmet, a cosmopterygid) laying eggs on the maturing female seed spikes. Nymphs of a seed bug *(Kleidocerys)* may often be found in dry seed spikes that have remained on the plant through the winter.

A dying cattail stem may signify the presence of a stalk borer, usually one of the aforementioned moth species that fed in the leaves or seed spike. Other common borers include snout beetles such as *Sphenophorus pertinax,* a billbug; and *Suphisellus puncticollis,* a burrowing water beetle.

The cattail mosquito *(Coquillettidia perturbans)*, one of the most abundant mosquitoes in midsummer, is the chief vector of eastern equine encephalitis, often fatal to humans. The larvae attach to the roots and rhizomes of cattail, as well as other aquatic plants, where they overwinter. Adult mosquitoes obtain the disease virus from birds, which are not affected by it, and transmit the virus by biting horses and people.

Vertebrate coactions with cattails are numerous, ranging from fishes to mammals. Bottom-feeding fish, especially carp, have been observed rooting at the bases of cattail clumps, thus separating the clump and possibly aiding the plant's vegetative reproduction. Painted turtles eat cattail seeds and stems.

For wetland birds, cattails provide nesting cover and materials. Among birds that suspend their nests amid the dense stalks and leaves, the three most common are marsh wrens, swamp sparrows, and red-winged blackbirds. Yellow-headed blackbirds also nest here. Ducks and other waterfowl marsh dwellers tend to nest in the outer edges of cattail growth rather than amidst the dense cover.

Dead cattail stems and leaves (the previous year's standing growth) provide the main building materials for many marshland dwellers. Most wetland birds that nest at water level or build platform nests use cattail materials either in whole or part. Such birds include grebes, least bitterns, mute swans, many ducks, Virginia and sora rails, and American coots. Blue-winged teal and black terns often nest atop inactive muskrat lodges, which mainly consist of cattail leaves and stems (beaver lodges are usually much larger, constructed of woody stems and branches). Eastern goldfinches often use cattail down for nest lining.

Floating fragments of cattail stems and leaves are often signs of muskrat activity. Starchy cattail rhizomes are the dominant food items for these marshland vegetarians, which dive to retrieve them from the mud at any time of year. They also eat the green stems, preferring the juicy pith or core. Any sizable cattail area is almost certain to host muskrats; these animals sometimes provide a significant control on cattail populations. Where sufficient numbers of muskrat exist, look for signs of its chief predator, the mink. This animal dens along stream or marshland banks (often under tree roots) or in deserted beaver or muskrat lodges.

Cattail rhizomes also provide food for beavers and, occasionally, geese.

Late summer, fall, winter. Large, vertically aligned orb webs of common shamrock spiders *(Aranea trifolium)* and orange-banded argiopes *(Argiope aurantia,* also called orange garden spiders) become especially common among the cattails in late summer and fall.

Ragged or unkempt cattail spikes that remain on the stem into the following spring are common sights in any cattail patch. These frayed-out spikes hang on for a reason—they have been threaded throughout with silken, almost invisible, webbing "tied" into place. The tiers are caterpillars of the aforementioned cattail moth *(Limnaecia phragmitella),* which feed on the seeds over winter and, in spring, make cocoons in the dry fluff or in the stems. You can find these caterpillars active inside the seed spike—sometimes only a few, sometimes fifty or more—on the

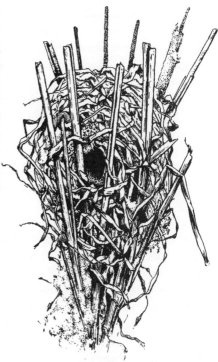

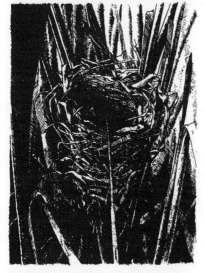

Dense cattail vegetation is favored nesting cover for many birds. American coots build platform nests (top left) just above the water surface. Marsh wren nests (top right) are dry, globular wads of plant material attached to the stems; the side entrance hole is often barely visible. Red-winged blackbirds construct suspended nests (bottom) several feet above the soil or water surface.

coldest days of winter, well insulated inside the downy mass. With practice, one can easily distinguish the moth-infested spikes from those spikes that are disintegrating naturally. Moth-infested spikes fluff out and generally "droop" from the stem, sagging like unkempt haymows; they look much grayer, more weatherbeaten, than the uninfested spikes. The aforementioned *Dicymolomia* pyralid moth also webs the seed spikes.

Birds observed feeding on cattail heads during these colder seasons—including black-capped chickadees and red-winged blackbirds, among others—are usually feeding on the moth caterpillars, not the seeds, which are too tiny and hairy to provide much food value. Food is often scarce for early spring migrants such as blackbirds; the cattail moth larvae may provide important protein for these early arrivals and for winter-resident birds as well.

Another type of coaction between the moths and the birds may also occur. One February day in a cattail marsh I found solitary corn grains stashed inside several of the moth-infested spikes I pulled apart; they were evidently bird (probably blue jay) caches. The spikes, held together by the caterpillar silk, provide a dry, long-lasting repository for food items cached by winter-resident birds. If you see a bird "feeding" on a cattail spike, observe closely: Is it delving for caterpillars or their cocoons? Or is it depositing or retrieving a food cache?

Mixed flocks of blackbirds and starlings often gather in dense communal roosts in summer and fall, frequently in cattail marshes. One study suggested that these flocks transport large quantities of nitrogen and phosphorous into the stands through the nutrients in bird excreta.

Lore: Some part of this plant is edible and nourishing at every season. In early spring, peeled, white cores of the young shoots and flower stalks can be eaten raw or boiled like asparagus. Later in spring the green, immature flower spikes can be boiled and eaten like corn on the cob. Later still, the prolific yellow pollen can be shaken from the male spikes and used as a protein-rich flour, usually mixed with wheat flour. Late-summer sprouts at the rootstock tips and the rhizome itself—which may contain up to 30 percent sugar and starch—provide excellent survival foods in fall, winter, and early spring. The food value of cattail is said to almost equal that of corn or rice.

Cattails rank with the peanut in number of their potentially commercial uses. Flour and cornstarch from the rhizomes, ethyl alcohol from the fermented flour, burlap and caulking from rhizome fibers, adhesive from the stems, insulation from the downy spikes, oil from the seeds, rayon from cattail pulp, and processed waste for chicken feed—these are only a few of the many products derived from the plants. The mature leaves, though inedible and possibly poisonous to livestock, have been used for paper pulp, matting, thatching, and chair caning.

Native peoples used the crushed rhizomes for poultices and cattail down for bandaging and mattress, pillow, and moccasin stuffing. The Chippewas bound and trimmed the leaves to make dolls and floating toy ducks for their children.

With cattails present, one need not starve, freeze, remain untreated for injury, or want for playthings.

Cedar, Northern White *(Thuja occidentalis).* Cypress family. Tree in swamps, wetland forests, also in dry limestone soils, uplands. Its flat, aromatic, scalelike leaves; shreddy, fibrous bark; and small, bell-shaped cones identify this conifer.

Other names: Arborvitae, canoewood.

Close relatives: Atlantic white cedar *(Chamaecyparis thyoides)*; junipers *(Juniperus).*

Lifestyle: This tree's two widely differing habitats—swamps and dry, calcareous uplands—have led some botanists to propose two genetic races (see *The Book of Forest and Thicket).* The trees are biologically similar in both habitats; soil chemistry (pH 7 and above) seems a more important factor for growth than amount of moisture. But the two different habitats result in different ecological associations. We focus here on the swamp cedars, one of the three dominant conifer species in northeastern wetlands (black spruce and tamarack are the others).

The presence of white cedar always indicates alkaline or basic soil environments. Because of its high-calcium favoritism, it is known as a *calciphile.* Stands of white cedar often develop from rich fen peatlands where moving surface or ground waters supply a steady flow of nutrients. White cedar is seldom found in acid bogs or black spruce muskegs (though black spruce trees may sometimes grow in a cedar swamp). Thus it often forms the terminal stage of plant succession in high-nutrient wetlands (as opposed to low-nutrient, acid wetlands where black spruce becomes the dominant tree).

In cedar swamps the trees may grow in pure stands of almost impenetrable density. This is a result of two common methods of vegetative reproduction: Layering occurs when lower branches become buried and produce vertical sprouts; tipping yields vertical branches arising from the buried trunk of a fallen tree, forming a straight row of trees along its length.

Tiny yellow male and bigger purplish female cones appear on the same tree in spring. Wind pollinates the erect female cones. Each cone scale releases two winged seeds in the fall. The cones hang empty on the tree through winter. Seed production begins at ten to fifteen years, and a tree will produce ample seed crops every three to five years.

White cedar thrives best in dense shade, but even in the best of conditions it grows slowly. An inch of trunk diameter is typically the work of ten to twenty summers. Though relatively short-lived, it may sometimes survive up to three hundred years. The root system is shallow and spreading, making the tree vulnerable to wind-throw. Its thin bark also makes fire an often fatal event.

Cedar trees often reproduce by sprouting from tipped-over trunks that become buried. Here, a horizontal trunk rests on an ancient cedar stump—possibly its own progenitor.

Close inspection of the leaves reveals tiny resin glands on the undersides, the source of cedar's aroma. Northern white cedar holds its leaves for two to five years.

Associates: Though often growing in extensive pure stands, northern white cedar also associates with balsam fir, speckled alder, black ash, red maple, and tamarack, among others. This tree is the only northeastern conifer that apparently lacks the symbiotic root-fungus association called *mycorrhiza*.

Spring, summer. Cedar swamps, though often hard traveling because of the dense growth and treacherous footing, host a large variety of plants, some of which are rarely found elsewhere.

Several calcium-tolerant species of *Sphagnum* moss often grow in cedar swamps, including *S. centrale, S. wulfianum, S. warnstorfii, S. girgensohnii, S. squarosum, S. fimbriatum*, and *S. russowii.* The flat thalluses of leafy liverworts often grow on the damp, exposed roots extending from cedar tree bases. Also look for patches of dwarf and wood horsetails. Ferns in cedar swamp habitats may include spinulose woodfern and oak fern. I have also seen large patches of bulblet fern growing in such areas.

Cedar swamps are also prime orchid habitat. Some of the likeliest species to look for include early or northern coral-root, ram's-head and yellow lady-slippers, tall northern bog orchid, blunt-leaf orchid, large round-leaved orchid, the calypso or fairy slipper (seldom found apart from white cedar), creeping or lesser rattlesnake plantain, broad-leaved and heartleaf twayblades, and white adder's-mouth.

Certain other flowers are more common in cedar swamp forests. These include starflower, goldthread, twinflower, naked miterwort, clintonia, creeping snowberry, and pyrolas, among others.

Insect species that feed on cedar foliage are fairly numerous, and signs of their presence are often conspicuous. Distorted branch tips are signs of tipdwarf mites *(Calipiterimerus thujae)*, which become most active in cool, humid weather.

Other foliage feeders include the cranberry spanworm caterpillar, an inchworm moth (see Cranberries); and the greenish, caterpillarlike larvae of arborvitae sawflies*(Monoctenus)*.

Dead twigs among green foliage and holes chewed in twig crotches are signs of the northern cedar bark beetle *(Phloeosinus canadensis)*. On barkless cedar logs, look for this engraver beetle's vertical galleries, from which horizontal galleries of the larval beetles wing out on either side.

In their northern range, black-backed woodpeckers often excavate nesting cavities in living or dead cedars. Swainson's thrushes and red squirrels often use strips of the fibrous bark for their nests.

Fall, winter. Mushrooms fruiting in cedar swamps include the depressed hedgehog *(Hydnum umbilicatum)*, orange-red with hanging "teeth" on the underside of the cap; and the orange-ring milkcap *(Lactarius thyinos)*, slimy orange-yellow, exuding an orange latex when cut or broken.

Several species of tiny moth caterpillars mine in the leaves. The commonest are the arborvitae leafminer *(Argyresthia thuiella)*, an ermine moth; and *Pulicalvaria thujaella,* a gelechiid moth. The larvae hatch in summer and feed in the leaf during the fall, causing brownish mines. They remain there over the winter and finally emerge as adult moths the following summer. Chalcid wasps (Chalcididae) often parasitize these miners.

Pendant, spindle-shaped bags of tough silk two inches in length and covered with cedar leaves and twigs indicate this tree's foremost insect pest, the evergreen bagworm *(Thyridopteryx ephemeraeformis)*. This psychid moth caterpillar feeds on the foliage, moving about and gradually enlarging its bag. Males become black, winged moths, but females never leave their bags, mating through an opening at the base of the bag and laying eggs therein. The caterpillars feed throughout spring and summer, but the attached bags containing overwintering eggs are most conspicuous in later seasons, when yellow-bellied sapsuckers and other woodpeckers often feed on them.

Also numerous and most obvious in early fall are the aforementioned leafmining insects.

Among seed-eating birds, pine siskins are frequent, and the seed cones are also clipped by red squirrels.

Snowshoe hares relish the foliage of low cedar branches in northern areas. The hares may deplete young cedar growth during cyclical population highs.

Cedar foliage ranks as the most important and preferred winter food for white-tailed deer. For moose, however, it is nonnourishing "starvation food," consumed only as a last resort. Most winter deer browsing occurs in dense cedar swamps, where the deer yard up (congregate) for shelter during periods of heavy snow cover. Flat-bottomed browse lines on cedar trees, where the animals have browsed as high as they can reach, are familiar sights in cedar swamp forests. Overpopulations of deer may result in gradually declining stands of cedar; the deer quickly crop sprouts and seedlings, leaving nothing to regenerate.

All year. A common crustlike growth on the trunks in cedar swamps is the spreading leather lichen *(Sticta amplissima)*, a flat, gray-green rosette with a smooth or wrinkled upper surface and wavy-edged extensions.

Fungous infections cause much heartwood decay in this species. Two signs of it are prominent on trunks of living trees: bracket-type conks and deep excavations by woodpeckers. Balsam butt rot, also called brown cubical rot *(Polyporus balsameus)*, produces tough, woody "shelves" low on the trunk, weakening the tree and making it vulnerable to wind-throw.

Another common excavation in living trees consists of honeycomb galleries that riddle the heartwood, leaving it partially exposed at the trunk base. These galleries are hollowed by black carpenter ants *(Camponotus pennsylvanicus)*, efficient wood destroyers that enter the tree through a wound or rotted area.

Carpenter ants attract pileated woodpeckers, which often feed in cedar swamps. They excavate characteristic oblong holes in the trees to get at the heartwood ant galleries.

Lore. The name *cedar* is a stolen misnomer for this tree. Northern white cedar is actually a cypress, a relative neither of the true cedars *(Cedrus)* of Eurasia nor of the famed cedars of Lebanon *(C. libani)*.

An even-bottomed cedar browse line indicates winter feeding by white-tailed deer, which crop foliage as high as they can reach. Northern white cedar provides favored, highly nourishing food for deer.

Its other common name—arborvitae, meaning "tree of life"—has better credentials. For this tree (or perhaps black spruce, nobody knows for sure) proved exactly that to the men of Jacques Cartier's Canadian exploring expedition of 1535. Suffering from scurvy, they drank a tea brewed from the leaves of an ever-green tree, and their symptoms disappeared.

The brownish, tealike color of many north-ern lakes and rivers results in large part from tan-nins leached by decaying cedar roots and trees.

Native Americans used cedar teas and poul-tices for ailments ranging from headache and rheumatism to burns. The leaf oil has antiseptic and expectorant properties but is a toxic heart stimulant in any pure quantity; the active ingredi-ent is thujone. Oil extracts have shown antiviral effects against venereal warts.

Northern white cedar and white birch were the two most sacred trees to the Chippewa peo-ples. Both bore important mystical connections to their teacher-deity-trickster figure Winabojo, who wore cedar as a head ornament because of its beauty. American natives used this tree pri-marily for birchbark canoe frames and ribs. It split easily, didn't shrink or warp, and separated along its annual growth rings when log ends were pounded (a feature known as *ring shake* or *wind shake,* making cedar undesirable for many mod-ern construction purposes).

Carpenter ants often riddle dead portions of cedar trees with honey-comb galleries. Usually such exca-vation begins only after the wood has already been infected or killed by heartwood fungus.

Because of its durability in contact with soil and moisture, cedar proves an ideal wood for posts, shingles, fishing floats and lures, telephone poles, railroad ties—and, still, canoes.

Chokeberries (*Aronia* spp.). Rose family. Thicket-forming shrubs in bogs, swamps, wet woods, occasionally in dry uplands. Identify chokeberries by their small-toothed leaves showing a row of tiny glands along the upper midrib; their compound clusters of small, white flowers in spring; and their small, applelike fruits in the fall.

Two or three species exist, depending on the classifier. Red chokeberry (*A. arbutifolia*) bears bright red fruit and leaves in the fall; black chokeberry (*A. melanocarpa*) bears black fruit and lustrous leaves that do not turn red; and purple chokeberry *(A. floribunda),* possibly a hybrid or variety of either of the fore-going species, bears purplish-black fruits and intermediate characteristics. Although black chokeberry grows farther north and east, all of the chokeberries overlap in large parts of their ranges. Black and purple chokeberries are somewhat more tolerant of dry and mesic habitats. Some botanists lump all the chokeberries in the genus *Pyrus* (the apples) because of their close similarities; others, for the same reason, include them in *Sorbus* (the mountain-ashes), with which they occasionally hybridize.

Other names: Choke-pear, dogberry. Chokeberry should not be confused with chokecherry *(Prunus virginiana).*

Close relatives: Apples *(Pyrus);* mountain-ashes *(Sorbus);* cherries *(Prunus);* hawthorns *(Crataegus);* roses *(Rosa);* avens *(Geum);* cinquefoils *(Potentilla);* spiraeas *(Spiraea).*

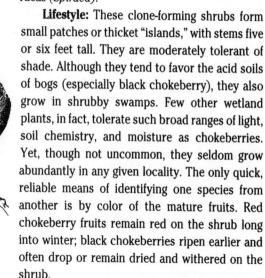

Lifestyle: These clone-forming shrubs form small patches or thicket "islands," with stems five or six feet tall. They are moderately tolerant of shade. Although they tend to favor the acid soils of bogs (especially black chokeberry), they also grow in shrubby swamps. Few other wetland plants, in fact, tolerate such broad ranges of light, soil chemistry, and moisture as chokeberries. Yet, though not uncommon, they seldom grow abundantly in any given locality. The only quick, reliable means of identifying one species from another is by color of the mature fruits. Red chokeberry fruits remain red on the shrub long into winter; black chokeberries ripen earlier and often drop or remain dried and withered on the shrub.

The white flowers are bisexual and insect pollinated, though self-pollination also occurs. The fruit is not actually a berry (like blueberry), but is rather a pome (like apple).

Chokeberry, adaptable to many environments, presents problems for plant classifiers. Leaf midribs (inset) bear tiny glands, which are visible close-up, providing a good identity mark.

Associates: Look for chokeberry in the shrub-carr of coniferous or hardwood swamps. Shrub associates may include red-osier dogwood, poison sumac, mountain-holly, and highbush blueberry.

Gray dogwood is a common associate in dryer patches. Tamarack, pin oak, and swamp white oak are among the trees often found as chokeberry neighbors.

Spring, summer. The flowers are pollinated by many types of insects, including gall gnats (Cecidomyiidae). Probably the foremost pollinators are small, ground-nesting andrenid bees, such as *Andrena* and *Panurginus,* and bumblebees *(Bombus).*

Small capsulelike or pouchlike galls on the leaves are the nursery feeding chambers of tiny mites *(Eriophyes).* Caterpillars of the praeclara underwing *(Catocala praeclara),* a noctuid moth, feed on the foliage; these caterpillars tend to be plumpest in the middle, tapering toward both ends.

White-tailed deer consume chokeberry twigs and foliage to some extent.

Fall, winter. The fruits, though eaten by several birds and mammals, do not rank as major wildlife foods. Ruffed and sharp-tailed grouse, ring-necked pheasants, black-capped chickadees, and cedar waxwings consume them, as do black bears, red foxes, cottontail rabbits, fox squirrels, and white-footed mice.

Lore: The chokeberries, so puzzling to taxonomists, provide a useful reminder: The system of pigeonholing organisms into genera and species is basically artificial. Constructed by humans to serve the beholder's convenience, it is a scheme we apply to a continuum, rather than an absolute order or pattern inherent in nature. Most of the time this scheme proves useful because it may outline and clarify some actual biological boundaries. But exceptions to these rules abound, the more so the closer we look. Chokeberries remind us that scientific taxonomy is only the least imperfect of the tools we have fashioned to help us classify and understand organisms.

Chokeberry fruits, though sweetish, are dry and astringent. They can be edible if correctly prepared, as for sauce or jelly.

Red chokeberry is sometimes used for landscape plantings because of its attractive reds in autumn and winter.

Cinquefoils *(Potentilla* spp.) Rose family. Herbs and shrubs in various wet, mesic, and dry habitats. This genus includes many flowering herbs, but both wetland species are low, woody shrubs.

Marsh cinquefoil *(P. palustris)* has a sprawling stem and maroon flowers. Shrubby cinquefoil *(P. fruticosa)* grows in dense, hip-high thickets, displaying shreddy bark and yellow flowers in summer and fall. Both cinquefoils show the characteristic five-to-seven-fingered compound leaves of this genus.

Other names: Five-finger (all cinquefoils); purple cinquefoil, purple marsh locks, cowberry, purplewort, meadownuts, bog strawberry *(P. palustris)*; prairie weed, bush cinquefoil *(P. fruticosa)*.

Close relatives: Strawberries *(Fragaria)*; avens *(Geum)*; spiraeas *(Spiraea)*; roses *(Rosa)*; cherries *(Prunus)*; apples *(Pyrus)*; chokeberries *(Aronia)*; mountain-ashes *(Sorbus)*; hawthorns *(Crataegus)*.

Lifestyles: Both wetland cinquefoils favor mineral-rich swamps and fens; don't look for them in bogs. Both species also flower at about the same time, but marsh cinquefoil is lower, more solitary and inconspicuous. It often occupies wetter ground than the bushy and colonial shrubby cinquefoil, which seems to prefer higher and drier portions of fens.

Both species have bisexual, insect-pollinated flowers that may also self-pollinate if no insect lands at the right time. Marsh cinquefoil flowers share certain characteristics with such unrelated white-flowered species as anemones and flowering dogwood: The conspicuous color resides not in the flower petals (which, in marsh cinquefoil, are small and pointed), but in the larger, underlying sepals or bracts. This arrangement does not occur in most other cinquefoils.

Shrubby cinquefoil is also unusual. It is one of the few woody plants that begins flowering in summer and continues to do so into late fall. From June or July onward all stages of floral development are visible on the plant as individual flowers open, mature, and set seed. Flowering, especially in woody plants, requires a huge energy expenditure, good nutrition, and ample resting periods. Shrubby cinquefoil, however, has refined this biological process so that the plant requires no respite once flowering begins. Repeated growth "flushes" occur throughout the season, resulting in frequent branching, which produces a very bushy shrub. The hairy, pear-shaped seeds, often held on the flower head long into winter, are *achenes*. Shrubby cinquefoil, highly intolerant of shade, is also very cold tolerant.

Cinquefoils and strawberry *(Fragaria)* are so closely related that they sometimes hybridize. Note the similarity of their disk flower forms. But this form also frequently appears in unrelated plants such as buttercups and frostweeds. Some botanists pose this similarity as an example of *Müllerian mimicry*—certain flowers have independently evolved the shallow bowl or disk form because of its general efficiency in hosting nonspecialized insect pollinators.

Still, because of their unlike flower colors, marsh and shrubby cinquefoils probably attract different insect pollinators at least some of the time. Many yellow flowers are not yellow to insect eyes but reflect ultraviolet "bee purple," invisible to human eyes. Flowers we perceive as purple are often greenish to them.

The color spectra we see, in other words, are not necessarily the ones that attract insects.

Associates: Marsh cinquefoil, characteristic of pioneer sedge mats, often associates with the sedge *Carex lasiocarpa,* three-way sedge, cattails, and buckbean in such habitats.

Shrubby cinquefoil occupies more advanced fen habitats in company with the moss *Campylium stellatum,* various sedges, speckled alder, shrub willows, and tamarack, among others.

Summer. Shrubby cinquefoil's chief pollinators probably include andrenid and halictid bees as well as honeybees *(Apis mellifera).*

If you see ants on a shrubby cinquefoil, look for a small, green, sluglike caterpillar. This is possibly the larva of a dorcas copper butterfly *(Lycaena dorcas),* which secretes a substance that attracts ants.

Round galls on the leaf stems are caused by cynipid wasp larvae, probably *Gonaspis potentillae* or *Diastrophus.*

Birds and mammals generally show little interest in cinquefoil seeds or foliage. Meadow voles sometimes cache the rhizomes of herb cinquefoils.

Lore: Because shrubby cinquefoil can also colonize drier, rocky uplands and is not grazed by cattle, it is often treated as an invasive nuisance weed, especially on western rangeland. Elsewhere, however, its long flowering season and compact growth form have made it a popular yard ornamental. This usage dates back to the eighteenth century in Europe, and many horticultural varieties of the plant have been developed.

Cinquefoil's astringent roots and leaves achieved popularity as a folk medicine for such ailments as diarrhea, sore throat, and catarrh. Native tribal use was apparently infrequent.

The roots can be made edible by boiling or roasting. Steeped, the dried leaves of shrubby cinquefoil make a decent, harmless tea.

Coontail *(Ceratophyllum demersum).* Hornwort family. Submersed herb in ponds, slow streams. Its narrow, forked leaves growing in feathery whorls with teeth along one edge of the forked segments, plus its bushy leaf clusters (like a raccoon's tail) at or near the stem ends, identify coontail.

Other names: Hornwort, hare's-tail.

Close relatives: Hornwort *(C. echinatum).*

Lifestyle: Usually growing in dense beds—literal underwater "forests"—

coontail bears superficial resemblances to the similarly feathery stonewort *Nitella*, water-marigold, water-milfoils, bladderworts, and fanwort. But coontail is the only submersed aquatic showing teeth on its finely cut leaf edge. Like bladderworts, these plants have no roots, though their lower ends are usually grounded in mud, and they float just beneath the water surface throughout the growing season.

Tiny unisexual flowers appear at the leaf bases. When the (male) stamens mature, they detach and float to the surface, where they release pollen. The pollen "rains" down on the female flowers, which produce fruits *(achenes)* bearing several long spines. Depth, turbidity, and movement of water all affect pollination success in this exclusively water-pollinated plant. Chances of sexual reproduction are much better in shallow waters, where coontail growth is dense.

But seed production is relatively uncommon. Like most aquatic plants, coontail mainly reproduces vegetatively. As fall arrives, the branch tips become bunchy and turn very green. Soon they detach from the dying branches, float for a while, then sink to the bottom. These *turions* (winter buds) remain alive over winter, rising again in spring to produce new branches. Coontail requires less light than many submersed aquatics and can therefore grow at greater depths (down to eighteen feet). It is highly adaptable to changes in water oxygen content and pH, though it favors alkaline waters.

Associates: *Spring, summer.* Plant associates in dense coontail beds are relatively infrequent, though duckweeds commonly float in mats above them. Most submersed aquatics host *epiphytes*—smaller plants, mainly algae, that are not parasitic, but use the larger plants as surfaces to grow on. But many investigators have noted the sparsity of epiphytes on coontail. It is apparently allelopathic to blue-green algae. Sulfur has been isolated from coontail in various experiments, and some researchers believe that this element accounts for the plant's relative lack of algal epiphytes. Yet the leaves sometimes bear a stiff, limy coating, presumably precipitated by calcium-secreting phytoplankton.

Coontail branches bear spiny fruits resulting from waterborne pollination. This plant's leaves, showing teeth only on one side, provide good identity marks.

If epiphytes are sparse on this plant, however, small

aquatic invertebrates are not. Fine-branched coontail provides havens for large populations of worms, snails, crustaceans, and insect larvae. *Melicerta,* a case-building rotifer visible to the naked eye, attaches to the branches, sometimes in huge numbers. Wheel snails *(Planorbis, Gyraulus)* may enhance the growth of coontail by chemical conditioning of the water, probably by means of their nitrogenous excretions. One investigator found that coontail leaves grazed by snails lived longer than ungrazed leaves.

Though many waterfowl, plus American coots and muskrats, consume the plant and its seeds, sources differ on coontail's value as a choice wildlife food (even though it surpasses corn in calcium and protein content). Because this plant may harbor up to 50 percent more small organisms than most other aquatic plants, its main food attraction for waterfowl may be its plentiful animal residents.

Lore: Toxic metals in solution are insidious water pollutants resulting from industry. Many aquatic plants have been tested for their ability to reduce water pollution by removing pollutants and concentrating them in their tissues. Coontail shows a remarkable potential for chromium accumulation, which might make it an effective means for helping remove this toxic metal from our wetlands. Such uses require careful management, however. The plants must be periodically harvested and safely disposed of; otherwise, the toxic material merely recycles into the food chain.

The fact that many edible aquatic plants can apparently concentrate toxic materials should make us cautious about collecting them from questionable locales (and few locales are not these days) for food. Coontail's coarse foliage makes it an unlikely viand in any case.

Cotton-grasses *(Eriophorum* spp.). Sedge family. Herbs in bogs and fens. Recognize cotton-grasses by their grasslike form and tufted, cottony seed-heads, solitary or clustered at the top of the plant. About eight species occupy mainly bogs in our area, though green-keeled cotton-grass *(E. viridi-carinatum)* also resides in rich fens. Three of the most common bog species are tall cotton-grass *(E. angustifolium),* tawny cotton-grass *(E. virginicum),* and dense cotton-grass *(E. spissum).*

Other names: Cotton-sedge; sheathed cotton-sedge *(E. spissum).*

Close relatives: Bulrushes *(Scirpus);* spike-rushes *(Eleocharis);* nut-grasses *(Cyperus);* sedges *(Carex).*

Lifestyle: A pleasing aspect of many bogs is the "cotton field" vista of these white-tufted plants rising above the sag-and-swell surface of the sphagnum-moss ground layer. Dense bog meadows of cotton-grasses are also seasonal features of northern tundra landscapes. Various species of cotton-grass flower and fruit from spring through fall. The downy "cotton" actually consists of soft, persistent bristles that develop on the bisexual flowers, which are wind pollinated. The seeds *(achenes)* are also dispersed by wind.

In many northern bogs, cotton-grasses form *tussocks* (round, bunchy, sodlike clumps bearing many stems of the plant). Tussocks are the result of the simultaneous growth and restraint of new shoots, or *tillers,* on a single plant. Buds at the leaf bases develop into new shoots, but the persistent leaf bases of old shoots slow the plant's lateral spread. The result is a sort of pot-bound growth form without the pot. Each tiller produces new tillers and a new pair of leaves annually. Leaves die back in the fall but may remain intact on the plant for years, eventually producing the tussock's bushy appearance. In undisturbed bogs, individual tussocks may survive for a century or more. Often they assume a crescent shape; as winds bend the old, bushy growth permanently to the leeward side, tussock expansion occurs mainly on the unshaded windward side.

Their sequential leaf growth apparently enables cotton-grasses to recycle their own nutrients. As old leaves age, many of their mineral constituents translocate into the new leaf growth, thus reducing the plant's dependence on soil nutrients in the unfertile bog environment. Young flowering shoots contain relatively high levels of phosphorus and potassium.

This is one of the few plants that can invade disturbed habitats as well as colonize undisturbed ones. *E. spissum* thrives especially well following a passage of fire.

Cotton-grass, not a grass but a sedge, is one of the most visibly distinctive plants of many bogs. This plant recycles many of its mineral constituents, a probable adaptation to the nutrient-poor bog environment.

Associates: Typical bog companions of cotton-grasses include sphagnum mosses and heaths, including blueberries, leatherleaf, bog-rosemary, Labrador-tea, and laurels. Black spruce and tamarack are frequent tree associates. In arctic alpine-tundra areas, white mountain-avens *(Dryas octopetala),* a prostrate dwarf shrub, often establishes itself on cotton-grass tussocks.

Spring, summer. Cotton-grasses have few animal users. A northern butterfly, the Jutta arctic *(Oeneis jutta)*, and perhaps other *Oeneis* species as well, feed as caterpillars on this and other sedges and grasses. Arctic butterfly caterpillars, feeding often at night, are stout-bodied and hairy with lengthwise stripes. The grayish-brown adult insects often alight on tree trunks.

Certain aphids *(Prociphilus)* feed on the sap of cotton-grass roots and secrete honeydew. Mound-building ants *(Lasius minutus)*, common in bogs, relish the honeydew and rarely appear above ground.

Do songbirds such as yellow warblers that use downy plant materials for their nests ever raid cotton-grass tufts for this purpose? The possibility bears investigation. Hoary redpolls feed on the seeds to some extent.

In arctic and subarctic regions, brown lemmings often burrow into cotton-grass tussocks. Calving caribou are said to feed selectively on cotton-grasses in spring and sometimes eliminate them by overgrazing in localized areas.

Lore: The "cotton" was apparently used by pioneer families for pillow stuffing. But its collection for such purposes must have been even more laborious than picking regular cotton; poultry feathers were much more efficiently gathered.

Cotton-grass tussocks are long-lived, gradually enlarging over decades of slow growth. Bog heaths often germinate on the tussocks (lower left). The flower head (lower right) is pollinated by wind.

Cranberries *(Vaccinium* spp.). Heath family. Small creeping and trailing shrubs in bogs, sedge fens. Small cranberry *(V. oxycoccus)* and large cranberry *(V. macrocarpon)* are the two common species. Both display alternate evergreen leaves less than an inch long; pinkish flowers with reflexed (bent-back) lobes; and red, persistent berries. Leaves and fruit of small cranberry are smaller than those of *V. macrocarpon*. Their fruits are often spotted and their leaves pointed; large cranberry leaves are blunt-tipped. Small cranberry flowers and fruits develop somewhat earlier than those of large cranberry.

Other names: American cranberry, marshberry, sourberry, bounceberry *(V. macrocarpon)*; fenberry (England), northern cranberry, marsh whortleberry *(V. oxycoccus)*.

Close relatives: Blueberries *(Vaccinium)*; lingonberry or mountain-cranberry *(V. vitis-idaea)*; huckleberries *(Gaylussacia)*; leatherleaf *(Chamaedaphnae calyculata)*; bog-rosemary *(Andromeda glaucophylla)*; laurels *(Kalmia)*; azaleas *(Rhododendron)*; Labrador-tea *(Ledum groenlandicum)*. The so-called highbush cranberry or cranberry viburnum *(Viburnum trilobum)* is an unrelated shrub.

Lifestyle: Cranberries and blueberries bear few obvious resemblances in plant form, habit, or fruit color, yet they both belong to the same genus because of their similar flower anatomy. The flowers are bisexual and insect pollinated. From pollination to seed set requires about eighty-five days in both cranberry species.

Small cranberry, cushioned in sphagnum moss ("on an acre of sponges," said Thoreau), requires extremely acid habitats (pH 2.9 to 3.8). Large cranberry has a somewhat broader pH tolerance (4.8 to 6.1) and often grows in sedge fens, which precede the development of more acidic peatlands. The two species often occur in close proximity, however, inhabiting localized pockets of varying acidity in the same bog. Clone plants may form along the length of the prostrate stems, so even one cranberry shrub may occupy considerable space.

Associates: Like most heaths, cranberries intimately associate beneath the soil with root fungi *(mycorrhizae)*. Their most common surface plant associates include sphagnum mosses and bog heaths, as well as sedges, bog birch, tamarack, and black spruce.

Spring, summer. Several insect species

Low, sprawling, large cranberry usually hides most of its stem deep in the sphagnum moss. Unlike their blueberry relatives, cranberries hold their fruits on the plants for months.

that feed on these plants have become pests in the artificial bog habitats constructed by the commercial cranberry industry. In early spring, look for the nymphs of recently hatched leafhoppers, slender jumping insects that suck plant sap. The brownish-colored blunt-nosed leafhopper *(Scleroracus vaccinii)* is the vector of a microplasma that causes false-blossom disease, a serious problem for commercial growers. Streaked, abnormally erect flowers and small, misshapen fruits are symptoms of this disease.

Moth feeders on the leaves include the cranberry spanworm *(Ematurga amitaria)*, an inchworm caterpillar. The cranberry or black-headed fireworm *(Rhophobota naevana)*, the yellow-headed fireworm *(Peronea minuta)*, and the spotted fireworm *(Choristoneura parallela)*, all tortricid moth caterpillars, web the leaves. Tiny leafmining caterpillars include *Nepticula paludicola* and *Coptodisca negligens,* which produce blotch mines.

Cranberry is the larval food plant of a small, darkish butterfly, the bog copper *(Lycaena epixanthe)*. The caterpillars are green and sluglike. Adult butterflies lay their eggs in summer on leaf undersurfaces near the shoot tips; the eggs remain over winter, and the caterpillars transform into new adult butterflies in summer. These butterflies are never seen far from bogs.

Dead or dying plants may indicate insect feeding on the roots. The cranberry girdler *(Chrysoteuchia topiaria)*, a moth caterpillar, girdles or severs the vine beneath the surface. The cranberry rootworm *(Rhabdopterus picipes)*, a beetle larva, feeds on rhododendron leaves in its adult stage.

The chief flower pollinators include solitary bees (Andrenidae, Halictidae), bumblebees *(Bombus)*, and honeybees *(Apis mellifera,* probably cranberry's least efficient pollinator and nectar remover).

Late summer, fall. A bright red, blisterlike appearance on the leaves is probably azalea leaf gall, common on many bog heaths (see Leatherleaf).

The pointed sallow *(Epiglaea apiata)*, a noctuid moth caterpillar, feeds on the leaves, sometimes becoming a late-season pest. *Epipsilia monochromatea,* a noctuid feeder on sundew plants, changes its diet to cranberry leaves in late summer.

Fruit feeders include a moth caterpillar called cranberry worm or sparganothis fruitworm *(Sparganothis sulfureana)*. Flooding the bog is a means of effective control against many cranberry pests, but these larvae can withstand submersion for almost six months. The cranberry fruitworm *(Mineola vaccinii)*, a pale green pyralid moth caterpillar, eats into berries near the stem, then closes the hole with silk; a single larva can devour the pulp of two or three berries.

Though they are not major wildlife foods, cranberry fruits are consumed by shorebirds, including Hudsonian godwits and gamebirds such as ruffed and sharp-tailed grouse, ring-necked pheasants, and northern bobwhites. Mourning doves, American tree sparrows, and a few other songbirds also feed on them. Waterfowl rarely consume them, if ever.

Eastern chipmunks eat the fruit occasionally. Rodents (voles and lemmings), I have noted, typically eat only the seeds, leaving neat piles of halved berries in their runways.

Lore: Cranberries are nourishing, healthful fruits, rich in vitamin C and pectin. Noted for their rot resistance and low spoilage, they persist red and ripe on the vine after snow disappears in early spring. This is my favorite time of year to collect them, when other fruits are sparse in the wild. ("They cut the winter's phlegm," wrote Thoreau.) It's not uncommon to find new flowers along with mature fruits from the previous year on the same plant in spring. To me, the tart taste of a cranberry conjures the acid tangs of black spruce, tamarack, Labrador-tea, and sphagnum moss—a sense of the bog itself. Sugar helps; prepared as sauce, jelly, or beverage, the fruits are too acid to consume without it.

New England Indians, who used the fruit in meal cakes (sweetened with maple syrup) and as a pemmican ingredient, introduced the Pilgrim colonists to cranberries. Indians also used the astringent berries as a medicine for dysentery and a poultice for wounds and skin inflammations. In modern medicine, cranberry juice is sometimes prescribed for urinary tract infections and hypoglycemia.

The French explorer Champlain noted hundreds of acres of "red currants" growing in New England coastal bogs in the early 1600s. Early colonists named them "crane-berries" because of the supposed resemblance of the flower to the neck of a crane (actually, heron). Sailing masters carried casks of the fruit on long sea journeys to prevent scurvy. But cranberry culture, strictly a New World enterprise, only began about 1817 in Massachusetts. Selective breeding for productivity and fruit size dealt exclusively with *V. macrocarpon*, the large cranberry. Cape Cod continues to supply about two-thirds of the nation's crop; the other big cranberry-growing states are New Jersey and Wisconsin. Cranberry farming involves leveling, sanding, and ditching bogs, flooding them in winter, and harvesting the fruit with machines.

Soundness of the berries is easily tested: The good ones bounce. Modern, steplike grading machinery that sorts the fruit relies on this characteristic. Cranberry was one of the first fruits to be commercially canned. Long regarded as a traditional holiday food, cranberry represents a textbook success story of American advertising, which publicized the fruit for year-round consumption and launched the cranberry juice industry.

Dogwood, Red-osier *(Cornus stolonifera)*. Dogwood family. Thicket-forming shrubs in swamps, fens, along shorelines. Red-osier is easily identified by its red stems and branches and opposite leaves.

Other less common shrub dogwoods in wetlands include silky dogwood *(C. amomum)*, roughleaf dogwood *(C. drummondi)*, and pale or narrowleaf dogwood *(C. obliqua)*. Although the very common gray dogwood *(C. racemosa)* colonizes both wet and dry habitats, it generally occupies drier sites than red-osier (see *The Book of Forest and Thicket*).

Other names: Red-stemmed dogwood, kinnikinnick, squaw-bush, waxberry cornel, dogberry-tree, gutter-tree, grey willow, river cornel, red cornel.

Close relatives: Flowering dogwood *(C. florida)*; bunchberry *(C. canadensis)*; gums *(Nyssa)*.

Lifestyle: Lending year-round color to shrub-carr wetlands, this dogwood reddens most vividly in early spring where it is openly exposed to sunlight. Although it can tolerate light shading, stems and branches in shaded sites tend to be greener. Degree of redness, caused by anthocyanin pigments in the bark, is determined by light intensity.

Red-osier stems often crowd along pondside margins, but the clones seldom spread very extensively. Red-osier thickets tend to be smaller and less dense than gray dogwood or alder thickets. The white, flat-topped flower clusters, bisexual and insect pollinated, are replaced in the fall by whitish or bluish *drupes* ("part of the pendant jewelry of the season," wrote Thoreau).

In the fall, note the fruit stems *(cymes)*. Sometimes, I have noted, they replicate on a miniature scale the entire form of the shrub.

Associates: Red-osier dogwood is a member of the shrub-carr community that often includes willows and buttonbush. Such fen plants as sensitive fern, blue-joint grass, wild mint, and meadowsweet are also frequent associates. In many places, red-osiers thinly border speckled alder thickets on the drier, landward side.

Spring, summer. The flowers, with abundant nectar, attract many insects, but andrenid and halictid bees and syrphid flies are probably the foremost pollinators. Bumblebees *(Bombus)* also visit the flowers frequently. Long-horned beetles (Cerambycidae) crawl on the flower heads and probably also aid in pollination.

Small masses of white, bubbly froth in the angles of twigs and branches indicate spittlebug feeding. Nymphs of the dogwood spittlebug *(Clastoptera proteus)* are sap-suckers; the adult insects, similar to leafhoppers, are called froghoppers (Cercopidae).

Tiny shield bearer moth caterpillars *(Antispila aurirubra, A. cornifoliella)* make blotch mines in the leaves. Larger moth caterpillars also feed on the foliage. Common ones include the dimorphic bomolocha *(Bomolocha bijugalis)* and the dark-spotted palthis *(Palthis angulalis)*; these are both noctuid moths. The crocus and false crocus geometers *(Xanthotype sospeta, X. urticaria)* are inchworm caterpillars, as is the dogwood probole *(Probole nyssaria)* and the fragile white carpet moth *(Hydrelia albifera)*.

Red-osier thickets often host nests of birds that build near water. These may include alder and willow flycatchers, gray catbirds, yellow warblers, and American goldfinches.

White-tailed deer and moose browse the foliage.

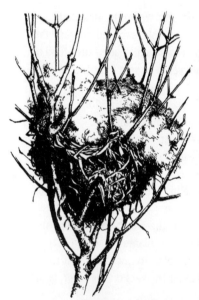

Vacated goldfinch nests in shrub dogwoods often provide fall and winter lodging for white-footed mice, which stuff the nests full of cattail down. Note how the branching of this shrub provides ideal support for nests.

Fall, winter. "I like the red dogwood because he feeds October robins," wrote Aldo Leopold. Red-osier fruits are relished by many birds, including American black ducks, mallards, wood ducks, ruffed and sharp-tailed grouse, northern bobwhites, ring-necked pheasants, wild turkeys, woodpeckers, and eastern kingbirds. Songbird feeders include American robins, gray catbirds, cedar waxwings, warbling vireos, northern cardinals, and grosbeaks. White-footed mice often "recycle" old nests of yellow warblers and goldfinches in red-osier, adding piles of plant down to the nest cup.

Cottontail rabbits and muskrats gnaw the stems, and beavers often cut them for their winter food caches. White-tailed deer relish the twig tips of red-osier, one of their preferred, most nourishing winter foods. Look for raggedly bitten-off twig ends. A practiced eye can identify previously winter-browsed dogwoods even in summer by the adventitious growth that compensates for the nipped twigs.

Lore: Red-osier and other shrub dogwoods were widely used among American natives—not for food, but for medicine, utility, and pleasure. Bark teas provided a wash for sore eyes and, taken internally, an effective cure for diarrhea. Red dyes of various shades could be made by boiling red-osier with certain other barks and herbs. Indians used the flexible branches for basketry and as frames for drying hides. The dried and grated inner bark provided the chief ingredient of kinnikinnick (Indian tobacco), which was smoked by itself or mixed with regular tobacco in pipes. (The Chippewa, according to old records, "are great smoakers"; *bois rouge*, as French explorers called the shrub, "is held by them in the highest estimation for their winter smoaking.")

Osier is a French word meaning "willow bed." Shrub dogwoods were often mislabeled as willows by early explorers and pioneers.

Red-osier has the widest range of any American dogwood, spanning all of northern North America.

Duckweeds (*Spirodela, Lemna, Wolffia, Wolfiella* spp.). Duckweed family. Small, floating herbs in quiet or standing waters. Most duckweeds blanket the water surface in colonies; they have no true leaves or stems but only a flat, green plant body called a *thallus* (described by one naturalist as "a flake of vegetation"). Thalli float on or (in *Lemna trisulca*) just beneath the surface. *Spirodela* and *Lemna* have dangling rootlets; *Wolffia* and *Wolfiella* have none.

Other names: Duck-meat; big duckweed *(Spirodela polyrhiza)*; common duckweed *(Lemna minor)*; watermeal, ducks-meal *(Wolffia)*.

Close relatives: None.

Lifestyle: Few ponds, ditches, or quiet waters are without duckweeds in greater or lesser profusion. Though tiny duckweeds are flowering plants, actual flowering is uncommon to rare. They reproduce mainly by dividing ("budding off") from the leaflike thallus and, in many species, by forming *turions* (winter buds). Some ten species of its four genera grow in east-central North America.

The two most common species are greater duckweed *(Spirodela polyrhiza)*, with purplish undersides and up to ten dangling rootlets; and lesser duckweed *(Lemna minor)*, smaller with only one rootlet. Since the entire lower surface of thalli can absorb nutrients, rootlets may have the greater functional importance of stabilizing the thallus and keeping it upright. Some waters may host only one duckweed species, but most sizable duckweed populations contain two or more genera.

Greater duckweed, the largest species (all of one-quarter inch long), favors acid-neutral or alkaline, mineral-rich waters. Compact surface mats of this species may contain 100,000 to 200,000 plants per square yard. Often, upon examination of the oval-circular plants, one may see budded but not yet separate plants consisting of two or three developing thalli. Even after their separation, the parent and budded-off plants tend to stay together, forming small colonial aggregations. New budding thalli develop from clefts in the edge of the parent thallus.

In midsummer to late fall, the plant begins producing turions (up to six from one thallus) in like manner. These tiny, kidney-shaped buds detach and immediately sink to the bottom, where they remain all winter. In the spring, each turion expels a gas bubble, which causes it to rise to the surface, where it rapidly develops into a new duckweed thallus. Turion formation requires a combination of bright sunlight and high water temperature.

Lesser duckweed, about one-eighth inch long and more oval in shape, is probably the most common species. It tolerates a wider range of water chemistry, flourishing best in slightly acid conditions (pH 5.1 to 6.7). Unlike other duckweeds, it commonly grows in cold springs as well as the usual duckweed habitats. Each thallus may bud off ten or more thalli before dying. A thallus's average life expectancy is about a month. Compact mats may contain 300,000 to 800,000 plants per square yard of surface. This duckweed seems to flower more frequently than the others, producing tiny white blooms from the thallus margin. Even in this species, however, flowering isn't common, so count yourself lucky if you see it. This species also produces turions.

Less frequently seen but almost as common is the star, ivy, or ivy-leaved duckweed *(L. trisulca)*, which floats not on, but suspended below, the water surface. Its oblong thallus is longer, producing chainlike clones that interlock, forming netlike lattices or sheets. Easily overlooked, it often "lurks" just beneath the aforementioned duckweed species. Thalli may dangle one rootlet or none.

Wolffia or watermeal species are not only the smallest duckweeds but also the smallest known flowering plants (though they hardly ever flower). Seldom measuring over 1/32 of an inch in diameter, the green, floating thallus is thick and grainy. One million to two million plants may occupy a square yard of water surface. *Wolffia* favors acid-neutral waters, often thriving between and among the other duckweed species. It has turions but no rootlets, sinks in the fall, and rises again to the surface in spring.

Wolfiella thalli are longer than broad (6 x 2 millimeters). Flowering in this genus occurs rarely, if at all.

Thick blankets of duckweed can shade pond bottoms, preventing adequate photosynthesis and making life difficult or impossible for submersed plants and animals. Because these plants themselves are so widely consumed by animal herbivores, however, this is often a problem of only intermittent duration.

Associates: *Spring, summer, fall.* Although the larger duckweed species may form pure masses, greater, lesser, and star duckweeds plus watermeal can often be found growing together in any extensive duckweed "blanket." The larger duckweeds may benefit tiny watermeal by stabilizing its position in the mat, preventing wind and wave breakup of the colony.

Other surface-floating plant associates may include mosquito fern, liverworts, and water-lilies. Light-loving green algae are usually scarce beneath a dense duckweed cover, but more shade-tolerant blue-green algae may flourish. Some researchers have suggested that a *commensal* relationship (one that benefits one and harms neither) may exist between blue-green algae and the larger duckweeds: Nitrogen-fixing blue-greens such as *Nostoc, Gloeotrichia,* and *Anabaena,* attaching to duckweeds, may benefit from physical support and shading—and possibly the host duckweed derives a shot of nitrogen. Other submersed plants that are tolerant of duckweed shading include bladderworts and coontail. Star duckweed often occurs in cattail marshes and amid stands of wild-rice.

Duckweed mats host a large variety of small fauna that feed, lay eggs, or shelter amid the plants. Many of them secure themselves to the thallus rootlets or undersides, where they snare and capture passing food organisms or particles. Protozoans, rotifers, insect larvae, and crustaceans are often abundant. One study found thirty-seven insect species associated in some degree with *Lemna* alone. The shading and canopy of profuse duckweed growth may also inhibit the growth of certain submersed or bottom-dwelling creatures, such as mosquito larvae. (One study, however, found that only a combined surface growth of *Lemna* and mosquito fern *[Azolla caroliniana],* not the duckweed alone, provided enough density for this effect.)

Abundant insect feeders on duckweeds include the pond-lily aphid *Rhopalosiphum nymphaeae,* which sucks the plant juices, and the even tinier collembolans or springtails *Podura aquatica* and *Sminthurus aquaticus.* Springtails, those flealike jumpers sometimes seen in leaping profusion atop duckweed and algae mats, create small holes in the upper thalli surfaces, where they feed and lay eggs.

A few small moth caterpillars also consume portions of the thallus. Two closely related pyralid moths that construct portable cases from thallus fragments are *Munroessa icciusalis* and *Synclita obliteralis;* nibbled edges of the thallus often indicate these feeders. Another case builder that uses duckweed is the caddisfly larva *Limnophilus combinatus.*

Larvae of a shore fly (Ephydridae) and lemna flies *(Lemnaphila scotlandae)* bore into the thalli, emerging as adult flies, which continue to feed on the plant. They eat characteristic parallel channels in the thallus, laying a yellowish egg on its upper edge. These and species of long-legged flies (Dolichopodidae) plus *Culex* and *Anopheles* mosquitoes may often be seen standing or walking on the duckweed mat.

Another mining larva is that of the duckweed weevil *Tanysphyrus lemnae,* a rhyncophorous beetle. The larva eats out linear blotch mines beneath the thallus epidermis. Adult weevils chew circular holes in the thallus (one insect can destroy many thalli) and lay eggs in its upper surface. The duckweed beetle *(Scirtes tibialis),* one of the tiny marsh beetles (Helodidae), also feeds on the plants.

Several other aquatic creatures do not feed on duckweed but often attach their eggs to it. These include the aquatic bug *Trepodates pictus,* wheel snails *(Planorbis)*, and pond snails *(Lymnaea)*, all of which glue their eggs in jellylike masses to thallus undersides. Ostracod crustaceans such as *Cypris* often deposit eggs on duckweed rootlets, as do *Hydroporus* predaceous diving beetles. Bright green nymphs of a water strider *(Mesovelia bisignata)*, long-legged spiderlike bugs that dart over the water surface, are commonly seen; the adult striders oviposit in duckweed thalli.

Tiny carnivorous beasts may cling to thallus undersides. Tentacled freshwater jellyfishes are called hydras. The green hydra *(Hydra viridissima)* and *H. vulgaris,* with gray, orange, or brownish bodies, are the most common ones. Groups of blackish planarian flatworms also shelter and scavenge on duckweed undersides.

Duckweeds are favored foods of several vertebrates. Among fishes, carp consume them in quantity, as do green frogs and probably other amphibians.

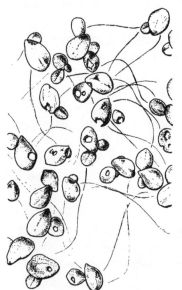

Close examination of floating duckweed thalli often reveals evidence of much insect feeding activity. Most of the holes seen here were probably made by duckweed weevils.

These plants derive the name duckweed, of course, from their value as relished, highly nutritious waterfowl foods. Surface-feeding ducks such as American black ducks, mallards, blue-winged and green-winged teals, American wigeons, and wood ducks especially favor them. But diving ducks, including buffleheads and ring-necked ducks, also feed on duckweeds, as do mute swans and American coots, common moorhens, sora rails, and ring-necked pheasants. Though all duckweed species are eaten, lesser duckweed is by far the most frequently consumed, mainly in summer and early fall when duckweeds are most abundant. Also, comments one biologist, "when waterfowl eat this saladlike fare, they doubtless obtain considerable numbers of minute animal organisms associated with it."

Probably the only mammals that occasionally consume duckweed are muskrats and beavers. These animals may also play an important role in the plants' dispersal and distribution. Very often a muskrat or beaver moving to a new pond will carry numerous duckweed thalli in its matted fur. Feathers and legs of waterfowl probably also transport the plant to new waters.

Lore: Like certain green algae species, duckweeds have been proposed as an abundant, easily grown source of human food—an idea not without precedent. A species of *Wolffia* has been cultivated and harvested in parts of Burma, Thailand, and Laos for human consumption. In dry weight, this meal contains about 20 percent protein, more than in similar quantities of peanuts or alfalfa. A much more frequent usage, however, is as animal feed, especially for poultry and hogs. Although duckweed's nutritional value is unquestioned, practicable harvesting and processing methods have yet to be devised for any large-scale duckweed "farming."

Elderberry, Common *(Sambucus canadensis)*. Honeysuckle family. Shrub in swamps, along ditches and shorelines. Recognize common elderberry by its opposite compound leaves (usually seven toothed leaflets); its stout, warty twigs; its flat-topped white flower clusters in early summer; and its flat-topped clusters of small, purplish-black fruits on red stems in the fall.

Other names: Common elder, American elder, Canada elder, black-berried elder, sweet elderberry, elder-blow.

Close relatives: Red elderberry *(S. pubens*—see *The Book Of Forest and Thicket)*; viburnums *(Viburnum)*; honeysuckles *(Lonicera)*; twinflower *(Linnaea borealis)*. Elderberries are unrelated to box elder *(Acer negundo)*, a maple.

Readily identified by its compound leaves, opposite branching, and warty bark, common elderberry is one of the most common wetland shrubs. It provides food for many birds and mammals.

Lifestyle: It grows fastest in full sunlight, but common elderberry is also shade tolerant. Multi-stemmed clones grow from underground branching runners, forming waterside thickets of arching stems with few branches. The conspicuous surface warts on the bark are *lenticels,* corky-tissued gateways for admitting air into the interior of stems and branches. Their presence identifies the plant in any season.

The bisexual flowers are insect pollinated, producing the BB-shot-sized drupes, often in masses.

Associates: Shrub willows, red-osier dogwood, and buttonbush are frequent associates.

Spring. In cool, wet weather of early spring, look for a tough, rubbery, brown fungus on dead elderberry stems. This is probably Judas ear or brown ear *(Auricularia auricula),* a jelly fungus that is cup shaped, somewhat like a human ear. Oriental chefs prize it as a delicacy.

Summer. Insect visitors to the flowers are pollen feeders and collectors; the flowers produce little nectar. Honeybees *(Apis mellifera),* halictid bees, and syrphid flies are common pollinators. Pollen-eating beetles may include small dermestids such as *Attogenus piceus,* soft-winged flower beetles (Malachiidae), tumbling flower beetles (Mordellidae), and long-horned beetles (Cerambycidae).

In elderberry flower clusters, look for occasional swollen florets, indicating larval feeding of the elder flower midge *(Youngomyia umbellicola).*

A large, beautiful long-horned beetle feeding in the flower clusters is the elder borer *(Desmocerus palliatus),* also called cloaked knotty horn; it is shiny, metallic blue with a contrasting reddish-yellow band. This insect spends most of its life cycle on and in elderberry. The pollen-eating adult, also eating notches out of leaves, lays its eggs on the stems close to the soil. The larvae burrow into the stems, work down into the roots, and finally pupate in the soil, emerging as adults. Their boring sometimes causes a dieback of branches.

Rolled leaf margins with whitish or brownish velvetlike patches are signs of mites *(Eriophyes).*

Deformed buds with curly, leaflike extrusions are caused by the elder bud gall gnat *(Asphondylia sambuci)*. Swollen linear sections of stem result from larval feeding of another gall gnat, the elder stem midge *(Neolasioptera sambuci)*.

The elder shoot borer moth or spindle worm *(Achatodes zeae)* bores into new shoots, often causing their ends to blacken and fall off. This larva also attacks corn *(Zea mays)*, working in the tassel or spindle. The adult noctuid moth displays orange-spotted forewings.

Dead stems or branches, hollow from decay of the thick, white pith, are often used as nesting chambers by various hymenopterans, including carpenter bees *(Ceratina)* and spider and potter wasps (Pompilidae, Vespidae). Partitioned mud cells may hold dead insects or spiders stocked by these wasps.

Gray catbirds and (especially for second nestings) indigo buntings frequently nest in common elderberry.

Late summer, fall. The aforementioned Judas ear fungus may also appear on dead stems in the fall.

Fruits of common elderberry are relished by more than forty species of birds, making these shrubs good places to look for fall migrants fueling up for long southward flights. All thrushes, especially American robins, Swainson's thrushes, and veeries feast on the fruits. Among other frequent feeders are ring-necked pheasants, gray catbirds, brown thrashers, European starlings, yellow-breasted chats, and rose-breasted grosbeaks. Robins and catbirds often raid the fruits before they are fully ripe. Birds are probably the plant's chief seed dispersers.

Fox and red squirrels, woodchucks, and white-footed mice also relish the fruits. White-tailed deer and elk feed on the foliage and twigs.

Winter. This is the season to look for vertical, zipperlike scars on elderberry stems, indicating egg deposition of the black-horned tree cricket *(Oecanthus nigricornis)*.

Elderberry is one of many plants that host the splendid cecropia or robin moth *(Hyalophora cecropia)*, North America's largest moth; its wingspan may extend almost six inches. The

Vertical, zipperlike lines on elderberry stems are egg scars of black-horned tree crickets; they are also a common sight on blackberry canes. Note elderberry's characteristic warts on the bark.

large, green caterpillar spins a brown, spindle-shaped cocoon in the fall, and attaches it lengthwise to a twig. This cocoon bleaches to a grayish color and remains on the twig all winter. The magnificent adult moth emerges in spring.

Lore: The only humanly edible parts of this plant are the fruits (with considerable sweetening) and flower clusters (said to make fine fritters when fried in batter). The bark, roots, leaves, and unripe fruits are toxic, causing severe distress to the eater; these parts all contain hydrocyanic acid, a source of cyanide poisoning. The processed fruits, of course, make tasty jellies, pies, syrups, and wines. They can also be dried and stored for later use; reconstitute them in boiling water. Elderberry fruits are extremely rich in vitamin C, and they also contain vitamin A, calcium, iron, and potassium.

American natives apparently did not use the fruits to any large extent. But many tribes did use other parts of the plant for strong, desperate medicines. The Onondaga, for example, drank a bark concoction to remedy poisoning by water-hemlock. ("It lets a man spew," according to one old account.) Buds and leaves also helped evacuate "both upwards and downwards." Applied externally, poultices of elder leaves and bark helped ease burns, rashes, and skin inflammations.

Pith-hollowed sections of stem were long used for spiles after maple trees were tapped for sap ("elder quill") and for making whistles and blowguns. An ancient reed instrument, the sambuca or sambuke (from which the plant supposedly derives its generic name) may have been made from elder stems. Crushed bark and leaves have a rank odor, which is said to be an effective insect repellent; one eigh-teenth-century gardener recommended whip-

Cecropia moths spin large cocoons in the fall and attach them to elderberry and many other shrub and tree species. The large, colorful adult moth emerges from the now somewhat shriveled cocoon in spring.

ping cabbages and turnips with young elder twigs to prevent insect ravages. The old, hard wood of closely related European elder *(S. nigra)* was much used for making skewers, combs, and shoemaker's pegs. Elderberry's first commercial cultivation originated in the 1920s when a New York wild clone was isolated for genetic selection, but elderberry cultivation has never been a major fruit industry.

Medieval tradition claimed that Judas Iscariot hung himself from an elder (the supposed origin of the aforementioned Judas ear fungus). According to one antique botanist, elder was also "employed to cure every ill that flesh is heir to." But since the names *elder* and *alder* may have derived from the same Anglo-Saxon word, references to this specific shrub in human history remain questionable at best.

Ferns Order Filicales. Cinnamon fern *(Osmunda cinnemomea)* and royal fern *(O. regalis)* in the royal fern family; sensitive fern *(Onoclea sensibilis)* and marsh fern *(Thelypteris palustris)* in the polypody family. Spore-bearing herbs in swamp, fen, and shoreline areas. The true ferns are land dwellers, and many species occupy moist or marginal wetland habitats. The four species mentioned are probably the most common and conspicuous of these.

Both *Osmunda* ferns often form lush, junglelike thickets. Recognize cinnamon fern by its arching, vaselike growth habit and circular growth clusters; its cinnamon-brown, clublike sporestalks in spring; and the woolly tufts at its leaflet bases.

Royal fern, one of the tallest ferns (up to six feet), has widely spaced, locust-like leaflets; its brownish, densely clustered spore leaflets grow at the topmost ends of the regular leaves.

Identify sensitive fern by its broad, leathery, triangular leaves (not delicate or lacy as in most ferns); its prominent network of veins on leaflet surfaces; and its foot-high, wandlike spore stalks, which hold the bead-shaped spore cases in dark brown spikes. These stalks remain standing conspicuously in winter after the leaves have decayed.

Marsh fern, small and delicate, has a twisting growth form. As in many ferns, it bears its spores on the upper leaflet undersides; the leaflet margins curve over the rows of fruit dots. Marsh fern favors soft mud habitats.

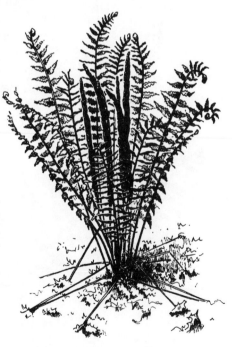

Cinnamon fern, often standing more than three feet tall, grows in a characteristic vase-shaped form, with its spore stalks in the middle.

Sensitive fern spore stalks remain standing long after the leaves disappear. This fern often occupies the same habitats as marsh fern.

Other names: Bead fern, oak-leaved fern, oak fern (*Onoclea sensibilis;* true oak fern is actually *Gymnocarpium dryopteris*); swamp brake, breadroot, fiddleheads *(Osmunda cinnemomea)*; regal fern, king fern, royal osmund, ditch fern, snake fern, locust fern, buckthorn brake, flowering fern, male fern (*O. regalis;* a polypody wood fern, *Dryopteris filix-mas,* is also called male fern); marsh shield fern, beaver-meadow fern, swamp fern, snuffbox fern, quill fern *(Thelypteris palustris).*

Close relatives: Interrupted fern *(Osmunda claytoniana);* for sensitive and marsh ferns, all ferns in the polypody family.

Lifestyle: Ferns are among the few plants in this book that reproduce by spores rather than seeds. The basic scheme is an alternation of sexual and nonsexual generations. *Gametophytes,* the sexual forms that develop from spores, are so inconspicuous in the soil that they are seldom seen. The visible plants that we know as ferns are the asexual *sporophytes,* the spore-producing generation that rises from fertilized gametophytes.

Most fern species have distinctively shaped spore cases, which appear at specific locales on the sporophyte. In many species they develop on leaflet undersides, as in marsh fern. Others, like cinnamon and sensitive ferns, bear separate spore stalks (fertile leaves). Still others, like royal fern, develop modified portions of their regular leaves for spore growth. *Osmunda* spores are green, in contrast to the brown spores of the other genera.

Marsh fern, a sprawling, usually low-growing plant, often shows slightly twisted leaves and leaflets. This is one of the most common ferns in many wetlands.

None of these four ferns are evergreen. Sensitive fern is highly vulnerable to cold (whence its name), but so are they all; their fronds (leaves) rapidly die off after the first touch of autumn frost. Late spring frosts may kill the entire new leafage of these ferns, forcing them to start new leaves.

Royal, cinnamon, and sensitive ferns generally favor medium acid to neutral soils, often bordering boggy areas. Marsh fern is more typically a fen species. Their habitats overlap considerably, however, and all four species may be found growing in proximity. Royal and cinnamon ferns often thrive in inches of standing water; sensitive and marsh ferns seem to prefer their "feet" out of the water.

All four ferns thrive best in full sunlight but are widely tolerant of shade. Probably more often than by spores, they reproduce by budding new stalks from the creeping rootstocks (rhizomes). Royal fern, however, relies much more than many ferns on spore reproduction. Its rhizome (as well as that of cinnamon fern) grows in a circular shape, producing individual clumps. Royal and cinnamon ferns, especially, may show stout, tussocklike bases consisting of the old, matted rhizomes of many years. Cinnamon fern has one of the largest creeping rhizomes of any American fern. The horizontal rootstocks are annually renewed with new fronds at one end as they die off at the other ("It is believed that they can live forever," writes fern botanist Boughton Cobb). Thus in many wetlands, some of the fern plants may have rhizomes that long predate the oldest forests of the region.

Associates: I often find royal and cinnamon ferns growing in close proximity. Marsh and sensitive ferns likewise can often be seen together on the same marshy ground. Marsh fern often becomes a persistent weed in cultivated cranberry bogs. Sedges are usually frequent plant associates of these ferns.

Spring, summer. Relatively few insects or wildlife species habitually feed on these ferns.

Some observers have recorded the downy wool from cinnamon ferns in the nest lining of yellow warblers. Brown thrash-

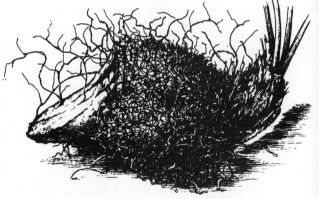

The old, matted, underground rhizome of a cinnamon fern is an accumulation of fibers and plant bases spanning many years. New ferns bud from the living portion (right), while the oldest portion (left) continually dies off and decays.

ers and veeries sometimes nest on or near the ground in the central "vase" of a cinnamon fern clump.

Late summer, fall. The osmunda borer moth caterpillar *(Papaipema speciosissima)* feeds in stems and rhizomes of royal and cinnamon ferns. In sensitive fern, the closely related sensitive fern borer moth *(P. inquaesita)* does the same. The adult noctuid moths, stout-bodied and orange-winged, emerge fairly late in the season.

Lore: *Osmunda* is among the most ancient fern genera, dating back to the Cretaceous period when the great reptiles abounded. These ferns have evolved few changes in many millions of years. Their generic name is said to be derived from the Saxon god Osmunder. Another legend holds that "a certain Osmund, living at Loch Tyne, saved his wife and child from the inimical Danes by hiding them upon an island among masses of flowering ferns, and that in after years, the child so shielded named the stately plants after her father."

"Heart of Osmund," or "bog onion," the central rhizome crown of royal and cinnamon ferns, is edible in early spring. Cinnamon fern "fiddleheads," the curled fronds emerging in early spring, can also be cooked as greens. The wiry, matted roots and rhizomes of cinnamon fern are often used in greenhouse orchid culture as a germination medium called osmundine. Royal fern's stem contains a mucilage that was once extracted and used in folk medicine for treating coughs and diarrhea.

Gentians *(Gentiana* spp.). Gentian family. Herbs with varying soil moisture preferences. Gentians, flowering in late summer and fall, have opposite leaves and erect, vaselike, blue flowers, usually in terminal clusters. Wetland species include fringed gentian *(G. crinita)*, smaller fringed gentian *(G. procera)*, soapwort gentian *(G. saponaria)*, closed gentian *(G. andrewsii)*, and narrow-leaved gentian *(G. linearis)*.

Other names: Bottle gentian, blind gentian *(G. andrewsii)*.

Close relatives: Marsh-pinks *(Sabatia)*; centauries *(Centaurium)*; bartonias *(Bartonia)*; buckbean *(Menyanthes trifoliata)*; floating hearts *(Nymphoides)*.

Lifestyle: Among our most beautiful wildflowers, the fringed gentian is blue as "the male bluebird's back," wrote Thoreau. Its color is "the nearest to true blue of almost any wildflower," wrote botanist F. Schuyler Mathews. Deepest blue probably belongs to the closed gentian, though all of the gentians occasionally produce white flowers, too.

Wetland gentian species differ somewhat in their flower forms. Fringed gentian species show four flared-out petals with fringed edges; other gentians open only slightly or, as in closed gentian, hardly at all. They differ, too, in their growth scheme. Unlike the vast majority of wildflowers, the fringed gentians are annuals *(G. procera)* and biennials *(G. crinita)*, relying solely on wind-scattered seed for survival. The other wetland gentians are perennials, tending to persist longer in a given locale.

Even the fringed gentians seem to begrudge opening for very long. They open in direct sunlight, but a cloudy day shuts them tightly. Wetland gentians apparently tolerate a broad range of soil chemistry. Fringed gentians favor fens and wet meadows, but these and other gentians also appear (rarely) in acid bogs. Seldom, however, do they grow in great abundance anywhere.

Though technically bisexual, all gentian flowers develop mature pollen-bearing anthers before the female parts mature, a timing sequence known as *protandry.* This mechanism, seen in many wildflowers, actually amounts to sequentially unisexual flowers, one sex succeeding the other. Protandry thus prevents self-fertilization; by the time a (female) pistil becomes ready to receive pollen, the pollen–bearing anthers of the same flower have usually withered, and pollen must come from younger flower heads. Sometimes the fall season advances so far before pollen–bearing ceases that the female parts never catch up before frost occurs (in which case the flower ends up, by default, as unisexual male).

Associates: *Late summer, fall.* Look for wetland gentians amid swamp, fen, and bog vegetation such as sedges, grasses, marsh fern, and sphagnum mosses.

Compared with many flowers, gentians are relatively inhospitable to insects. Tubular gentian flowers, however, are especially adapted for bumblebee *(Bombus)* pollination; many "bumblebee flowers" are likewise blue. This powerfully built insect can shoulder its way past the entrance obstacles that discourage smaller, less efficient pollinators. Even the closed gentian admits the forceful entry of a bumblebee; the bee pries head–foremost into the flower, then backs out, combing the pollen from head and thorax into the baskets on its hind legs. Closed gentian is one of the riches of all flowers in nectar quantity (up to 45 milliliters) and sweetness (40 percent sugar). As with many deep, tubular flowers, bees sometimes perforate holes in the flower base from outside, thus short–

circuiting the conventional frontal route to the nectar—a route that, in gentians, always offers resistance.

Lore: The name is said to derive from one King Gentius of ancient Illyria (500 B.C.), who used the roots of European yellow gentian *(G. lutea)* medicinally. "It is too remarkable a flower not to be sought out and admired each year," wrote Thoreau. Poet William Cullen Bryant thought so, too, and penned his famous lines to "The Fringed Gentian," making this plant on of America's foremost literary flowers.

In the years since Thoreau and Bryant admired them, however, gentians have suffered grievously from the loss and shrinkage of wetland habitats. They are now uncommon to rare plants in many areas that formerly supported abundant gentian populations. The fringed gentians, being seed–grown annuals and biennials, are especially vulnerable to habitat changes; only one year's aborted growth can wipe out an entire population, since the seeds remain viable for only a short time. Although gentians are legally protected flowers in most places, the wetland habitats they must have to survive remain undervalued and underprotected.

Goldenrod, Bog *(Solidago uliginosa)*. Composite family. Tall herb in swamps, bogs, wet meadows. Its yellow, plumelike flowers in late summer and fall; its long, lancelike leaves at the plant base; and its stem-clasping leaf stalks identify this goldenrod. Another common wetland goldenrod is rough-leaved, square stemmed, or spreading goldenrod *(S. patula)*, with a four-angled stem and rough, sandpaperlike leaves.

Other names: Swamp goldenrod (for both species).

Close relatives: Asters *(Aster)*; boneset, Joe-Pye-weeds *(Eupatorium)*; ironweeds *(Vernonia)*; thistles *(Cirsium)*; bur-marigolds *(Bidens)*; sunflowers *(Helianthus)*; and all other composites.

Lifestyle: Most of the sixty or so goldenrod species of our area favor dry or mesic habitats, though many of these can adapt to wetter habitats as well. But only bog goldenrod and a few others consistently grow in wetlands, making these particular species fairly easy to identify. Bog goldenrod is probably the most acid-tolerant species, occupying poor to intermediate fen communities; the other wetland species favor richer fens.

Individual flowers of goldenrod, as in all composites, are tiny, compressed into composite flower heads. Two types of insect-pollinated flowers—ray and disk flowers—occupy each flower head. The radiating ray flowers (about five in bog goldenrod) are all unisexual female; the central disk flowers are bisexual. The numbers of insects attracted to goldenrods might lead one to conclude that their nectar is abundant, but goldenrods actually produce relatively little nectar compared with many other flowers. Their abundant pollen is probably the chief attraction. The seeds are *achenes,* each equipped with a small, feathery parachute for wind dispersal.

Goldenrods are cloning plants, forming colonies of stems from branching rhizomes. Although goldenrods often hybridize, this event probably occurs less commonly among wetland goldenrods than in more goldenrod-populous upland areas.

Associates: *Late summer, fall.* Common plant associates of bog goldenrod include sphagnum mosses, marsh fern, blue flag, Joe-Pye-weeds, tamarack, and bog birch.

Goldenrods attract a large variety of insect feeders. Bees and beetles feed on the

A bushy gall atop bog goldenrod stems results from feeding by a fly larva. The gall interrupts stem growth, causing leafy shoots and profuse branching to arise from and beneath the gall.

pollen, and various bees, bumblebees *(Bombus),* and the beelike syrphid flies (Syrphidae) consume nectar. Common beetles crawling over the flower heads may include the locust borer *(Megacyllene robiniae),* black and yellow-lined; in its larval stages it is a destructive pest in black locust trees. The banded longhorn *(Typocerus velutinus),* another beetle found in the flower heads, feeds as a larva in decaying birch and other trees. Soldier beetles, especially *Chauliognathus* species with black and yellow markings, are also common.

Lurking in the flower heads are also camouflaged predators of the bee and fly visitors. These are most often ambush bugs (Phymatidae; see Boneset) and crab or goldenrod spiders *(Misumena vatia)*; both are smaller than most of their insect prey.

Goldenrods host scores of gall-forming insects, chiefly midge larvae that cause stem swellings of various shapes and sizes. The familiar swollen ball gall, caused by the goldenrod gall flies *Eurosta solidaginis* and *Lasioptera solidaginis*, appears mainly on Canada goldenrod *(S. canadensis)*, an upland species. One of the most common galls on wetland goldenrods is a bushy "cabbage gall" that arrests growth at the top of the stem; the plant responds by sending out side branches just beneath the gall, giving the goldenrod a kind of top-heavy, bushy appearance. This gall insect is *Rhopalomyia solidaginis*, another fly larva.

The goldenrod leaf miner *(Cremastobombycia solidaginis)*, a tineid moth caterpillar, creates elongate, wrinkled mines on leaf undersides.

Goldenrods provide no significant food for birds or mammals.

Lore: Goldenrods have a long history of external and internal medicinal uses (mainly as astringents) by American natives and European physicians dating back to the Crusades. Bog goldenrod was valued by the Potawatomi, who used the thick rhizome for astringent poultices on wounds and boils.

Goldenrods contain diterpenes, which can be toxic to livestock (and presumably humans) when eaten in large quantities.

Grass-of-Parnassus *(Parnassia glauca)*. Saxifrage family. Herb in fens, wet meadows, along streams. Flowering in summer and fall, grass-of-Parnassus shows solitary flowers with green veins lining the five cream-white petals. A small leaf clasps the flowering stem.

Close relatives: Saxifrages *(Saxifraga)*; foam-flower *(Tiarella cordifolia)*; miterworts *(Mitella)*; alumroots *(Heuchera)*; mock-oranges *(Philadelphus)*; hydrangeas *(Hydrangea)*; currants, gooseberries *(Ribes)*.

Lifestyle: Neither a grass nor resembling one despite its name, this intriguing wildflower usually grows in small colonies, a resident of calcium-rich wetlands. Its bisexual, insect-pollinated flower is actually unisexually sequenced *(protandry)*, with male parts developing and declining before the female parts mature. Protandry virtually guarantees cross-pollination. The fruits are four-valved capsules.

Those green lines on the petals are nectar guides. They show up especially well to pollinating insects, who perceive a strong contrast between the lines and the whiteness of the petals, which weakly reflect ultraviolet light. These rays are

Green-lined, ultraviolet light-reflecting petals of grass-of-Parnassus help guide insects to the central nectaries. Note the central ring of stalked filaments (sham nectaries). The flower shown here appears in its later, female phase.

invisible to our eyes but are like neon to bees and other insects.

Note the stalked filaments (*staminoids*) bearing swollen heads that glisten like nectar droplets. If you touch one, however, you'll find it absolutely dry. These are sham nectaries (the real nectaries lie near their bases). The deceptive droplets are analogous to advertising hooks, which get the consumers into the store to discover the genuine goods.

Associates: *Summer, fall.* Fen associates of this plant may include sedges, shrubby cinquefoil, reed, and orchids such as showy lady-slipper, rose pogonia, and bog twayblade.

Flies, especially attracted by the false nectaries, are the chief pollinators. Small bees and butterflies, mainly skippers, also visit the flowers.

Lore: The similar Old World species *P. palustris* gave the plant its common name by supposedly having been first discovered growing on the slopes of Mount Parnassus in Greece.

Hollies (*Ilex, Nemopanthus* spp.). Holly family. Shrubs in swamps, shrub-carr.

Common winterberry (*Ilex verticillata*) has alternate leaves with short, bristly tips on the leaf teeth. The tips are perpendicular to the leaf surface. Winterberry has yellowish-white flowers and bright red fruits, which cluster close to the branches in autumn.

Mountain-holly (*Nemopanthus mucronata*) has smaller, untoothed leaves, each with a minute bristle at the apex. Yellowish flowers, crimson fruits, and short spur twigs on the branches help to identify it.

Other names: Northern holly, Michigan holly, redberry, blackhaw, Christmasberry, fever bush, black, striped, white, or false alder (*I. verticillata*); the alders (*Alnus*) are unrelated shrubs; catberry, bog holly, false holly, brick-timber (*N. mucronata*). Largeleaf holly or mountain winterberry (*I. montana*), an upland species, is also called mountain holly.

Close relatives: Other *Ilex* hollies.

Lifestyle: In spring and summer these cloning shrubs are easily overlooked in the general background greenery. Only in the fall, when their red fruits *(drupes)* blaze color into the swamp thickets, do they become highly visible. For winter identification of *Ilex,* look for a tiny black dot flanking each leaf scar; these are stipule scars, not always present but always diagnostic of this genus when they are.

Mountain-holly generally flowers earlier and fruits in summer, producing "the most beautiful of berries," opined Thoreau. Winterberry flowers in late spring and summer, fruiting in the fall; its fruits often remain on the plant into midwinter. The inconspicuous insect-pollinated flowers are generally unisexual on the same or different plants. Male flowers grow in clusters, while the female ones are solitary. The first frost blackens the leaves, which fall almost overnight.

Common winterberry fruits, crowded along the twigs, blaze bright red in autumn swamp thickets. Only in the fall do these shrubs become conspicuous. Branching sometimes appears opposite at branch tips because of crowded budding.

Both hollies are moderately shade tolerant and tolerant of flooding. Mountain-holly usually favors more acidic habitats adjacent to bogs; winterberry typically resides in shrubby swamps.

Associates: Winterberry plant associates include black ash, red maple, highbush blueberry, common elderberry, and poison sumac.

Look for mountain-holly among northern white cedar, tamarack, leatherleaf, speckled alder, black chokeberry, swamp rose, and the aforementioned blueberry and sumac. In some areas, both hollies may grow in close proximity.

Spring, summer. Bees and bumblebees *(Bombus)* are probably the chief pollinators.

The holly leafminer *(Phytomyza ilicis),* a fly larva, makes blotch mines and serpentine tunnels in the leaf undersides.

Late summer, fall, winter. Aborted fruits of winterberry result from the feeding of gall midge larvae *(Asphondylia ilicoides)*; adult midges lay eggs in the young fruit.

Although many bird species consume the bright fruits, these fruits are relatively low in fat content and are usually not a favored food. Birds often eat them later in the season or in winter when choicer fruits are gone. Frequent songbird consumers include eastern bluebirds; gray-cheeked, Swainson's, hermit, and wood thrushes; American robins; gray catbirds; northern mockingbirds; brown thrashers; cedar waxwings; and white-throated sparrows. Ruffed grouse, mourning doves, northern flickers, pileated woodpeckers, and eastern phoebes also eat the fruits. Hollies are probably dispersed chiefly by birds, since these feeders cannot digest the hard nutlets in the fruit.

Raccoons and white-footed mice consume the fruits and seeds; mice "run up the twigs in the night and gather this shining fruit," wrote Thoreau, "take out the small seeds, and eat their kernels at the entrance to their burrows." White-tailed deer browse the foliage and twigs.

Lore: The Christmas holly familiar to most people is the tree-sized, closely related American holly *(I. opaca)*; like many holly species (but unlike winterberry and mountain-holly), its leaves are thorny and evergreen.

The English holly of pagan religions, European history, and folklore is *I. aquifolium,* also thorny and evergreen. This holly has been cultivated for many ornamental holly varieties used for hedges and yard plantings. The word *Ilex* originally referred to the unrelated European holly oak *(Quercus ilex),* another evergreen.

American natives used winterberry bark internally and externally for astringent tonics and poultices and antiseptic medicines. All *Ilex* hollies contain the bitter compound ilicin. Holly fruits, toxic to humans, were once used to induce vomiting and expel worms.

These plants, so colorful in autumn, number among those threatened by wetland depletion during the past decades. Today they are legally protected in most states.

Horsetails *(Equisetum* spp.). Horsetail family. Herbs in various wet, mesic, and dry habitats. Recognize these unique plants by their rough, bamboolike, hollow and jointed stems, whorled branching, and catkinlike spore cones *(strobili)* atop the fertile stems. The most common wetland species are dwarf horsetail *(E. scirpoides),* rough or common horsetail *(E. hyemale),* wood horsetail *(E. sylvaticum),* marsh horsetail *(E. palustre),* and swamp or water horsetail *(E. fluviatile).*

Other names: Scouring rush, pipes, horse-pipe, ditch rush, shave-grass, scrubgrass, gunbright, mare's-tail, joint-grass, bottle-brush.

Close relatives: None.

Lifestyle: Horsetails, allied to ferns, are one of the most ancient plant families on Earth, their fossil history better known than that of any other plant group. They are the sole survivors of a lush Carboniferous vegetation that included the long-extinct, tree-sized calamites, whose spore deposits produced some of the world's biggest coal beds. Viewing at ground level amid a stand of horsetails, you can gain some idea of what the Paleozoic forests must have looked like.

Their spore reproduction methods are much like ferns (see Ferns). Instead of fruit dots on leaves or spore stalks, however, they produce spores in stem-top solitary cones that look armored with polygonal scales. Ripe spores germinate into separate unisexual gametophytes, which produce a new sporophyte, or cone-bearing, plant.

Horsetails also reproduce by cloning from creeping rhizomes, which may extend in spreading networks hundreds of feet outward and many feet downward. Rough horsetail can also sprout new stems from old stem fragments containing a node (joint) even while floating in water; probably some of the other species can do this too.

The five species mentioned all produce both fertile and sterile stems, but they differ in several other characteristics. Dwarf horsetail, the smallest, curls in twining, prostrate mats; all the others are erect. Both dwarf and rough horsetails are unbranched. Sterile stems of wood horsetail show lacy, delicate branch whorls (the plant resembles a miniature tree), but its fertile stems are whitish and unbranched. Marsh and swamp horsetails have numerous ascending branches. Dwarf and rough

Dwarf horsetail, smallest of these jointed plants, is sprawling and evergreen. It often forms a low ground cover in shady cedar swamps, along with mosses and liverworts.

horsetails are evergreen. The latter species grows tallest, to five feet. The most aquatic species is swamp horsetail, which grows in quiet waters with mud bottoms. The others usually occupy marginal shoreline habitats.

The rough-textured surface of horsetail stems results from the plants' uptake of silica in solution. It becomes crystallized in the plant tissues. Rough horsetail has the grittiest stem, and swamp horsetail has one of the smoothest ("like small bamboos from Oriental jungles," wrote Thoreau).

The tiny spores come equipped with two ribbonlike devices called *elaters*, which are extremely sensitive to atmospheric humidity. They coil around the spore, only uncoiling in dry air; their movements help disperse the spores. You can observe this action with a hand lens by placing an opening spore cone on a sheet of paper. Breathe lightly on the released spores and watch the "dance of the elaters."

Associates: *All year.* Horsetails can be found in almost any wetland that isn't too acid. Most of them like room to spread out, and pure stands or patches of them are typically seen growing among sedges. Dwarf horsetails thrive in damp shade with bryophytes.

These plants remain quite free of insect herbivores, probably owing to their tough, grainy tissues.

Tundra swans and snow geese sometimes eat the stems and rhizomes, and smooth young shoots of swamp horsetail are consumed by muskrats. Moose also eat the plants, especially in winter.

Lore: Despite the fact that cattle seem to relish swamp horsetail, most horsetails are toxic, especially to horses and probably to humans (though this is not well documented; in direct contradiction, records exist of Indian and French colonial travelers who considered the plants "excellent horse feed"). The plants have a laxative effect, which apparently helps prevent serious poisoning. (Toxicity is said to result from a disturbance of the body's thiamine metabolism.)

American natives and folk practitioners used horsetails for astringent poultices and, in decoctions, for kidney and urinary problems. But these plants (so named from their fancied resemblance to a horse's tail) were best known as readily available scouring pads. Their abrasive roughness proved effective for scouring out pans and kettles, for sanding and polishing wooden and metal objects, and for scrubbing floors. They were collected in bundles as a stock kitchen item for pioneer homesteaders in the days before steel wool or soap pads. They can still serve much the same purpose for camp chores.

The fully opened blue flag displays its large, fused sepals marked with nectar guides for incoming insect visitors. The flower's sexual parts lie just beneath the curled-up style roofing the sepals.

Irises, Wild (*Iris* spp.). Iris family. Herbs in marshes, fens, wet meadows, and upland areas.

Recognize the larger blue flag (*I. versicolor*) by its showy, purple-veined blue flower. Yellow iris (*I. pseudacorus*) has a large, all-yellow flower. Both irises raise erect, straplike, bluish-green leaves, which resemble cattail leaves, though shorter.

Other names: Blue iris, wild iris, fleur-de-lis, flower-de-luce, flag lily, snake-liver (*I. versicolor*); water flag (*I. pseudacorus*).

Close relatives: Blackberry-lily (*Belamcanda chinensis*); blue-eyed grasses (*Sisyrinchium*); crocus (*Crocus neapolitanus*); gladiolus (*Gladiolus*).

Lifestyle: Some twelve *Iris* (not all of them wetland) species grow wild in east-central North America, but these two are by far the most common.

The spectacular flowers are, more literally than most flowers, exhibitionistic "flags" that capture the attention of pollinating insects. Each flower is bisexual. While a single flower stalk may produce several flowers, the flowers bloom sequentially, not all at once. Lines called nectar guides adorn the largest, tonguelike part, which consists of three fused sepals. The three upright parts are the petals, and the curved structures above the sepals hold the sexual parts. An insect pushing beneath this curved entrance (actually the female flower) is "combed" of pollen as it enters, and it also brushes against the pollen-bearing anthers. The female parts face away from the anthers, so the chances of self-pollination are reduced. The fruit, a three-lobed capsule, splits to release the stacked seeds. These can float on water, thus aiding in dispersal.

Irises rise from thick, creeping rhizomes that branch and spread. They typically appear in small, cloning patches, seldom in large, pure stands.

New plants usually produce only leaves for the first year or two, so a flowering iris represents more than a season's effort. Irises thrive best in full sunlight, but they can also tolerate light shade.

Associates: Wetland irises thrive in areas dominated by sedges, rushes such as *Juncus effusus,* the similar-leafed sweet-flag, and other plants that favor wet, mineral-rich habitats.

Spring, summer. Flower pollinators are usually large insects such as bumblebees *(Bombus);* smaller halictid and other solitary bees, including *Synhalonia frater;* mason bees *(Osmia destructa)*; digger bees *(Clisodon terminalis)*; and syrphid flies *(Rhingia rostrata).*

Common insect residents in iris flowers include thrips (Thysanoptera) and the flower beetle *Trichiotinus piger,* a pollen feeder. Flag weevils *(Mononychus vulpeculus),* which puncture holes in the nectaries and also eat the seeds, occur frequently. Short-horned grasshoppers (Acrididae) consume iris petals, and hairy moth caterpillars such as the agreeable tiger moth *(Spilosoma congrua)* feed first on leaves, then on the petals. Larvae of a picture-winged fly *(Chaetopsis aenea)* feed on the flower buds before they open.

Blue flag seed capsules, reflecting earlier alignment of the spectacular flowers, release floating seeds.

Several nonpollinating nectar feeders are frequent flower visitors. These include two orange-brown, medium-sized butterflies: Harris' checkerspot *(Melitaea harrisii)* and the bronze copper *(Lycaena thoë).* Several yellowish skippers— tawny-edged *(Polites themistocles)*, Peck's *(P. peckius)*, the long dash *(P. mystic)*, and the hobomok *(Poanes hobomok)*—are also common visitors.

"The burnished dragon fly is thine attendant," waxed Longfellow about "Flower-de-Luce." So it is, but also look on the leaves for folded tips forming boxlike chambers, the nurseries of *Clubiona* spiders (see Cattails). Larvae of a fly, *Agromyza laterella,* mine in the leaves and create bunchy galls. Hairy, yellowish caterpillars of the Virginia ctenucha *(Ctenucha virginica),* a wasp moth, also feed on the leaves.

Iris borer caterpillars *(Macronoctua onusta),* noctuid moths, enter leaf tissues in spring and work their way down into the rhizome, which they eat out, leaving only a papery skin. Ragged-looking leaves and rotted tissue at the leaf bases may indicate the presence of this moth, iris's chief pest. Most of the damage results from the soft-rot bacteria carried and transmitted by these large, pinkish caterpillars.

Late summer, fall. Watch for the aforementioned iris borer moths. They appear now as blackish, thick-bodied adult insects hovering near old iris leaves. There they lay eggs, which remain over winter and hatch in spring.

The tortricid moth caterpillar *Olethreutes hebesana* bores into iris seed capsules.

Iris seeds are not relished by waterfowl, but certain marsh birds such as common moorhens eat them. Muskrats sometimes consume plant parts.

Lore: Irises and rainbows have ancient connections. In Greek mythology, Iris was the rainbow, a messenger goddess designated to transport women's souls to the Elysian fields after death.

Colonial France's blue national flag during the years of early American exploration was nicknamed the *fleur-de-lis* because of its iris symbol. The significance of this flower for the French originated as far back as the first century A.D., when it adorned the banners of Gaul. Louis VII, the Crusader king, adopted the flower (probably *I. germanica*) as his personal emblem, and the *fleur-de-Louis* became the "flower of chivalry" with "a sword for its leaf and a lily for its heart," wrote John Ruskin. Napoleon later discarded the symbol as a royal anathema (and replaced it with some iris pollinators, golden bees).

From *I. germanica* plus several other Old World species came genes for the hundreds of cultivated and bearded irises that flower today in garden splendor.

Yellow iris, also a European native, escaped from colonial cultivation into our wetlands. In early Christianity, yellow iris became associated with the Virgin Mary. One botanist has listed this species among those hardy plants likely to flourish after a nuclear holocaust.

Like all irises, the native *I. versicolor* is toxic to humans and cattle. Rhizomes contain irisin, an acrid substance used to produce the drug iridin, and are exceedingly bitter.

American natives brewed small fragments of the rhizome for drastically powerful cathartics and emetics. They also used them as poultices for external wounds and sores. Various tribes used the leaves as sources of green dye and for weaving mats and baskets. The Ojibwa carried pieces of the root as charms against snakebite, believing the scent protected them.

Larger blue flag is the official flower of Tennessee and the province of Quebec.

Jack-in-the-pulpit *(Arisaema triphyllum)*. Arum family. Herb in wet and mesic woodlands, swamps. Recognize this plant by its three-parted leaf or leaves, a striped floral leaf *(spathe)* forming a hooded canopy over the enclosed clublike *spadix*, and its cluster of scarlet berries in the fall.

Other names: Indian turnip, wild turnip, marsh-pepper, bog-onion, brown dragon, starchwort, wake-robin, dragon-root, cuckoo-pint.

Close relatives: Green dragon *(A. dracontium)*; arrow-arum *(Peltandra virginica)*; skunk-cabbage *(Symplocarpus foetidus)*; wild calla *(Calla palustris)*; sweet-flag *(Acorus calamus)*; philodendrons *(Philodendron)*; breadfruit *(Artocarpus communis)*; calla lily *(Zantedeschia aethiopica)*.

Lifestyle: There are three distinct forms or varieties of this familiar species, one of them favoring more mesic woodland habitats (see *The Book of Forest and Thicket*).

The flowers are usually unisexual, but it's impossible to tell male from female without prying open the "pulpit" base to examine the spadix. Female flowers are round and berrylike on the spadix; the male pollen-bearing flowers are threadlike.

The plants arise from an underground stem called a *corm*. In any given year, a corm may produce either a male or female plant. The plants have no sex chromosomes as such. Which sex "happens" apparently depends on the size of the plant, hence the amount of food accumulated in the corm. This sex "decision" occurs in the fall, when the corm sprouts the plant that will appear aboveground the following spring. Individual corms may also bud off new corms, thus forming new plants; some corms survive for twenty years or longer.

A large plant bearing two compound leaves is almost invariably female. Small plants bearing only one leaf are male or asexual. Once a corm becomes large enough to produce a female plant, it may continue producing females for years (unless or until it becomes depleted from a poor growing season or insect attack). So Jack-in-the-pulpit adapts itself remarkably to varying environmental conditions, changing its sex (and thus its energy needs, since male plants require less) to meet the circumstances of a particular growing season.

The lowermost chamber housing the spadix often traps small insects, because the slippery internal walls may prevent them from climbing out. This situation is probably an incidental consequence of the floral structure and not a capture mechanism, as in pitcher-plants. Still, though not technically considered an insect-trapping plant, Jack sometimes accumulates a sizable corpse litter in its basal floral chamber.

Jack-in-the-pulpit adapts its size, coloration, and sex to environmental circumstances. It also traps insects inside the lower chamber housing the club-shaped spadix.

The insect-pollinated flower produces no nectar. Spadix bases, however, produce a fungus-like odor that certain insects find irresistible.

Naturalist Hal Borland believed that shaded plants show darker stripes on the green spathe than plants exposed to open sunlight. He suggested that the darker stripes aided the flower's heat conservation in its cooler sites.

Associates: *Spring, summer.* Jack-in-the-pulpit occupies the same shady, wet woodland habitats as its relatives skunk-cabbage and green dragon.

Some populations of the plant bear a bright yellow rust fungus on leaves and flowers. This is *Uromyces ari-triphylli,* a basidiomycete (club fungus). Once parasitized with this spore-producing rust, corms remain infected for as long as they live.

Pollinating insects are mainly fungus gnats (Mycetophilidae) and dark-winged fungus gnats (Sciaridae), attracted by the odor. A species of thrips (Heterothripidae)—tiny, barely visible insects—feeds in the flowers.

This plant's chemical defenses make its foliage and corms extremely unpalatable to most insects and mammals.

Fall. The scarlet berries attract a few bird feeders, probably the plant's chief dispersers. Ring-necked pheasants, wild turkeys, and wood thrushes consume these fruits. They rank low in quality, however, as a wildlife food.

Lore: Calcium oxalate crystals, found also in other arums, produce an intensely caustic, corrosive taste in leaves, corms, and fruits of Jack-in-the-pulpit. Meskwaki tribesmen made a war weapon of the fresh, grated corm; they added it to meat and offered it to their Sioux enemies, who ate it—and died in agony.

Thorough drying, however, rids the starchy corm of this substance. It then becomes safely edible, either sliced thinly or powdered into flour. Native tribes collected and dried the corms for food. They also used it in internal medicines for colds and bronchial ailments and externally for poultices on aches and sores.

This plant's common name was originated by a clerical-minded New Englander, one Clara Smith of Medford, Massachusetts. She sent a "flowery" verse to poet John G. Whittier for his approval. He tinkered with it, finally publishing it under his own famous name about 1884. Thus "Jack" suddenly became a good (if somewhat plagiarized) New England Calvinist flower.

Jewelweeds (*Impatiens* spp.). Touch-me-not family. Herbs in wet, shady areas, around shorelines, springs. Recognize jewelweeds by their succulent, translucent stems; horizontal, pendant, rear-spurred orange or yellow flowers; and smooth, alternate leaves. Two species are common: spotted jewelweed (*I. capensis*), with orange-yellow flowers sometimes spotted with brown and a long, bent-back spur; and pale jewelweed (*I. pallida*), with pale yellow flowers and a short, right-angled rear spur. Spotted jewelweed usually grows only in wet habitats; pale jewelweed may also occupy somewhat drier sites.

Other names: Touch-me-not, silver-cap, wild balsam, lady's eardrops, snapweed, wild lady's-slipper, silverleaf, celandine.

Close relative: Garden balsam (*I. balsamina*).

Lifestyle: Unlike the vast majority of wildflowers, jewelweeds are annuals, reproducing solely from seed each spring. Each flower produces about 2.5 milliliters of nectar, containing about 40 percent sugar, in a day. Pale jewelweed usually begins flowering shortly before spotted jewelweed in summer and holds each flower for two or three days, about a day longer than spotted jewelweed. Both species continue flowering until the first frost.

Though technically bisexual, jewelweed flowers are actually sequentially unisexual *(protandrous)*; that is, the male flower parts develop and decline before the female parts mature. The male phase generally lasts a day or two longer than the female phase. This differential timing helps ensure cross-pollination, especially important for an annual relying exclusively on seed for its survival.

But jewelweeds have it both ways, for they also produce small, green, inconspicuous flowers that never open. These *cleistogamous* flowers are entirely self-pollinated. Many jewelweeds, especially those growing in dense shade or drier soil, produce more of them (late in the season, typically) than of the conspicuous open flowers, which tend to be more numerous in sunnier places and optimal habitat conditions. In some jewelweed populations, cleistogamous flowers are indeed the major seed producers.

These two methods of seed production give the plants some growth options. The expelling force of the explosive seed capsules varies depending on the type of flower that produced it; seeds from the open flower are tossed farther from the parent plant than seeds from the closed flower. Researchers speculate that the short-tossed seeds from closed flowers are more likely to land in a spot similar to the parent's habitat—and thus thrive. The farther-tossed seeds, carrying genes from two parent plants, are better equipped to survive in conditions perhaps somewhat different than those of the parent site. Such reproductive options provide the best possible survival chances for plants that, given only one season's failure of seed production (since the seed remains viable for only one spring), could disappear from their habitats.

The oval seed capsule, held straight under tension, splits and coils suddenly when triggered, throwing the released seeds up to four feet or more from the plant. Often just a breeze or a slight tap on the capsule is enough to send the seeds catapulting (hence the name touch-me-not) when they're ready to go.

Jewelweed leaves, too, are fascinating works of the plant kingdom. They are unwettable, beading water on their surfaces as if coated with oil. The "oil" is actually a thin film of air trapped by a surface of microscopic hairs, especially on the leaf underside. Immerse a leaf in water and watch it turn silver, owing to its air "coating." Pick it up and it will be perfectly dry. The adaptive value of this efficient waterproofing remains unknown.

Plants in a colony are usually all the same age, since jewelweed seeds germinate more-or-less simultaneously in any given area (they require at least 140 days of winter stratification, or "cold treatment"). Heights and timing rates for sexual flower development vary within populations, however. Both species often overlap in habitat, but they seem never to hybridize; they reject or abort each other's pollen tubes.

Jewelweed seed capsules on the plant (top) curl explosively, sometimes hurling the seeds (bottom left) several feet away. In contrast to most wildflowers, jewelweed colonies spring entirely from the previous year's seed.

Jewelweed populations illustrate the ecological self-regulating mechanisms known as *density dependence;* that is, their vigor and mortality are importantly influenced by how densely they grow. Shading and competitive crowding of stems tend to thin them out, thus enhancing the colonial welfare.

Associates: *Summer, fall.* Jewelweeds often

form dominant herb canopies that may suppress or shade out the establishment of perennial herbs. This situation—an annual species achieving persistent habitat dominance over long-lived perennials—is unusual in plant ecology.

Other common plants in mineral-rich jewelweed habitats may include sedges, rushes, skunk-cabbage, and marsh marigold.

A twining, parasitic vine that often taps into jewelweeds (and many other plants) is dodder *(Cuscuta gronovii)*. Beginning as rooted plants, these yellow-orange, threadlike vines twist around jewelweed stems and penetrate them with tiny suckers. Eventually dodder receives its full nourishment from the parasitized plant. Look for twisted, stringy mats of dodder lying atop the jewelweed canopy ("like a tangled mass of golden yarn," wrote one botanist), intermeshed with the plants. Dodder lacks leaves but produces tiny masses of white flowers along the vines (see illustration for Vervain, Blue).

Insect pollinators are primarily bees—bumblebees *(Bombus)*, honeybees *(Apis mellifera)*, leafcutting bees (Megachilidae)—and a wasp, the eastern yellowjacket *(Vespula maculifrons)*. Spotted jewelweed seems to attract more insect species than pale jewelweed, perhaps because of its larger flower spur and landing platform. Bumblebee and yellowjacket nectar thieves cut holes in the rear spurs. Secondary thieves also feeding at these holes often include honeybees (which may alternate their robbing with entering a flower the "right way" and pollinating it); green metallic-colored halictid bees *(Augochlora, Augochloropsis)*; and ants *(Crematogaster;* brownish in color, they look like their abdomens are turned upside down). Syrphid flies that also rob the nectar include *Rhingia nasica* and *Platycheirus* (naturalist Edwin Way Teale observed syrphid flies clinging to jewelweed flowers at night). Metallic bluish or green blow flies *(Lucilia, Phaenicia)* also feed here, as do the skeletonizing leaf beetles *Diabrotica undecimpunctata* (spotted cucumber beetle) and *D. longicornis* (northern corn rootworm). Despite all of this nectar thievery and bypassing of the front gate, the apparent impact on seed production remains insignificant.

Another important pollinator is the ruby-throated hummingbird, which feeds on the abundant nectar. Jewelweed produces one of the most important summer hummingbird flowers in the eastern United States. Patches of jewelweed are good places to watch for these tiny, colorful birds.

Grasshoppers and katydids feed on jewelweed buds and flowers, as do brightly colored soldier beetles (Cantharidae).

A succulent, roundish gall at flower or bud bases indicates the presence of *Cecidomyia impatientis,* gall gnat larvae.

Insect foliage feeders are also numerous. Probably the foremost is *Rhabdopterus praetexus,* a leaf beetle that skeletonizes the leaves, sometimes defoliating entire plants. It apparently feeds quite exclusively on jewelweeds.

Leaves showing small puncture marks or linear blotch mines are signs of the jewelweed leafminer *(Agromyza borealis).* The yellowish adult female insects, which hover like syrphid flies, puncture the leaf surface when they lay their eggs; the hatched, feeding larvae create the mines.

Yellowish, hairy caterpillars of the Virginia tiger moth *(Spilosoma virginica)* commonly feed on jewelweed leaves. Another caterpillar feeder is the white-striped black moth *(Trichodezia albovittata),* an inchworm; adult forms are striking in appearance—black with a white bar across the forewings. Sawfly larvae *(Aglaostigma semiluteum),* resembling caterpillars, may also be seen.

Swellings at leaf bases or midrib folds are caused by another gall gnat larva, *Lasioptera impatientifolia.*

Stems of jewelweed also have their specialists. Caterpillars of *Olethreutes agilana,* a tortricid moth, bore into the stems. Marsh weevils *(Smicronyx quadrifer)* begin feeding in the aforementioned parasitic dodder, then move into stems of the host plant—an unusual procedure among plant feeders. Larvae of the gall gnats *Lasioptera fulva* and *Mycodiplosis impatientis* produce swollen stem galls.

Major seed eaters include nymphs of the stink bug *Acrosternum hilare.*

Gamebirds, including ruffed grouse, ring-necked pheasants, and northern bobwhites, also relish the seeds. White-footed mice and short-tailed shrews often cache the seeds in their nests.

Lore: In the wetland muds of early spring, I have found seedling carpets of jewelweed to be reliable indicators of soft, saturated ground too miry to support a safe step. Knowing this has helped me avoid some instances, at least, of "bogging down." Later in the season, when many of these spots become drier, the correlation isn't so reliable.

Jewelweed is also a well-known friend in another respect—again I speak from personal experience. The juice of its stem and foliage provides quite effective relief for skin rashes and insect bites. Mashing the plant, then applying the pulpy mass to poison ivy, poison sumac, or nettle rashes reduces the inflammation and relieves pain and itching (a remedy that has now been authenticated by medical science). Immediate application of jewelweed after skin exposure to poison ivy or poison sumac may also help neutralize the oily urushiol, which causes contact dermatitis.

At least one of the effective compounds in jewelweed is tannin, an astringent acid found in many plant leaves and tree barks. Although jewelweeds do not invariably grow in or near the same habitats as poison ivy, often they do; so the remedy for exposure may be close at hand. Certainly one should learn to identify both these plants: one to avoid, the other to provide relief for nonavoidance. American natives and pioneers were well aware of jewelweed's benefits as a skin treatment. They also drank it as a decoction for stomach cramps and various other ailments. The boiled juice of the plant produced a useful orange-yellow dye.

Young shoots can be eaten as a cooked green with plenty of rinsing and boiling, but other greens are tastier and require less preparation.

Joe-Pye-weeds *(Eupatorium* spp.). Composite family. Tall herbs in swamps, marshes, wet thickets. Flowering in summer and fall, Joe-Pye-weeds show pinkish-purple, domed or flat-topped flower clusters; whorls of three to seven long, toothed leaves; and often purple-streaked or purple-spotted stems.

The most common wetland species include spotted Joe-Pye-weed *(E. maculatum)*, hollow Joe-Pye-weed *(E. fistulosum)*, and Joe-Pye-weed *(E. dubium)*, an eastern coastal species.

Other names: Gravel-root, Indian-gravel, kidney-root, trumpet-weed, king or queen of the meadows, skunk-weed, marsh milkweed, quillwort, purple boneset or thoroughwort.

Close relatives: Bonesets *(Eupatorium)*; ironweeds *(Vernonia)*; thistles *(Cirsium)*; asters *(Aster)*; goldenrods *(Solidago)*; bur-marigolds *(Bidens)*; sunflowers *(Helianthus)*; and all other composites.

Lifestyle: Their floral characteristics place Joe-Pye-weeds in the same genus as boneset (see Boneset), but their flower colors and leaf arrangements are much different. Joe-Pye-weeds also resemble ironweeds in form, again with leaf and flower differences.

Many composites, such as asters and daisies, have both disk and ray flowers. Joe-Pye-weeds are among those members of this huge family that, like thistles and others, have only disk flowers; in other words, if you pull off all the ray flowers ("petals") of a daisy, what remains is the central hub of disk flowers, which constitutes the sole flower head of Joe-Pye-weeds. The bisexual, insect-pollinated flowers come into bloom a few at a time in clusters atop the stem. Placement of their sexual parts often permits these flowers to self-pollinate as well, eventually producing furry heads of feathery achenes that are dispersed by wind in the fall.

The dead stalks often remain standing through winter, bleak swamp skeletons that imagination finds difficult to clothe with color. New stems arise in spring from horizontal, perennial rhizomes. These, with their roots, form a tough, tangled subsurface matrix that helps bind loose marsh soil into land.

Look straight down the stem of a Joe-Pye-weed and note how each leaf whorl is slightly rotated from the whorl above and below. This arrangement enables maximal light to reach each leaf. Joe-Pye-weeds require open sunlight and are not very shade tolerant.

Associates: *Summer, fall. Eupatorium* and ironweeds often share the same general habitats. Where boneset or ironweeds exist, chances are good that spotted or hollow Joe-Pye-weed may also reside. All of these plants favor mineral-rich sites, often occupying transitional zones of rank growth between cattails and swamp loosestrife on the water side and goldenrods or Queen Anne's lace on the landward side. Often too, as in ditches or swales, the zonation is not so distinct, and Joe-Pye-weed associates may include sedges, marsh fern, swamp thistle, and jewelweeds, among others.

Pollinating insects include various bees, flies, and—very often—butterflies, all attracted by the fragrant nectar deep in the tubular florets. Tiger swallowtails *(Papilio glaucus)* and fritillaries (Nymphalidae), plus many smaller butterflies, land frequently: patches of Joe-Pye-weed are excellent places to see or photograph these lepidopterans.

Deep inside the flower heads or just below them I have often observed tiny beetles, shiny black and convex on top. These are shining mold beetles (Phalacridae); one species *(Olibrus)* frequently feeds in the flower heads of composites. Caterpillars of the three-lined flower moth *(Schinia trifascia)* consume both flowers and seeds.

Larvae of *Dasyneura purpurea*, tiny gall gnats, create small galls in the flower buds.

Moth caterpillars and beetles that favor Joe-Pye-weed foliage, stems, and roots are generally the same ones that feed on this plant's close relatives (see Boneset). A common stem borer is *Papaipema eupatorii*, a noctuid moth caterpillar.

Tiger swallowtails and other large and small butterflies are common visitors to flowering Joe-Pye-weeds, which are some of the most common wetland wildflowers seen in summer and fall.

These are not major wildlife food plants. Mallard, ruffed grouse, wild turkeys, and swamp sparrows are among its few seed eaters.

Lore: Who was Joe Pye? His name has come down through oral tradition. Scholars have diligently tried to trace this legendary Indian herbalist and healer who supposedly befriended New England pioneers, but the name on the plant is really all that remains of him. He may have been a Mohegan who lived and practiced his homeopathic arts near Salem, Massachusetts, in colonial times. It is said that he brewed decoctions of the plant bearing his name to induce sweating in typhus fever.

The name *Eupatorium* memorializes another, much earlier healer. This was first-century Mithradates IV Eupator, king of Pontus (southern Black Sea), who reputedly used a plant of this genus for some ancient ache or pain.

Much later (1785), the Reverend Manasseh Cutler reported that an infusion of the plant "vomits and purges smartly." The names gravel-root and kidney-root resulted from the astringent rhizome's wide usage among natives and pioneers for urinary ailments. Forest Potawatomi, among other tribes, regarded the flowers as good-luck charms, especially effective for winning at gambling.

Labrador-tea *(Ledum groenlandicum)*. Heath family. Low shrub in bogs. Recognize Labrador-tea by its spicy-fragrant, leathery, evergreen leaves with inrolled edges. Leaf undersides are densely woolly and white or rust-colored.

Other names: Muskeg tea, country tea, marsh tea, Hudson's Bay tea.

Close relatives: Azaleas *(Rhododendron)*; laurels *(Kalmia)*; bog-rosemary *(Andromeda glaucophylla)*; leatherleaf *(Chamaedaphne calyculata)*; blueberries and cranberries *(Vaccinium)*.

Lifestyle: One of the many heaths that inhabit northern bogs, Labrador-tea is a welcome sight (and fragrance) in the dense, shrubby undergrowth of these unique environments. It seldom grows much taller than three feet.

The thick, furry coat on the leaf undersides (see illustration for Bog-rosemary) was once believed to be a desert adaptation for conserving water in an often frozen environment. Researchers now believe, however, that this physiological drought theory does not hold water; bog plants, dormant in winter, have few problems with water stress except sometimes in early spring, when leaves begin to function and roots may still be frozen. Though leathery evergreen leaves in bogs certainly resemble desert plant adaptations, they are probably adapted for nutrient, not water, deficiencies. And fuzzy leaf undersides probably protect from cold, allowing the leaves to function longer into fall and earlier in spring. Another theory, however, simply regards these adaptations as typical characteristics of the heath family rather than basic survival strategies (see Bog-rosemary).

Though technically evergreen, the leaves actually turn brownish in the fall, persisting on the plant into the following year. The wool is white on new leaves and turns rusty-brown as they age. Thoreau remarked upon "the perfect tent form" of the plant's upper leaves.

The fragrant white flower clusters topping the plant in spring are bisexual and insect pollinated. Look closely at the seed capsules; they resemble miniature rockets, with dead, swept-back petals and the persistent style.

Labrador-tea is shade intolerant, though somewhat less so than its frequent associate, leatherleaf. This slight difference in shade tolerance enables Labrador-tea to replace leatherleaf in bogs where trees or taller shrubs are invading.

Associates: Sphagnum mosses, leatherleaf, bog-rosemary, pale laurel, and black spruce are Labrador-tea's common plant associates. Others include blueberries and small cranberry. The symbiosis with subsurface mycorrhizal fungi, as in most heath plants, enables vital nutrient absorption into the roots (see Blueberries).

A greenish-yellow foliose lichen *(Cetraria pinastri)* sometimes grows on stems and branches.

Spring, summer. Flower pollinators include bumblebees *(Bombus)*, other bees, and syrphid flies (Syrphidae).

Like most bog heaths, Labrador-tea has few insect pests. Its tannins and other chemicals not only show remarkable resistance to bacterial and viral infections, but also seem able to neutralize the effects of microbe enzymes that do manage to invade.

A red or yellow fungus *(Exobasidium vaccinii)* often colors and distorts the leaves (see Leatherleaf).

All year: White-tailed deer and moose are known to feed on Labrador-tea, probably mainly during winter months when choicer browse is scarce.

Seed capsules of Labrador-tea resemble fireworks as they arc from the stem. A handful of Labrador-tea leaves will lend the fragrance of a bog to your pocket.

Lore: To me, the strong odor of Labrador-tea carries unique associations. Its leaves seem to hold and condense the acid pungency of the heath wetlands, a bitter-fragrant bog perfume that conjures instant mental pictures of this rigorous yet lush environment. Thoreau described the leaf odor as "between turpentine and strawberries" and like "the peculiar scent of a bee."

Long used as a tea (and sometimes tobacco) substitute by natives and other residents of northern regions, the fragrant leaves make an agreeable brew—best taken, however, in small quantities. Too much at once can be toxic, causing headache, vertigo, and symptoms of intoxication. "In Canada," reported E. Delamare in 1888, "it is used to put a head on small beers." The toxic substance is acetylandromedol, found also in bog-rosemary and leatherleaf.

The tea has also been used medicinally as a tonic, diuretic, and astringent treatment for intestinal upsets and bronchitis. Damp poultices of the leaves are said to provide effective relief for skin ulcers, burns, and insect bites. Twigs and decoctions of the leaves were also used as insect repellents, both on the skin and in stored clothing. Linnaeus stated that the leaves mixed in stored corn kept mice away. A brown dye made from the plant was once used to color woolens.

Lady-slippers (*Cypripedium* spp.). Orchid family. Herbs in a variety of habitats (see *The Book of Forest and Thicket*). Identify these orchids by their ballooning, pouch-shaped lower petal *(labellum)* and a large top sepal reaching above the flower. The three most common lady-slippers are pink lady-slipper *(C. acaule)*, yellow lady-slipper *(C. calceolus)*, and showy lady-slipper *(C. reginae)*.

Other names: American valerian, stemless lady's slipper, moccasin-flower, Indian-moccasin, squirrel-shoes, nerve-root *(C. acaule)*; whippoorwill's-shoe, Indian-shoe, yellows *(C. calceolus)*; queen's lady-slipper *(C. reginae)*.

Close relatives: Lipped orchids *(Platanthera, Pogonia, Arethusa, Calopogon, Spiranthes, Liparis)*, and others (see Orchids, Lipped).

Lifestyle: These spectacular orchids vary widely in their habitat requirements. Most adaptable in its moisture tolerances is pink lady-slipper, which flowers in both bogs and dry, sandy uplands. Its main requirement is sterile, acid soil—wet or dry. Yellow lady-slipper grows in both wet and mesic sites, favoring more neutral soils, including swamps and fens; it especially thrives in limestone areas. Showy lady-slipper, with its two-tone flower—white with streaked rose-purple labellum—is one of our largest, most beautiful native orchids. It dwells much more consistently in wetlands than the previous two orchids, usually growing in fens and swamp openings and tolerating only light shade.

These bisexual, insect-pollinated flowers are deceptive in the extreme. Luring pollinators by color and an odor from the sepals and lateral petals, they offer little or no nectar. The insect (usually a bee) enters the pouch through a front slit (in pink lady-slipper) or a circular opening at the top (in the two others). Fine, slanting hairs on the pouch's smooth-walled inner surface nudge the insect toward the sticky, overhanging female stigma, a constricted passage from which it cannot backtrack. It continues to squeeze through the passage, finally brushing against the pollen-loaded anthers. The exit passage is narrow and complex; the pouches sometimes become traps for insects that miss their cues on where to go.

Unlike many of the lipped orchids, lady-slippers are *obligate outbreeders;* that is, they cannot (or only rarely) self-pollinate. The flower's interior arrangement of sex organs requires that pollen be brought from another flower for fertilization to occur. The fruit capsules split to release clouds of powdery, wind-dispersed seeds. Only a few of them ever find the right combination of habitat and symbiotic fungus to grow and thrive.

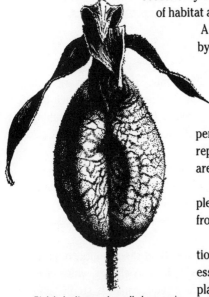

A germinated seed *(protocorm)* must be joined by a mycorrhizal soil fungus *(Rhizoctonia)* before it can absorb nutrition. The initial growth process may require two years or more, and the plant may not produce a flower for several more years. Lady-slippers, like trilliums and a few other wildflowers, represent long-term habitat investments and are hardly the quick creatures of a summer.

The subsurface plant forms a radiating complex of spaghettilike roots and round tubers, from which the new shoots arise in spring.

Associates: *Spring, summer.* The aforementioned mycorrhizal fungus is an absolutely necessary orchid partner. It functions as and in place of root hairs; without it, orchid roots cannot absorb soil nutrients. Many botanists believe that the relationship actually consists of orchid parasitism on the fungus.

In bogs, pink lady-slipper usually occupies

Pink lady-slipper, also called moccasin-flower, displays a pink, veined pouch. This frontal view shows the cleft by which insects enter the flower; they exit by a tortuous passage behind. Unlucky visitors become trapped in the pouch.

hummocks of sphagnum moss and other drier areas. Plant associates often include cranberries, pitcher-plant, leatherleaf, tamarack, and black spruce.

Look for colonies of yellow lady-slipper in northern white cedar swamps, also in sedge fens and shrubby swamps with poison sumac, shrubby cinquefoil, and red-osier dogwood.

In more open fens, the showy lady-slipper often appears among marsh fern, sedges, horsetails, and grass-of-Parnassus, also tamarack and northern white cedar.

The flower colors and odors attract mainly bees. Midsize, ground-nesting andrenid and halictid bees, honeybees *(Apis mellifera)*, and smaller bumblebees *(Bombus)* are the chief pollinators. Large bumblebees that get trapped sometimes bite their way free, leaving a mutilated pouch. Yellow lady-slippers are frequently pollinated by the solitary *Andrena* and small carpenter *(Ceratina)* bees. Common pollinators of showy lady-slipper include leafcutting bees *(Megachile)*.

Often inhabiting the pouch sacs are pollinator predators, the foremost being crab spiders (Thomisidae), which attack and devour entering insects.

Foliage of yellow lady-slippers is sometimes infested by spider mites (Tetranychidae). Other foliage feeders include slugs, which may eat large, oval holes in the leaves and even defoliate plants.

Their relative infrequency makes orchids insignificant food plants for birds and mammals. White-tailed deer, however, apparently aid the germination of showy lady-slippers in cedar swamps, where deer often yard up in winter. By trampling and aerating the soil and overbrowsing the trees, thus creating forest openings, the deer help plant the orchid seeds. Old winter deeryards may display colonies of this spectacular orchid.

Lore: Orchids (especially lady-slippers) are ancient sexual and erotic symbols; the word *orchis* means "testicle" in Greek. Not only the scrotum shape of the labellum but also the roots and testiclelike tubers suggested uses as aphrodisiacs (the "doctrine of signatures" held that plant parts bearing some resemblance in shape to human body parts signaled the plants' appropriate medicinal usage). Does some residual belief in orchid charms and powers lie behind our particular selection of these flowers as bodily adornment for ceremonial occasions involving courtship and marriage? May some such urge also drive the seemingly irresistible impulse in many humans to pick every available wild orchid in sight? That many species of our native orchids are not now extinct probably owes more to the difficulty in accessing orchid habitat than to legal protection or the forebearance of "flower lovers."

For some at least, the picking of lady-slippers can be a physically unpleasant experience. *Cypripedium* (especially showy lady-slipper) may produce a skin rash similar to that caused by poison ivy, in this case caused by a volatile oil and the resinoid cypripedin.

Sedative properties of *Cypripedium* roots were well known to native peoples and American pioneers alike. Root teas were taken to calm the nerves; ease insomnia, depression, and menstrual disorders; and treat epilepsy. The Chippewa applied the dried, powdered roots to aching teeth; other tribes used root decoctions for kidney and stomach ailments. Root foragers heavily harvested yellow lady-slippers during the last century for medicinal uses; their populations have probably never fully recovered.

Laurels (*Kalmia* spp.). Heath family. Low shrubs in swamps, bogs, marginal wetlands. Sheep laurel (*K. angustifolia*) and pale laurel (*K. polifolia*) are low evergreen shrubs with leathery leaves. Sheep laurel has opposite or three-whorled leaves; pale laurel leaves are usually opposite with bright white undersides and incurled edges. Pale laurel also has characteristic two-edged twigs. The distinctive saucer-shaped laurel flower is usually reddish purple or deep pink in color.

Other names: Lambkill, wicky, dwarf laurel, sheep-poison, calf-kill (*K. angustifolia*); bog laurel, swamp laurel, American laurel, bog kalmia (*K. polifolia*). *Kalmia* is unrelated to the true laurels (Lauraceae), sprigs of which crowned ancient poets and heroes.

Close relatives: Azaleas (*Rhododendron*); bog-rosemary (*Andromeda glaucophylla*); Labrador-tea (*Ledum groenlandicum*); leatherleaf (*Chamaedaphne calyculata*); blueberries and cranberries (*Vaccinium*).

Lifestyle: Sheep laurel bears its flowers in clusters along the stem, and the plant is usually surmounted by a leaf cluster. Flowers of pale laurel bloom at the twig tips; this is a smaller, more straggling shrub than sheep laurel, and it flowers earlier in spring. Pale laurel seldom grows outside bogs; sheep laurel has a much wider moisture tolerance and often thrives in upland acid soil as well as in wetlands.

When not in flower, pale laurel much resembles its close relative bog-rosemary in its narrow, leathery, edge-curled leaves with white undersides. But whereas bog-rosemary has a blue-gray cast to its alternate leaves, pale laurel leaves are opposite and shiny green on top (see illustration for Bog-rosemary). This is one of those bog heaths whose leaves were once believed to indicate a condition of physiological drought (see Bog-rosemary, Labrador-tea).

Bisexual laurel flowers have a delicate spring-loaded mechanism that is easily tripped and released by a nectar-foraging insect. The ten spokelike stamens are arched outward, their pollen-bearing anthers held under tension in small pockets ringing the flower center. The slightest disturbance releases them, flinging a sticky string of pollen inward on the forager. After a few minutes, the stamens reset themselves in their tensile positions. You can test this mechanism with a pin or blade of grass.

The flowers develop into rounded capsules that release wind-dispersed seeds.

Associates: Pale laurel occupies relatively drier portions of the sphagnum moss community in bogs. Its common shrub associates include other bog heaths such as leatherleaf, Labrador-tea, and late low blueberry. Black spruce is its foremost tree associate.

Bog laurel flowers "explode" their pollen onto alighting insects. At top, the spring-loaded flower has pollen-bearing stamens held under pressure. At bottom, the stamens have been released. They will soon reset themselves in their outer-rim "pockets."

Sheep laurel's wider range of habitats gives it a larger variety of plant associates. It is apparently allelopathic in some degree to black spruce.

Spring. Bumblebees *(Bombus)* are the main laurel pollinators.

Sheep laurel has two common leaf-mining moth caterpillars: *Parornix palmiella,* a gracillariid, that creates blotch mines, and *Coptodisca kalmiella,* a shield bearer moth (see Leatherleaf).

In early spring, look for brown elfins *(Incisalia augustinus),* small, orange-brownish butterflies flying around sheep laurel, one of its larval food plants. They lay eggs on the new shoot tips. The northern blue *(Lycaeides argyrognomon),* another butterfly, may likewise be seen around pale laurel.

Several inchworm moth caterpillars feed on sheep laurel from spring extending into summer. These include the heath probole *(Probole nepiasaria),* the red-fronted emerald *(Nemoria rubrifrontaria),* and the mottled gray carpet *(Cladara limitaria).*

Summer. In this season, the aforementioned butterflies feed as caterpillars on the leaves. Brown elfin caterpillars are fat and yellowish-green. Northern blue larvae are translucent green, secrete honeydew, and are often attended by ants.

Lore: Laurel foliage is poisonous when eaten by livestock or humans. The toxic compound, as in bog-rosemary and azaleas, is acetylandromedol. Native Americans made cautious use of the leaves and twigs in tonics for various ailments; they were well aware of these plants' dangerous properties.

Linnaeus named the genus in tribute to Swedish botanist Peter Kalm, one of the first scientists to examine and study the flora of eastern North America.

Leatherleaf *(Chamaedaphne calyculata).* Heath family. Low shrub in bogs, often forming the dominant shrub cover. Its leathery, evergreen leaves are usually yellowish and scaly on their undersides. One-sided rows of small, white, bell-shaped flowers dangle from the uppermost twig ends in spring.

Other names: Cassandra, dwarf cassandra.

Close relatives: Azaleas *(Rhododendron)*; laurels *(Kalmia)*; bog-rosemary *(Andromeda glaucophylla)*; Labrador-tea *(Ledum groenlandicum)*; blueberries and cranberries *(Vaccinium).*

Lifestyle: Leatherleaf and sphagnum mosses are the dominant plants in most North American bogs. Acres of dense, wiry, knee-high leatherleaf clothe the hollows and hummocks of peat bogs or crowd the edges of marshes and fens where the chemical transition to acid wetland has begun. These are long-lived clonal shrubs, spreading mainly by adventitious roots and epicormic branching (that is, roots and branches arise from previously dormant buds low on the stem). The typical density is about two hundred stems per square meter; depressions in the shrub crown surface often mark the boundaries between separate clones. Leatherleaf is shade intolerant, requiring open sunlight to survive.

A leatherleaf stem shows distinctive zone patterns of growth. From the top of the upright vertical stem arises an arching, horizontal twig with smaller leaves. This twig produces the flowers and fruit, then sheds its leaves and dies. In the meantime, another lateral top branch sprouts at an angle from the parent stem; this branch produces the annual growth increment. Since the "knees" of the lateral bud growth persist, you can age the shoot by simply counting the number of straight stem portions between knees. Over a long period, this form of growth produces a horizontal orientation of the clone so that individual stems tend to lean and recline in one direction.

Leatherleaf flowers are bisexual and insect pollinated. A heavy snow cover in winter seems to encourage full flowering in spring; long exposure of bare stems to cold winds apparently inhibits flowering. Flowers, fully formed in their buds by autumn, typically appear early in spring, sometimes before all the snow is gone. In contrast to the dangling blueberrylike flowers, the seed capsules point upward.

As with Labrador-tea, the leaves can be considered evergreen only in the fact that many of them persist longer than a year, but never more than two growing seasons. New brownish, olive-green leaves grow in spring and throughout summer. About one-third of them fall in their first autumn, while the rest remain into the following growing season. Leaves turn reddish bronze in the fall, giving many bogs a subtle reddish hue when viewed from a distance.

Leatherleaf plants show zones of annual stem growth. The branch at top right, with smaller leaves, has produced this season's flowers and seeds. Like the previous year's fruiting branch (bottom right), it will wither and die. Next year's flowering branch will sprout from the leafy branch at top left.

Associates: Typical leatherleaf associates include sphagnum mosses, cottongrasses, pitcher-plant, sweet gale, and bog heaths such as Labrador-tea, bog-rosemary, pale laurel, blueberries, and cranberries. Tamarack and black spruce are common tree associates.

Blueberry invasion into leatherleaf generally indicates passage of a severe fire in years past (leatherleaf can survive lighter burns). Leatherleaf often first appears on the mats formed by accumulations of hairy-fruited sedge and other sedges, replacing these fen plants quite gradually. Leatherleaf "islands" may form on sphagnum hummocks, providing stable shelter for the germination of tamarack and tall shrubs—which will shade out the leatherleaf in time.

Spring, summer. In shallow pools near leatherleaf, look for bog beacon mushrooms *(Mitrula elegans)*, golden-orange "candles" that grow from leatherleaf's submersed dead leaves.

Leaves showing round, bright red blisters on their top surfaces are commonly seen on leatherleaf as well as on other bog heaths. A whitish fungus mats the underside of such swellings. This is red leaf spot or azalea leaf gall *(Exobasidium vaccinii)*, a club fungus.

Like most bog heaths, leatherleaf suffers relatively few foliage feeders. Probably the most common one is a leaf-mining insect, a tiny shield bearer moth caterpillar *(Coptodisca kalmiella)*; on lower leaves, look for serpentine mines that wind from the midrib outward. Later in the season, the caterpillar cuts two oval pieces from the leaf, one from each surface, and seals them together to form a case for itself. Then it drops to the sphagnum moss, where it pupates.

Other feeders include *Plagiognathus repetitus,* a plant bug (Miridae); the heath spittlebug *(Clastoptera saintcyri),* whose sap-sucking nymphs create frothy masses on the twigs; and leafhoppers *(Scleroracus, Macrosteles).* Cyphon marsh beetles, oval, somewhat hairy insects, also feed on the leaves.

Bumblebees *(Bombus)* are the flowers' chief pollinators.

Dense leatherleaf makes excellent nesting cover for several waterfowl and shorebirds. I have found mallard and American black duck nests on leatherleaf-sphagnum hummocks. Ring-necked ducks also nest here, as do common snipe.

Fall, winter. The aforementioned *Coptodisca* moth lays its eggs on persistent leaves in autumn. The eggs overwinter here and hatch in spring.

At the tips of dead twigs, look for the ragged mesh webs of *Dictyna* spiders.

In areas of its range, sharp-tailed grouse use leatherleaf fruits and buds as staple winter foods.

Cottontail rabbits and snowshoe hares feed on the twigs and bark, and white-tailed deer also browse the twigs and foliage.

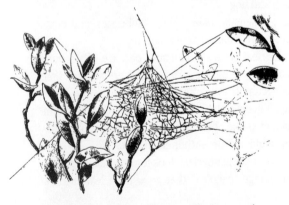

*The irregular meshwork of **Dictyna** spiders is commonly seen in bogs. These spiders often web the twig tips of leatherleaf and blueberry stems.*

Lore: The leaves have been used for tea and fever tonics by a few native tribes. As with other heath teas, however, only small quantities should be taken.

Fossil evidence shows that this plant genus originally developed in drier, more mesic habitats than where it now thrives. Such evidence has led some botanists to discount the plant's apparent leaf adaptations for survival in the physiological drought conditions of bogs. These features, they believe, were developed earlier and merely carried over into the wetter bog environment (see Bog-rosemary, Labrador-tea).

Water in northern wilderness lakes is often stained brown by tannins. The chief source of these plant by-products is decomposing leatherleaf and northern white cedar vegetation.

Lobelia, Great *(Lobelia siphilitica)*. Lobelia family. Herb in swamps, wet ground. Identify this lobelia by its height (up to three feet) and its blue flowers in showy spikes. The flowers are lobed, showing two erect "ears" above and a divided lip below, with a white-striped flower tube. Other blue-flowered wetland lobelias are smaller plants; they include water lobelia *(L. dortmanna)* and brook lobelia *(L. kalmii)*.

Other names: Great blue lobelia, blue cardinal-flower, high-belia.

Close relatives: Cardinal-flower *(L. cardinalis)*; bellflowers *(Campanula)*.

Lifestyle: This is the blue version (though not quite so spectacular) of red cardinal-flower; great lobelia flower structure is much the same but on a somewhat smaller scale (see Cardinal-flower). One difference is that insect-pollinated great lobelia has a solid "landing platform"—the lobed, lower lip of

Great lobelia flowers, marked by their two upright ears, attract bumblebee pollinators. Note how the stamens protrude through the slitted top surface of the flower tubes before bending into the flower again.

the flower; cardinal-flower, being hummingbird pollinated (on the wing), has no such surface. The two species sometimes hybridize, producing deep reddish or crimson-purple flowers and varying petal sizes and shapes. Occasional white-flowered variants also appear.

The bisexual flowers are *protandrous* (that is, the male parts mature first), thus encouraging cross-fertilization, but self-fertilization also occurs. A unique feature of the flower tube is a top slit, which extends to its base and through which the stamens protrude. Numerous seeds spill from the fruit capsules when ripe.

Lobelias are relatively short-lived perennials, often lasting only two or three years. This lobelia never entirely dies back during its lifetime, for it overwinters beneath the snow as a small, green rosette of leaves. This is a fen or swamp species, preferring alkaline or acid-neutral soils.

Associates: Great lobelia often associates with its red-flowered counterpart, cardinal-flower. Cardinal-flower usually begins flowering a bit later in summer than great lobelia, but the latter lasts longer, so the two have a period of overlap. I often see great lobelia associated with other blue-flowered plants, including blue vervain, skullcaps, and monkey-flower. Boneset is also a frequent associate.

Summer. As with most blue-flowered plants, bumblebees *(Bombus)* are the chief pollinators. Andrenid and halictid bees (Andrenidae, Halictidae) also collect pollen from the flowers.

Masses of small, oval, black bugs feeding on flowers and foliage may be negro bugs (Corimelaenidae), which in some years appear in great numbers on a variety of plants.

Elongate swellings on the stem indicate the presence of gall gnat larvae *(Lasioptera).* Seedpod weevils *(Gymnaetron)* develop as larvae in the seed capsules.

This lobelia is sometimes grazed by white-tailed deer.

Lore: Great lobelia once numbered among those many plants that were alleged to cure syphilis, hence its specific Latin name. (They never had such powers; as is now known, early stages of the disease often progress into a remission of outward symptoms.) American natives also used root decoctions in poultices for wounds, inflammations, and skin cancers, and drank a leaf tea (usually in mixture) for treating colds and other ailments. The acrid, milky juice of all lobelias is toxic, so home remedies using lobelia are ill-advised.

Some botanists see the slitted flower tube of lobelias as an evolutionary landmark, representing the tendency toward development of multiple flowers (specifically, the strap or ray flowers) found in the most advanced plant family, the composites. Taxonomists generally rank the lobelia family just below the composites.

Loosestrife, Purple *(Lythrum salicaria).* Loosestrife family. Tall herb in marshes, swamps, wet edges. Its spire of magenta flowers, with six petals, and its opposite or three-whorled, stalkless leaves mark this attractive, ubiquitous plant. Almost all loosestrife species in our region are wetland plants. This is the most common purple-flowered loosestrife. The yellow loosestrifes *(Lysimachia)* belong to a different family, the primroses.

Other names: Spiked loosestrife, spiked willow-herb, long purples, black blood.

Close relatives: Swamp loosestrife *(Decodon verticillatus)*; clammy cuphea or blue waxweed *(Cuphea petiolata)*; crape myrtle *(Lagerstroemia indica).*

Lifestyle: Charles Darwin spent much time and effort analyzing the insect pollination scheme of purple loosestrife. The bisexual flowers display three separate forms *(trimorphism),* each on a separate plant or clone. Each form is based on the length (short, medium, or long) of male and female floral parts. Darwin's experiments proved that pollen from a stamen of one length functions best on a pistil of the same length (see diagram). The flowers can also self-fertilize; this happens in the medium-length form more often than in the others. A single plant may produce three thousand individual flowers. Thirteen hours of daylight are required for flowering to begin. Blooming begins at the bottom of the spike and moves upward as the season progresses. The last flowers of the season bloom at the very top.

Purple loosestrife produces prolific seed. Each seed capsule contains about one hundred seeds, which are gradually dispersed by wind in the fall and winter. In water, the seeds immediately sink. Not until they germinate do they rise and float, dispersed as tiny seedlings.

Most perennial wetland herbs reproduce mainly by spreading rhizomes, but purple loosestrife colonies originate largely from seed. Each stem dies back to its base in the fall; new stems arise in spring from root buds, which form only slightly larger clones each year. In addition, new plants can sprout from broken green stems that have fallen.

Purple loosestrife thrives in fen areas but can also tolerate slightly acid soil. It does best not in water but on land that rises no more than inches or a few feet, at most, above the water table. Thus, in dense vegetation along watercourses, its zonal growth tells you quite accurately where land begins. The plant prefers full sunlight but can tolerate light shading.

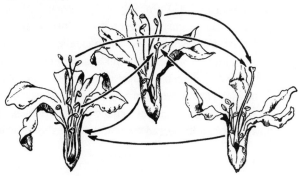

The three heights of purple loosestrife sex organs guide pollen flow to female organs of the same height as the male sources. Swamp loosestrife and pickerel-weed display a similar trimorphic scheme.

A purple loosestrife flower spike shows sequential zonation. At the bottom, flowers have disappeared and the seed is setting. Flowers bloom in the middle. At the top, flower buds wait to open. Many other flowers occurring on spikes show a similar sequence.

Associates: Purple loosestrife associates include cattails, reed canarygrass, cordgrass, water-parsnip, shrub willows, and other fen dwellers. In most places, its colonial growth quickly gains competitive superiority over many native wetland herbs and crowds them out. Zonal wetland grasses such as blue-joint and cordgrass are frequent victims of such takeovers.

Summer. Major flower pollinators include bumblebees *(Bombus)*, honeybees *(Apis mellifera)*, leafcutting bees (Megachilidae), and carpenter bees *(Xylocopa, Ceratina)*. Butterfly pollinators, such as the European cabbage butterfly *(Pieris rapae)*, the common sulphur *(Colias philodice)*, and the wood nymph *(Cercyonis pegala)* are also frequently seen.

Insect foliage feeders are not numerous. The pearly wood-nymph *(Eudryas unio)*, a forester moth, is probably the major leaf eater; the adult moths resemble bird droppings when at rest.

Biological control agents (mainly various beetle species) have been used with unimpressive results to control this plant in Europe.

Birds rarely consume the seeds. Indigo buntings sometimes use purple loosestrife for nesting cover (mainly for second nestings in summer), as do red-winged blackbirds. Birds probably play some role in dispersing the plant by carrying seeds in mud clinging to their feet.

Muskrats seem to avoid using the plant even for lodge building.

Lore: An alien species from Europe, purple loosestrife arrived on our shores sometime before 1850, probably via immigrant gardeners and ships' ballast. Until the turn of the century, however, it remained localized and nonaggressive. This plant thrives in disrupted wetland habitats, so subsequent dredging and development of inland waterways, canals, and ditches provided numerous highways for its travel. It soon began spreading across the continent, competing with and often eliminating much of our native wetland vegetation by its dense, colonial growth. Today thousands of wetland acres have been taken over by this colorful loosestrife, and its spread continues. It remains essentially unstoppable. Unlike most alien plants, which tend to spread from urban areas outward, purple loose-strife apparently began its march in rural areas.

The situation is an easy one for environmentalists to deplore. This plant, like few others, stirs our alien prejudice. Our native cattails, for example, are almost as rudely aggressive and competitive in many wetland areas as purple loosestrife. Yet, because cattails obviously "belong here," they seldom evoke the same out-raged feelings against their existence.

Plants, after all, go and grow only where habitats invite them. And once they begin to establish themselves, a series of complex adjustments involving the entire habitat community also begins. There are winners and losers. But the weight of evidence shows that after a vigorously aggressive phase, invasions usu-ally run their course. What usually happens is that community self-regulating mechanisms—herbivory, parasitism, diseases—begin to limit and restrict the invasive dominance of a species. Eventually it becomes integrated into changed but relatively stable community structures that display their own survival strate-gies. This process operates on its own schedule, requiring time and seasons. With the spread of purple loosestrife, we have (at least) new opportunities to witness the phases of an ever-recurring ecological process. We can watch it affect, change, adapt, and refit both its own elements and those of invaded communities into new arrangements of energy efficiency. The point is that we might as well study this process rather than simply deplore it; we have few alternatives.

Despite its aggressive habit and low wildlife value, purple loosestrife is not universally despised. Gardeners and landscapers use it for colorful plantings (deep rose and clear pink varieties are popular); and beekeepers rank its dark honey high in taste and sweetness.

The first-century Greek physician Dioscorides bestowed the name *lytron,* sig-nifying blood or gore from a wound, on this plant. As "dead men's fingers" and "long purples," it appears in Shakespeare's plays.

American natives didn't know the plant, of course, but purple loosestrife teas were popular European folk remedies for stomach upset and sore throat. They were also used for cleansing wounds. Modern pharmacology has found that the plant contains antibiotic properties; as an astringent, it also stops bleeding.

Loosestrife, Swamp *(Decodon verticillatus).* Loosestrife family. Arching shrub or herb in swamps. Recognize swamp loosestrife by its arching growth habit; its lavender, bell-shaped summer flowers tufted in the upper leaf angles; and its paired or three-whorled leaves.

Other names: Water-willow, whorled loosestrife, swamp willow-herb, grass poly. These plants are unrelated to true willows *(Salix)* and willow-herbs *(Epilobium)*.

Close relatives: Purple loosestrife *(Lythrum salicaria)*; clammy cuphea or blue waxweed *(Cuphea petiolata)*; crape myrtle *(Lagerstroemia indica)*.

Lifestyle: This is our most common native loosestrife, quite unlike the alien purple loosestrife in habit and appearance. Botanists can't decide whether it's shrub or herb; it has woody stems, but unlike those of true shrubs, they die back in the fall. Most elect to call it "shrubby" and let it go at that.

Its distinctively ridged, arching stems, three to nine feet long, are thickened and spongy at the base; ridged stems in plants can support more weight than round ones of the same diameter. On land, stem tips root where they touch the mud, sending up another arching stem in a sort of looping, leapfrog growth that may extend one plant over many feet. More often, however, these are land-building plants of the shoreline edge. Typically arching over the water, their tips float, expand, and send down roots. Dense tangles of their roots trap, anchor, and build up sediments, in which other emergent vegetation takes root. Led by vanguard loosestrife, the shoreline advances, in some places by a foot or more each summer.

The flower is bisexual, insect pollinated, and (like its close relative) trimorphous (see Loosestrife, Purple). It produces urn-shaped seed capsules. Like most wetland plants, however, swamp loosestrife reproduces most vigorously by the vegetative means mentioned. "Those in the water do not generally bloom," noted Thoreau.

Associates: Look for swamp loosestrife on shrubby shoreline edges. Buttonbush and shrub willows are frequent associates. On offshore edges, swamp loosestrife roots trap soil, providing rooting areas for arrowheads, pickerel-weed, and rushes.

Summer, fall. Dodder *(Cuscuta)* is a parasitic seed plant that often twines around swamp loosestrife, tapping into its stems (see Jewelweeds and illustration for Vervain, Blue). Dodder vines draping and enmeshing swamp loosestrife in the fall resemble heavy, yellow cobwebs when seen from a distance. This parasitism seems to affect loosestrife abundance very little.

Bumblebees *(Bombus)*, honeybees *(Apis mellifera)*, and other bees are the usual pollinators. Tiger swallowtail butterflies *(Papilio glaucus)* often alight on the flowers and pollinate them.

A large, green caterpillar with a rear "horn" found feeding on the leaves may be a hydrangea sphinx moth *(Darapsa versicolor)*.

Mallards, American black ducks, blue-winged and green-winged teals, and wood ducks eat the seeds. Muskrats relish the thickened submersed stems.

Lore: Swamp loosestrife is generally a good indicator of soft, unstable ground—places to step carefully if you're exploring a swamp or water's edge.

Maple, Red *(Acer rubrum).* Maple family. Tree in swamps, lowland and upland forests.

Recognize red maple by its smooth, light gray branches and beechlike bark on young trunks; its lobed, opposite leaves with whitish undersides; its reddish twigs, leafstalks, and buds; and its bright red foliage in autumn. Other maples favoring lowland or riverine habitats are silver maple *(A. saccharinum)* and box elder *(A. negundo).*

Other names: Scarlet maple, swamp maple, soft maple, water maple.

Close relatives: Sugar maple *(A. saccharum)* and all other maples.

Lifestyle: Red maple occupies a wide range of habitats and successional stages within those habitats (see *The Book of Forest and Thicket).* A common resident of upland deciduous forests, it also resides in wet woodlands and swampy locales—and in fact these are its favored habitats.

One of the earliest trees to flower in spring, red maple produces its gauzy, reddish flowers before its leaves emerge. Unisexual flowers usually occur on separate trees or on separate branches of the same tree. Bisexual flowers are not uncommon, however. Male flowers tend to be orange-red and, in most stands, outnumber female flowers, which are even redder. Flowers are cross-pollinated by both wind and insects; the bisexual flowers can also self-pollinate.

The winged seed keys *(samaras)* fall in late spring. They often germinate quickly but may remain viable for at least two years. One study found that red maples on moist sites tend to reproduce mainly by seed, and vegetative sprouting from stumps or roots occurs more frequently on upland sites. Stump or root sprouts often appear as small groups of saplings.

In the fall, this tree blazes into full color. Individual stands or trees vary in degree of autumnal redness depending on weather, day length, and soil acidity. Also, male trees tend to turn redder than female trees, which more often show yellow-orange hues.

Fire, cutting, and browsing stimulate vigorous sprouting from the shallow, spreading roots. Red maple branches are somewhat brittle, easily broken by wind and ice. Red maple is shade tolerant but less so than sugar maple. It sometimes hybridizes with silver maple, which typically occupies alluvial floodplains rather than swamps.

Associates: In deciduous swampland, look for red maple in association with speckled alder, black ash, and hollies. In conifer-hardwood lowlands, it also associates with spruces, balsam fir, and yellow birch. It is common in shrub-carr that has developed on old sedge mats. Red maple thickets often replace northern white cedar in swamps where the latter has been logged out.

Spring, summer. White, hairy, bell-shaped mushrooms growing singly or in clusters on trunks may be silky sheath mushrooms *(Volvariella bombycina).*

Red maple flowers are pollinated by a variety of bees and flies, as well as a few moths.

On the leaves, flat, circular "target" galls with bright red margins are larval dwellings of the maple leafspot midge *(Cecidomyia ocellaris).* Bladderlike pouch galls on upper leaf surfaces are caused by maple bladdergall mites *(Vasates quadripedes),* which overwinter on the bark. Crimson patches on the leaves indicate *Eriophyes* mites.

Caterpillar feeders, mostly moths, number into the hundreds on maple foliage. Few of them, however, specialize exclusively on red maples. Only a small sampling can be given here. Some of the most common ones include the following: green-striped mapleworm *(Dryocampa rubicunda),* a royal (saturniid) moth, also called the rosy maple moth; noctuid moth caterpillars such as the American and retarded dagger moths *(Acronicta americana, A. retardata),* the maple zale *(Zale galbanata),* the maple looper *(Parallelia bistriaris),* and the Baltimore bomolocha *(Bomolocha baltimoralis);* inchworm moths such as the lesser maple spanworm *(Itame pustularia),* the crocus geometer *(Xanthotype sospeta),* the large maple spanworm *(Prochoerodes transversata),* the beggar *(Eubaphe mendica),* and the three-spotted fillip *(Heterophleps triguttaria);* and the maple leafcutter or casebearer *(Paraclemensia*

*Two common types of gall on red maple leaves, both caused by mites, include (top) pouch galls of maple bladdergall mites (**Vasates quadripedes**) and (bottom) red erineum gall (**Eriophyes**).*

acerifoliella), an incurvariid moth—it first mines in the leaf, then cuts two circular pieces from a leaf to form a turtlelike case, which it carries about.

Alder blight aphids *(Prociphilus tessellatus)*, whose alternate host is alder, feed on red maple leaves in summer (see Alder, Speckled).

Leaf stems are the specialty of maple petiole borers *(Caulocampus acericaulis)*; these are sawfly larvae that tunnel inside the leaf stalks, causing leaves to wither and drop.

Red maple seeds mature in spring, when most birds are seeking insect protein rather than seed diets. Yet birds such as ruffed grouse, grosbeaks, and purple finches consume them. Red squirrels relish them, and eastern chipmunks, voles, and white-footed mice cache them along with seeds of other maples.

Fall, winter. Clusters of white-waxy, umbrella-shaped mushrooms growing from wounds in the trunk may be marble-caps *(Hypsizygus tessulatus)*; fruiting in summer and fall, they indicate heartrot in the tree. Small, slimy, bright green mushrooms growing on leaf litter beneath red maples are probably parrot waxycaps *(Hygrocybe psittacina)*. They turn reddish-orange and bright yellow as they age.

In the fall, narrow-winged tree crickets *(Oecanthus angustipennis)* lay their eggs on the trunks, creating small vertical slits in the bark.

Red maples near beaver ponds are often cut by the animals, which eat the bark and store branch caches near their lodges for winter food.

Foliage, twigs, and sprouts are favored nourishing foods of white-tailed deer, whose feeding may deplete red maple populations where deer are abundant. The bark of saplings is also relished by elk and moose; look for long, vertical strips, some still attached, that are peeled from the bottom. These animals scrape upward with their lower incisors (they have no upper ones).

All year. Egg wounds in the bark made by the aforementioned narrow-winged tree crickets may permit entry of a canker fungus *(Cryptosporiopsis)* that often infects red maple. The vertical canker eventually appears as notchlike sunken areas surrounded by infolding callus growth, which soon covers the canker, leaving thickened, tumorlike warts. Sometimes a secondary canker *(Valsa ambiens)* may colonize the first one; this fungus is much more destructive and may severely injure or kill the tree.

Another common, quite destructive parasite is the false tinder fungus *(Phellinus tremulae)*, a hoof-shaped bracket on trunks that causes and indicates heartrot. This fungus causes more timber loss of deciduous trees than any other wood destroyer.

Lore: The timber industry classifies both red and silver maples as *soft maple,* in contrast to sugar or *hard maple*. Although red maple is valued for furniture and other items, it ranks lower in quality than sugar maple, as it is somewhat weaker and more brittle. The sugar in spring sap is more diluted, so this tree is rarely tapped for syrup-making if sugar maple is available. (Native tribes, however, used all species of tree maples for making syrup and sugar.)

Red maple bark was once used in making black ink and dyes. Potawatomi trappers boiled their traps in water containing the bark in order to remove human and previous animal scents.

Red maple is Rhode Island's state tree.

Marigold, Marsh *(Caltha palustris)*. Buttercup family. Herb in wet meadows, swamps, fens, along shorelines. Its glossy, bright yellow flowers, among the first of spring, and its roundish, glossy leaves identify this common wetland plant.

Other names: Cowslip, meadow-gowan, capers, soldier's-buttons, boots, meadow boots, drunkards, crazy bet, kingcup.

Close relatives: Buttercups *(Ranunculus)*; meadow-rues *(Thalictrum)*; goldthread *(Coptis trifolia)*; anemones *(Anemone)*; wild columbine *(Aquilegia canadensis)*; baneberries *(Actaea)*; hepaticas *(Hepatica)*; not related to bur-marigolds *(Bidens)* or garden marigolds *(Tagetes)*.

Lifestyle: This brightest herald of spring lacks petals; the golden-yellow flower consists of five to ten sepals. Like the petals of many buttercups, marsh marigold's sepals look wet and shiny. This waxy-yellow color can be scraped off with a fingernail, leaving colorless, translucent tissue. The yellow surface is "bee-purple," reflecting ultraviolet light from all but the very center of the flower (a black spot to a bee), thus providing a nectar guide.

Marsh marigolds grow in saturated soil, frequently in the shallow margins of ponds, brooks, and springs. You will usually need boots (or bare feet) to get a close look at them. Although partially shade tolerant, they thrive best in full sunlight; at night or on cloudy days, the flowers close.

The bisexual, insect-pollinated flowers mature their male and female parts at the same time, but their placement (the anthers numerous and opening outwardly, the pistils fewer and very short) aids cross-fertilization. The flower "has no scent but speaks wholly to the eye," observed Thoreau. (Actually the flower has two "scent marks" at the base, but not many humans can detect the odor.) The distinctive seed cluster radiates outward in papery pods. These split open along the upper side, somewhat like violets; they often hold their seed rows exposed before the seeds fall out.

Summer is the time when marsh marigold does most of its food manufacturing (via photosynthesis) and energy storage. After flowers and seeds are gone, the leaves enlarge. Broadly heart-shaped, they now resemble the leaves of skunk-cabbage, a frequent associate. (A quick way to tell them apart: Marsh marigold leaves are usually slightly toothed, while skunk-cabbage leaves have smooth, untoothed edges.)

Marsh marigold is one of those spring flowers that occasionally bloom again in the fall, when October day lengths correspond to their spring flowering period.

Associates: *Spring, summer.* Watercress and speckled alder are common associates. Skunk-cabbage and jewelweeds often border the muddy landward side of marsh marigold plants. I often find that marsh marigolds in wet soil shelter large *Conocephalum* liverworts beneath them.

The glistening yellow flowers are especially attractive to flies. Syrphid flies (Syrphidae),

Marsh marigold's splayed seedpods (almost empty here) succeed its brilliant yellow flowers. Note the toothed leaves, which will enlarge over summer, building energy for renewed flowering in the spring.

those beelike, often brightly colored hoverers, are probably the main pollinators; a common one is *Sphaerophoria menthastri.* Many other flies as well as bees (such as the halictids *Augochlorella* and *Lasioglossum*) also seek nectar and pollen here.

A 1962 Ontario study listed thirty-nine insect species that fed in the flowers. One of the most common pollen and aphid feeders is *Coleomegilla maculata,* a spotted lady beetle. Flower thrips (Thripidae), tiny sucking insects, are also common.

Gamebirds, mainly northern bobwhites and ring-necked pheasants, consume the seeds. Moose graze the plant, but apparently few other mammals feed on it.

Lore: Most botanists have given up trying to remind us that this is not a true marigold. Common names often bear their own blithe insistence, and the name *marsh marigold* seems to wear quite well on this flower. Marsh marigold grows all over the world; early English poets called it simply "gold"—and certainly its sudden splashes of color in early spring become a golden feast for the eyes. The plant's Latin name means marsh cup, and its flowers were once used for dyeing yarn.

Is this plant humanly edible? Yes, but . . . At flowering time, the young leaves (boiled in several changes of water) are said by some to taste better than spinach; others vehemently disagree ("I say it's spinach, and I say to hell with it!"). Marsh marigold leaves are rich in iron, and American natives used them (boiled) for treating anemia. The flower buds can be pickled.

But never should any part of this plant be eaten raw. (It's unlikely one would do so because of its exceedingly acrid taste.) Thorough cooking dispels bad taste and toxicity from the alkaloid jervine and the glucoside helleborin. The plant is also poisonous to livestock, but these animals usually avoid it.

Meadowsweet *(Spiraea alba).* Rose family. Shrub in marshes, swamps, ditches, along shorelines. Yellowish-brown twigs and stiff, wandlike stems (to four feet tall) topped by dense spires of white flowers characterize meadowsweet. This meadowsweet hybridizes and intergrades with a more eastern species, the broadleaf meadowsweet *(S. latifolia).* A similar, closely related plant with pink or purplish flowers is steeplebush or hardhack *(S. tomentosa),* often found in the same habitats as meadowsweet.

Other names: Narrowleaf meadowsweet or spiraea; white, wild, or willowleaf spiraea; pipestem; queen-of-the-meadow; Quaker lady.

Close relatives: Cinquefoils *(Potentilla);* avens *(Geum);* blackberries and raspberries *(Rubus);* roses *(Rosa);* cherries *(Prunus);* chokeberries *(Aronia);* mountain-ashes *(Sorbus);* hawthorns *(Crataegus);* shadbushes *(Amelanchier).*

Lifestyle: One of the most common summer-flowering shrubs in open fens and along pond margins, meadowsweet is also conspicuous—easy to see and identify. Its common name is misleading, for the flower does not appear in meadows and has little if any fragrance (at least to human noses.) The bisexual, insect-pollinated flowers mature their female parts first *(protogyny),* but these remain functional even after the male parts mature, so the flower can and does self-fertilize at times. The aggregated linear seeds, maturing in early fall, are *follicles.*

Meadowsweet also spreads by cloning; several stems in the same vicinity may all be one plant. You can number a stem's age by counting branches beneath the flower heads.

This shrub is intolerant of shade and requires full sunlight. It is an indicator of mineral-rich wetlands.

Associates: *Summer.* Meadowsweet, boneset, and Joe-Pye-weeds, all about the same height, are commonly found in the same places, often flowering together. Other associates may include sedges, purple loosestrife, blue-joint grass, and the aforementioned steeplebush. Speckled alder and willows are frequent shrub associates.

The nectar-secreting flowers attract many insects. Bumblebees *(Bombus)*, other bees, and wasps are important pollinators, as are adult long-horned beetles (Cerambycidae) and Virginia ctenucha moths *(Ctenucha virginica)*, blue-bodied, black-winged wasp moths. Enlarged, reddening flowers may indicate the presence of spirea flower midge larvae *(Itonida spiraeaflorae)*.

Meadowsweet hosts other gall gnat larvae as well, mostly in the flower and leaf buds, which are deformed in characteristic ways. Round bud galls include those caused by spiraea bud gall gnats *(Cecidomyia, Trishormomyia clarkeae)*. *Itonida spiraeina* produces an oval brown bud gall. The clustered bud gall larvae *(Parallelodiplosis clarkei)* create stem-top clusters. Discolored leaf buds are marks of *Asphondylia* larvae. Flask-shaped, swollen flower buds indicate *Eriophyes* mites.

Very common atop stems is a spiny, lettucelike gall called spiraea cabbage gall, produced by the gall gnat *Contarinia spiraeina.*

Leaves also display gnat larvae galls. The fringed ball gnat *(Cecidomyia)* causes fringed, distorted leaflets, and the cone-shaped leaf cone gall is produced by another *Cecidomyia* species. *Lasioptera spiraeafolia* creates yellowish-brown leaf blisters. A thickened midrib fold reveals the spiraea pod-gall gnat *(Rhabdophaga salicifolia)*, which sometimes swells leaflets to enormous size. Leaves rolled at the margins probably host *Parallelodiplosis spirae* larvae.

Other insect foliage feeders often include spring azure butterfly caterpillars *(Lycaenopsis argiolus)*, whitish, rose-tinted larvae; and the dark-spotted looper moth caterpillar *(Diachrysia aereoides)*, a noctuid species.

I have often seen *Crematogaster* ants on the plant, probably tending aphids.

A leafy stem-top gall, produced by one of many gnat larvae that cause galls on meadowsweet, halts further stem growth and often results in epicormic branching of this normally unbranched shrub.

Though not ranked as important wildlife food, meadowsweet twigs are eaten by snowshoe hares and white-tailed deer. Ruffed and sharp-tailed grouse consume the buds.

Lore: This plant's common name apparently originated not from *meadow* but from *mead-wort;* flowers of a similar species were once used to flavor home-brewed mead, or honey wine.

"The Shetlanders," states one source, "called it 'courtship and matrimony' because the smell changed once the leaves were trodden on," as they often were because the plant was sometimes strewn like straw to cover floors.

The mildly astringent leaves have been used for tea and tonic treatments for intestinal complaints. Cattle, it is said, relish them.

Milkweed, Swamp *(Asclepias incarnata).* Milkweed family. Tall herb (two to four feet) in swamps, ditches, along pond margins. Its domed, pink or purplish-red flower cluster atop the plant and its narrow, mostly opposite leaves and slender, erect seed pods identify this milkweed. Most other milkweed species occupy dry upland fields or woods.

Other names: Rose milkweed, white Indian hemp, water nerve-root, water silkweed.

Close relatives: Butterfly-weed *(A. tuberosa)* and other milkweeds; angle-pods *(Gonolobus);* black swallow-wort *(Cynanchum nigrum).*

Lifestyle: The small but complex flowers of milkweeds show distinctive bent-back petals with both male and female flower parts united in a single central structure called the *gynostegium.* Surrounding this organ are five clasping hoods enclosing five incurved, nectar-secreting horns. The pollen occurs in waxy masses called *pollinia,* which adhere to the legs of insects. Struggling to gain footing on the flower, an insect steps into one or more of the small clefts or slots in the flower base, where the pollinia ensnare the leg with filaments. Carrying these pollinia "saddlebags" as it leaves the flower, the insect similarly struggles in another flower, often breaking the pollinia and thus effecting cross-fertilization. Milkweeds are called *obligate outbreeders* because self-pollinated flowers (including flowers pollinated from others in the same cluster) are rarely fertile.

If each flower were to develop into a seedpod, the plant would be loaded with them. As it is, only about five pods (containing some fifty seeds) develop from about seventy-five or so flowers per plant. The control mechanisms are unknown. Each seed has a tuft of hairs, which assists dispersal by wind and water.

Swamp milkweed favors "wet feet," often rising in shallow water marginal to shores or swamp pools. In contrast to common milkweed *(A. syriaca)*, its rhizomes are small and produce few cloning stems. Like most milkweeds, it requires full sunlight.

Associates: *Summer.* Sedges, swamp loosestrife, and other rich-fen dwellers such as Joe-Pye-weeds, boneset, buttonbush, and shrub willows are common swamp milkweed associates.

The major pollinators are bumblebees *(Bombus)* and honeybees *(Apis mellifera)*, though other insects also pollinate the plant. Among these are sand-loving and thread-waisted wasps *(Tachytes, Sphex)* and butterflies, including the monarch *(Danaus plexippus)*, swallowtails *(Papilio)*, mulberry wing skipper *(Poanes massasoit)*, and black dash skipper *(Atrytone conspicua)*. I have also observed hummingbird clearwing moths *(Hemaris thysbe)* hovering like hummingbirds over the flowers as they sip nectar. Watch for all of these insects carrying the aforementioned yellow pollinia on their legs. Insects may get their feet or tongues trapped in the pollinia slots; the sight of dead insects hanging from milkweed flowers is not uncommon.

Milkweeds, like goldenrods, center a sizable community of insects that occur quite exclusively on these plants. Several of them (especially the beetles and bugs) display bright *aposematic* (warning) colorations; these insects sequester the milkweed toxins in their bodies and thus are often unpalatable or poisonous morsels to bird predators, who learn to avoid them.

Examples include the large milkweed bug *(Oncopeltus fasciatus)*, an insect that spends its entire life cycle on the plant. Egg masses on leaf undersides hatch into reddish nymphs, which cluster on the developing pods and finally metamorphose into large, black and red-banded adults. Milkweed bugs are primarily seed eaters, though

Red flower clusters of swamp milkweed attract many pollinating insects, such as this hummingbird clearwing moth. Insects sometimes become trapped by their legs in these flowers.

the adults also feed on the flower nectar. About a fourth of the adults migrate south from their northern range to warmer areas in the fall. In summer, the adults return north from their wintering areas and establish new annual populations.

The small milkweed bug *(Lygaeus kalmii)*, resembling its larger cousin but marked with a red X on its back, feeds on milkweed sap as a nymph and on sap and seeds as an adult.

Swamp milkweed leaf beetles *(Labidomera clivicollis)* are oval-shaped, convex, bluish insects strongly marked with orange-yellow. They consume both flowers and foliage, sometimes defoliating the stem. Look on leaf undersides for rows of their elongated eggs. In winter you may find these beetles hibernating in the shriveled, woolly leaves of dead but standing common mullein plants *(Verbascum thapsus)*.

The red milkweed beetle, also called eastern milkweed longhorn *(Tetraopes tetrophthalmus)*, is red with four black dots on the back. Its larvae bore into stems and roots, where they remain through the winter. The colorful adult insects make squeaking sounds.

All of these aposematic milkweed specialists bear resemblances in color, an instance of *Müllerian mimicry;* that is, each species, relying on birds' memory for color, ultimately tends to reinforce protection of the others.

Other foliage feeders include striped caterpillars of the aforementioned monarch butterfly (not as common on swamp milkweed as on upland species); and the delicate cycnia *(Cycnia tenera)*, a densely haired tiger moth caterpillar that feeds at night. *Rhyssomatus* weevils also eat the leaves, chewing holes in the stem for laying eggs; the larvae feed on the stem pith.

Contarinia gall gnat larvae create swollen midrib folds in the leaves. Another gall gnat, *Neolasioptera asclepiae*, produces stem swellings.

Threadlike stem fibers of this milkweed are very strong. Birds, including alder flycatchers, yellow warblers, and northern orioles, use it in nest construction.

White-tailed deer occasionally graze the plant, and muskrats eat the rhizomes sparingly. Mallards and common pintails have also been

Insects whose larvae feed on swamp milkweed lay eggs on the plant, often on leaf undersides. This typical egg mass (probably of a swamp milkweed leaf beetle) is only one discovery awaiting explorers of this intriguing plant.

recorded as eating the seeds, but bird and mammal food use of this plant is generally uncommon.

Lore: The alkaloid compounds containing cardiac glycosides, found in the milky latex of milkweeds, are toxic and distasteful to most vertebrates. This feature hardly prevented some notable masochistic attempts to find medicine in the plant. "The root tea is said to drive the worms from a person in one hour's time," reported an observer of the Meskwaki tribe. Indeed, such tea is strongly laxative and also induces vomiting. American colonists used it in various concoctions for a variety of ailments, but milkweeds remain dangerous plants to sample for experimental remedies.

With repeated boilings, young shoots, top leaves, and flowers are edible and, it is said, tasty, but the similarities of young plants to highly toxic dogbanes *(Apocynum)* and butterfly-weed *(Asclepias tuberosa)* advise against collecting them for food.

American natives also braided the stem fibers for strong cordage.

Mosses, Sphagnum *(Sphagnum* spp., Class Sphenopsida). Sphagnum family. Large, evergreen mosses in bogs, swamps, and fens. Growing in thick, cushiony, water-absorbent mats, sphagnums are alive and growing at their tops, brown and dead at the base of their stalks, which may extend several feet in vertical length. Their branches occur in whorls and are recurved (bent back).

Some thirty species in east-central North America range in color from bright green to reddish-brown to yellowish. In the shade, sphagnums tend to be green in color whatever the species. Although precise species identification often requires technical knowledge, many sphagnums occur in quite specialized habitats and thus can be "narrowed down" to one or a few likely species.

Other name: Peat moss.

Close relatives: True mosses (Order Bryales); liverworts (Class Hepaticae).

Lifestyle: Sphagnums are the dominant plants of waterlogged acid bogs, forming thick accumulations of peat. In grounded bogs, peat layers may extend tens or scores of feet beneath the bog surface. In floating or "quaking" bogs, sphagnums comprise the main mass of plant material that gives with every step (the sensation to a "bog trotter" probably comes as close to walking on water as humans can experience). But certain sphagnums also thrive in mineral-rich fens and cedar swamps. A few species grow submersed in shallow water, but most grow in large, compact cushions or wide, often saturated lawns above the water table.

Sphagnums have two basic types of cells: large, empty ones *(hyaline cells)*, which absorb water through surface pores; and narrow, green ones *(chlorophyll cells)* dividing the hyaline cells. The hyaline cells remain intact even on dead parts of the plant. A sphagnum plant may hold fifteen to twenty times its own weight of water, but hyaline cells are mostly filled with air when growing above the water.

Sphagnums perpetually grow at the top while dying at the bottom. As the plants add to their top mass, the weight forces the older portions deeper. Without light, these portions die, releasing tannins and acids that inhibit decay-causing bacteria. In this way, sphagnum denourishes and acidifies its environment, locking up plant nutrients in the dead mass of plant material that underlies the topmost living portions. Recycling of minerals released through decay, which occurs in most nonacidic environments, is thus halted. Thus the unique chemistry and ecosystem that is a bog—an essentially static environment.

In true bogs, the only sources of water are rain and snow. Flowage into a bog, either by surface or ground waters, brings mineral nutrients, which reduce the acidity and change the character of vegetation growing there. This can happen, but the usual sequence goes in the other direction: A mineral-rich fen deposits sedge peat, which begins to acidify the environment, enabling acid-loving sphagnums to become established. A mineral-poor fen, usually a floating mat, results as heaths and other acid-tolerant plants invade, but this complex still derives some nourishment from groundwater. Finally, the compacted peat seals off the groundwater flow; the peat eventually accumulates to such a depth that the bog mat is grounded. Surface-water inflow is now largely confined to the *lagg,* or moat, often surrounding a bog's outer margins. Fen-type plants often ring the bog, finding more mineral nourishment here than the bog can supply.

In northern regions, the final result of the fen-to-bog sequence (though most ecologists hesitate to call it a natural climax) is often spruce muskeg, dominated by sphagnums, Labrador-tea, black spruce, and often tamarack. In more southerly areas, succession may proceed to cover the open bog with thicket or mixed forest. Fire or flooding by surface inflow may interrupt these sequence patterns, and local changes in drainage conditions may also affect them. Many gradations exist. No two bogs are exactly alike in flora, chemistry, or appearance. Fens grade into bogs (or cedar swamps—see Cedar, Northern White), and bog edges grade into deciduous shrub-carr thickets and lagg fens.

The acidic environment (pH 2.7 to 6.5) produced and maintained by sphagnums involves a complex chemical process called *cation exchange.* Sphagnums attract positive ions (cations) of nutrient minerals from solution, resulting in the release of hydrogen ions, which increase acidity. Decomposition of peat substances by anaerobic bacteria also creates acid conditions.

A typical sphagnum bog displays a mosaic surface of hummocks and hollows that continuously recycles itself. Hummocks become hollows and vice versa; a fast-motion camera aimed over a bog and compressing decades into minutes would show a continuously heaving, agitated surface resembling choppy, irregular waves. A hummock begins when a sphagnum moss (usually *S. capillifolium,* a red species) establishes itself on a sedge tussock, on a lower branch of leatherleaf, or on a pad of haircap moss *(Polytrichum).* Water capillarity enables this and successive sphagnums to grow upward to the limit of capillary water movement against gravity (some twenty inches). When capillarity reaches the point where it is counterbalanced by gravity, the hummock ceases its upward growth, dries out, and begins to erode. Eventually it becomes a hollow—and the former hollows surrounding it build with new sphagnum growth. In actual fact, the cycle is seldom this regular; sometimes hummocks do not dry out and die but become hollows simply by virtue of the upgrowth of surrounding hummocks. But by whatever processes renewal occurs, the bog surface is never still.

Individual sphagnum species often occupy quite specific microhabitats and zonations. A given hummock, for example, may consist of three or four sphagnums: the reddish *S. capillifolium* and *S. magellanicum* and the green *S. recurvum* often grow at the lower levels and sides; brownish *S. fuscum* frequently caps the drier tops. Sphagnum hollows often consist solely of *S. recurvum,* green or yellowish-brown in color. This vertical zonation probably results from the differing cation-exchange and water-conducting abilities of the individual species.

The visible surface plant is a *gametophore;* that is, it produces *gametes* (sex cells). Its apex, a crowded, leafy tuft, is the *capitulum,* which contains young branches, the sexual organs, and the terminal bud. Each capitulum bears both

Typical bog topography features ever-changing mosaics of hummocks and hollows as sphagnum mosses build and decay. Bog heaths form the shrub layer above the sphagnums, and trees such as tamarack (left) and black spruce (right) thrive here.

kinds of unisexual cells: male sperm from stalked *antheridia* and female eggs from flask-shaped *archegonia*. The released sex cells unite (usually in early spring) to form a *sporophyte* generation in the capitulum, producing spores on stalked capsules. The spores, explosively released in summer, germinate into new gametophore plants. Spore production, however, is irregular in most sphagnums. Vegetative reproduction is much more common, as new plants develop from fragmented pieces of the gametophore.

Associates: Heaths, including blueberries, cranberries, leatherleaf, and Labrador-tea, are the primary plant associates of bog sphagnums. Other associates in bogs include cotton-grasses, tamarack, and black spruce.

On mature bog hummocks, look for true mosses such as haircaps *(Polytrichum)*, *Dicranum undulatum, Pohlia nutans,* and *Pleurozium schreberi. Cladina* and *Cladonia* lichens also reside here.

Common, more mineral-tolerant sphagnums in sedge fens include *S. warnstorfii, S. fuscum,* and *S. teres.* Northern white cedar swamps are favored habitats for *S. centrale, S. squarrosum, S. wulfianum,* and *S. warnstorfii,* among others.

Most of the following are associates of primarily bog sphagnums in their acidic habitats.

Spring, summer. The green alga *Closterium,* one-celled desmids, are often present in bog pools, sometimes tinting the water green. A leafy liverwort, *Cephalozia connivens,* is quite common; another, *Mylia anomala,* grows mainly on the shady sides of sphagnum hummocks. Massachusetts fern *(Thelypteris simulata),* resembling marsh fern, is uncommon though widespread.

A little brown mushroom called the moss murderer *(Lyophyllum palustre),* a false funnelcap, parasitizes sphagnum moss cells, digesting their remains after killing them. Look for it amid patches of dead sphagnums.

Other plants to look for include insect-trapping pitcher-plants and sundews. Three-leaved false Solomon's seal is often common here. A number of orchid species also favor sphagnum habitats. These include arethusa or dragon's mouth, grass pink, moccasin-flower, heartleaf twayblade, club-spur orchid, white-fringed orchid, green-fringed orchid, and rose pogonia. A midsummer orchid in sphagnum bogs is the yellow-fringed orchid.

A few invertebrates feed directly on decaying sphagnum. These include mites (Acarina) and springtails (Collembola). Many more species commonly occur in hummock, hollow, and pool habitats. The protozoans *Stentor,* microscopic trumpet-shaped animals, and shelled rhizopods are often abundant in sphagnum pools. Rotifers (wheel animalcules) are also common; they can withstand long periods of dessication when bogs dry out in summer. Look for planarian flatworms or turbellarians here, too.

Among insects, short-winged mold beetles *(Reichenbachia)* feed on mites and springtails deep in the mosses. Minute bog beetles *(Sphaerius)*, small, shiny-brown, oval-shaped insects, feed here too. In bog pools, whirligig beetles (Gyrinidae) and the bugs called water boatmen (Corixidae) are often present. Many bog insects are hard-bodied, resistant to the water acidity; the latter two insects can survive in bog waters of pH 3.5. Mosquito larvae—typically *Aedes* (the first in spring), *Anopheles,* and *Culex,* some twenty-one species in all—commonly live in bog pools. Certain crane fly larvae (Tipulidae) also reside here.

In northern bogs, watch for jutta arctic butterflies *(Oeneis jutta)*, grayish-brown, fast fliers often alighting on tamarack and black spruce trunks. Bog and purple lesser fritillaries *(Boloria eunomia, B. titania)* are orange-brown butterflies with black markings. Other butterflies and commonly seen moths are associated with heath or spruce food plants.

Two small, brown crickets are fairly common in sphagnum bogs: the marsh ground cricket *(Nemobius palustris)* and Say's bush cricket *(Anaxipha exigua)*.

Large ant mounds are quite common in the drier portions of sphagnum bogs, frequently favoring the tough caps of haircap moss growing atop sphagnum hummocks. Ant colonies often consist of *Lasius minutus.* The ants rarely appear on the mound surface; they mainly feed underground on honeydew secreted from root aphids *(Prociphilus)* present on cotton-grasses and a few other bog sedges.

No reptiles or amphibians reside exclusively in bogs, but several species favor them. Look for bog and spotted turtles, especially in the drainage channels or animal runways between sphagnum hummocks. Bog turtles, increasingly rare, are classified as endangered species in most states where they occur.

Snakes are usually uncommon in sphagnum bogs. Red-bellied snakes, less than a foot long, are probably the most frequently seen. The four-toed salamander, about three inches long with a black-spotted belly and tail constriction, is a secretive dweller inside sphagnum hummocks. It lays its eggs adjacent to bog pools.

Wood and carpenter frogs are probably the most frequent amphibian dwellers in sphagnum bogs. Wood frogs can tolerate acidity of pH 4. Carpenter or "sphagnum" frogs occur mainly in Atlantic coastal plain bogs.

Likewise, no bird species always nests in sphagnum bogs, but several are frequent and many others occasionally reside there. I have found mallard, American black duck, Nashville warbler, and white-throated sparrow nests atop or among sphagnum hummocks. Other ground nesters may include spruce grouse; sandhill cranes; common snipe; yellow-bellied flycatchers; Wilson's, Tennessee, and Connecticut warblers; and white-crowned sparrows. Probably palm warblers and Lincoln's sparrows are the most regular ground-nesting songbird dwellers. Nests are usually well camouflaged and difficult to find unless a parent bird flushes. Cape May warblers sometimes use sphagnum mosses for nest exteriors.

Many mammals traverse or venture into bogs, but only a few (usually shrews and rodents) typically live there. The northern water shrew sometimes runs atop the water surface in bog pools. Starnose moles, those curiously nose-tentacled mammals, burrow in saturated sphagnums. Meadow voles, short-tailed shrews, and bog lemmings, though not endemic bog dwellers, often create trails and runways in the sphagnum.

Late summer, fall. These are the seasons to look for typical bog mushrooms. Black earthtongue *(Geoglossum nigritum)* is a black, club-shaped, easily overlooked cup fungus protruding from the sphagnum. Gilled mushrooms may include spotted-stalk waxycap *(Hygrophorus tephroleucus)*, small, gray-capped, and also inconspicuous; the straight-stalked pinkgill *(Entoloma strictior)*, with brown, cone-shaped cap and pinkish gills; the sickener *(Russula emetica)*, with bright red cap and white gills; the waterdrop milkcap *(Lactarius aquifluus)*, brown-capped with a watery latex smelling like brown sugar; and the sooty milkcap *(L. lignyotus)*, with dark brown cap and white latex. The gartered galerina *(Galerina paludosa)*, a small, brownish, parasol-shaped skullcap mushroom, parasitizes selective cells of sphagnums; it doesn't kill them, but it withdraws nutrients. None of these species are safely edible.

Lore: Sphagnum bogs are the acidic counterparts of mineral-rich sedge fens (see Sedges); these are the two extremes of a continuum that shows multiple expressions and gradations. (Another continuum is the sedge-white cedar sequence; see Cedar, Northern White.) The varying vegetation of each extreme reflects differences in water sources, chemistry, and nutrient levels. Over time, sphagnum creates the conditions for its own spread and survival. In so doing, it also determines the kinds of plants it will compete with.

Sphagnum bogs can be seen as massive environmental air-conditioning systems. Bogs absorb heat very slowly in spring; they "help conserve the climate," as one bog ecologist has stated. They repeat this heating-and-cooling process on a smaller scale each day and night except in winter. They are temperature buffers as well as water sponges, storing and releasing heat, cold, and moisture in constant diurnal and seasonal cyclic patterns.

As local climate stabilizers, bogs may represent important cogs in the compensatory self-regulating systems that give us (somewhat) predictable seasons and weather reports. Thus the modern peat moss industry, which ditches, dries, and vacuum-mines vast acreages of sphagnum peat for agricultural and other uses, may have significant effects ranging far beyond the exploitation of another nonrenewable resource. Bog depletions on a worldwide scale may well invite unpredictable environmental consequences. Perhaps they have already begun to do so.

According to one estimate, the world holds about 223 billion dry tons of sphagnum, about half of this in Russia. From the small Canadian province of New Brunswick alone some six million bales (each seventy to eighty pounds dry weight) of sphagnum are exported annually. Almost half of U.S. boglands have now been drained for agricultural expansion; some ninety million acres remain. The largest surviving American bogs are located in Minnesota and Maine (sphagnum covers about 2.3 percent of the latter state). Most commercial horticultural peat comes from New Brunswick, Quebec, and Florida.

In Neolithic Europe (4000–2000 B.C.), bogs became sacred locales, sites of solemn rituals, human and animal sacrifices, and burials. These were fearsome places steeped in mythology and folklore.

The use of peat moss as fuel can be dated to Roman times but probably existed ages before that. American natives used dried sphagnum mainly as stuffing for pillows and mattresses and as absorbent diapers for children. As recently as World War I, German hospitals found sphagnum a useful antibiotic dressing for surgical incisions.

Today the primary use of sphagnum peat is by farmers and gardeners as a water-holding organic mulch, fertilizer, and conditioner for both dry and heavy soils. From peatlands come most of the commercial blueberry and cranberry crops. Europeans, especially, use sphagnum (often called *turf* there) for home insulation, for ballast in railroad beds, for "peatwood" (similar to plywood), and "peatcrete" (similar to concrete). Other uses, so far little developed in America, include chemical extractions (ethyl alcohol, waxes, resins for medical ingredients), sewage-treatment and composting additives, and energy production and fuel (sphagnum burning generates about one third of Ireland's electricity; two tons of peat release as much heat as one ton of coal or four tons of firewood).

Sphagnum bogs also produce methane gas; often a hollow rod inserted into a bog will nurture a flame. Small clouds of released methane sometimes spontaneously ignite, producing those mysterious, hovering "bog-lights" or "will-o-the-wisps" seen over a bog at night. Methane is one reason why many fires in drier bogs are notoriously difficult or impossible to extinguish once begun; some of them smolder for years.

Because of its antibiotic acidity, compressed and waterlogged sphagnum does not truly decompose. Instead it carbonizes, turning into "black butter"; this peat consists of about 60 percent carbon. In northeastern American bogs, one to three inches of peat take about a century of time to accumulate. Further compression, burial, anaerobic bacterial activity, and time result in the formation of lignite, which with increasing loss of gases and moisture becomes bituminous, or "soft," coal. (Anthracite, or "hard," coal is metamorphic bituminous coal, containing about 90 percent carbon; metamorphosed anthracite becomes graphite.) An inch-wide coal seam represents centuries of peat accumulation.

The preservative abilities of peat deposits are well known. Paleobotanists recover and analyze pollen grains from peat cores, discovering much about past vegetation and climates. Extinct animals such as mammoths and mastodons lie intact where they fell. And such well-preserved human remains as the eight-thousand-year-old Windover burials in Florida, Lindow man in England, and Tollund man in Denmark reveal much about our own cultural ancestry.

Nut-Grasses (*Cyperus* spp.). Sedge family. Grasslike herbs in wet, mesic, and dry habitats. Nut-grasses show flattened, two-ranked spikelets with leafy bracts at their bases; one or more whorled, grasslike leaves extending beyond the spikelet clusters; and three-angled stems. Some thirty-five species grow in east-central North America. Chufa *(C. esculentus)* and straw-colored cyperus *(C. strigosus)* are two of the common wetland nut-grasses.

Other names: Galingale, umbrella-sedge, nut-sedge, sweet-rush, flat-sedge, ground-almond, yellow nut-sedge or nut-grass, tiger-nut, earth-almond, earth-nut, rush-nut, Zulu-nut *(C. esculentus)*; false nut-sedge, long galingale *(C. strigosus)*.

Close relatives: Spike-rushes *(Eleocharis)*; bulrushes *(Scirpus)*; cotton-grasses *(Eriophorum)*; beak-rushes *(Rhyncospora)*; sedges *(Carex)*.

Lifestyle: Most sedges are virtually impossible to identify down to species level unless mature nutlets are present on the plant, and in the case of some *Cyperus* and *Carex* sedges, even distinguishing the correct genus can be difficult. Nut-grasses, especially the two species mentioned, appear somewhat bushier and coarser than the finer, more grasslike *Carex* sedges, owing to their larger, spiny-looking fruit spikelets.

The wind-pollinated flowers, in contrast to those of *Carex* sedges, are bisexual.

Underground parts of these plants differ extensively among species. Chufa, for example, has long, scaly stolons with enlarged tubers at the ends; *C. strigosus* rises from a fleshy, bulblike corm with rootlets beneath.

Associates: *Summer, fall.* Wetland nut-grasses are fen plants, inhabiting marshes, ditches, and shorelines. Typical associates include marsh fern, *Carex* sedges, shrub willows, and other fen dwellers.

Insect feeders are generally the same as for other sedges (see Sedges). A moth caterpillar borer *(Diploschizia impigritella)*, a glyphipterigid, commonly feeds in nut-grass stems and leaf bases.

Nut-grass tubers and nutlets, especially those of chufa, are relished by

Nut-grasses provide food for many birds, especially in winter floodings. Both seeds and tubers are relished by waterfowl and shorebirds. Triangular stems and grasslike leaves extending beyond the spikelets are good identity marks.

waterfowl, including American black ducks, gadwalls, mallards, common pintails, American wigeons, wood ducks, Northern shovelers, blue-winged and green-winged teals, canvasbacks, ring-necked ducks, and greater and lesser scaups. Geese and grebes also feed on the plants, as do American bitterns and other herons, king, sora, and Virginia rails, and ruffed grouse. Songbirds that eat the nutlets include American crows and American tree sparrows.

Muskrats are the only regular mammal feeders on the wetland species.

Winter. Much, if not most, waterfowl feeding on chufa occurs at this season, when mudflats are flooded and provide easy access to the plants by water birds.

Lore: Chufa tubers have long been valued for human food. Egyptian tombs of the third millennium B.C. contained remnants of them; the plant was apparently cultivated and regarded as a choice food. It is still grown today (mainly in Valencia, Spain) as an ingredient for an ancient but still popular rice-water beverage called *horchata.* The nourishing tubers can be eaten raw, cooked, dried and ground into flour, or roasted and ground into a coffee.

Probably native to Egypt, where the stem pith from another species *(C. papyrifera)* was used for making paper, chufa has grown worldwide for so long that it can hardly be classed as an alien species.

Chufa is not universally admired, however. In upland areas, especially in light, sandy soils, it can become a troublesome weed.

Oak, Pin *(Quercus palustris)* and **Swamp White Oak** *(Q.bicolor)*. Beech family. Trees in swampy lowlands, bottomland soils. These two common wetland oaks represent the two major oak groupings (see *The Book of Forest and Thicket*). Pin oak belongs in the red or black oak group, characterized by leaves with bristle-tipped lobes. Swamp white oak is a member of the white oak group, distinguished by rounded leaf lobes or teeth.

Recognize pin oak by its shiny green leaves, deeply cut leaf sinuses, stubby branchlets ("pins"), drooping lower branches, and shallow acorn cups. The related northern pin or jack oak *(Q. ellipsoidalis)* is an upland species.

Swamp white oak has thick, dark green leaves with wavy-toothed (rarely lobed) margins; and long-stalked acorns in pairs with swollen, slightly fringed acorn cups. Because of its rounded leaf teeth rather than lobes, swamp white oak is sometimes placed in the chestnut oak group.

Other names: Swamp oak, water oak, swamp Spanish oak *(Q. palustris)*; swamp oak *(Q. bicolor)*.

Close relatives: American beech *(Fagus grandifolia)*; American chestnut *(Castanea dentata)*; all other oaks *(Quercus)*.

Lifestyle: Both of these trees bear resemblances in leaf shapes to other oak species: Pin oak leaves resemble those of northern pin and scarlet oaks *(Q. ellipsoidalis, Q. coccinea)*; swamp white oak leaves are similar to leaves of chestnut and chinquapin oaks *(Q. prinus, Q. prinoides)*. Key differences, however, lie in their habitats; all except pin and swamp white oaks favor dry soil and upland sites.

Both oaks show limited continental distribution. Southern New England and the southern Great Lakes border their northern range, and neither oak extends as far south as the Gulf. Both these species have shallow root systems, both produce flowers along with their leaves in spring, and both bear unisexual, wind-pollinated flowers on the same tree.

Pin oak favors habitats that manifest *hydroperiods;* that is, they are seasonally rather than constantly wet. It tolerates heavy flooding during its dormancy in winter and early spring; it also tolerates excessive dryness on the same sites in summer. It is shade intolerant, grows quite rapidly, begins producing acorns at about age twenty, and seldom lives longer than a century. This tree's pyramidal form and thick trunk relative to the size of its branches are fairly distinctive. After leaf-fall you can easily see how its branches in the top half of the tree ascend and those in the lower half droop down, sometimes to the ground. Lower branches and twigs usually remain attached to the tree long after they die. The pin designation is variously ascribed to its short, spurlike branchlets or to the many knots of dead branches that extend pinlike into the trunk.

The small, bitter pin oak acorns mature and drop in the autumn of their second year (as with all red oaks). Leaves, which show hairy tufts in the angles of their veins, turn bright red in the fall; many often remain brown on the tree through winter.

Swamp white oak favors swampy borders and shorelines rather than the standing water of open swamps. Like pin oak, it tolerates changing water levels but not to the seasonal extremes endured by that tree. Its seedlings can tolerate medium shade. The tree grows quite slowly, begins producing acorns at about age twenty, and lives long (three hundred years or more). As do other white oaks, it matures its acorns each autumn, producing heavy crops every three to five years. The paired acorns are sweet and (humanly) edible.

This tree's form is somewhat shaggy, with upswept and down-curved branches and dead lower branches persisting—altogether a more "modest" version of pin oak. Small branches shed their bark somewhat like sycamore trees. Leaves and flowers emerge quite late in spring. Whitish and velvety on their undersides, the leaves give the tree its specific name *bicolor.* They turn yellowish-brown or orange in fall. This oak hybridizes with bur, chestnut, English, and white oaks *(Q. macrocarpa, Q. prinus, Q. robur, Q. alba).*

Associates: Pin and swamp white oaks sometimes grow in close proximity. Other common tree associates may include American elm, silver and red maples, northern hackberry, shagbark and shellbark hickories, and American basswood.

Spring, summer. All oaks host large insect populations. Many of them often occur on most of the twenty-five or so oak species of east-central North America. A complete listing of known oak insects would require many pages (the discovery of new ones may await *your* observations). Noted here are only some of the insects likeliest to be seen on each of these two oak species. (For other oak insects, see the accounts for Red Oak and White Oak in *The Book of Forest and Thicket.*)

PIN OAK. Leaf feeders prominently include two moth caterpillars that often defoliate this and other trees, usually without killing them. The forest tent caterpillar *(Malacosoma disstria)*, bluish in color, leaves silken mats on trunks and branches; during heavy infestations, look for large gray flesh flies *(Sarcophaga aldrichi)*, which parasitize the caterpillar cocoons. The gypsy moth *(Lymantria dispar)*, foremost insect pest of all northeastern oaks, is brownish and hairy. This tussock moth, an import from Europe, hatches very early in spring. It feeds on the leaves and disperses to other trees by swinging from silken strands. One of its main insect predators is a large, black, carabid beetle, the European caterpillar hunter *(Calosoma sycophanta)*. Both of these caterpillars feed in gregarious masses and are *irruptive* (that is, their populations undergo cyclic highs and lows). When they are feeding en masse, you can hear a constant rain of insect excreta and leaf fragments pattering down. In midsummer, watch for groups of excited, brownish, adult male gypsy moths fluttering around a stationary swollen female moth laying eggs on oak or aspen trunks; though winged, the female moth is flightless.

Other common moth caterpillar feeders on pin oak include the common lytrosis *(Lytrosis unitaria)*, an inchworm species; the oak leaftier *(Croesia semipurpurana)*, a tortricid moth, which folds over sections of leaves and feeds inside the folds; and leaf rollers *(Argyrotaenia quercifoliana, A. alisellana)*, also tortricids, which feed inside the tubular leaf rolls they create.

Resembling caterpillars, sawfly larvae also feed on the leaves: most prominently, the pin oak sawfly *(Caliroa lineata)*; the scarlet oak or slug oak sawfly *(C. quercuscoccineae)*; and *C. petiolata*. All are sluglike, gregarious feeders that skeletonize leaves, often working from the top of the tree down.

Over a period of some thirty million years, oaks have evolved complex host relationships with a family of small wasps called cynipids (Cynipidae), the so-called gall wasps. Some eight hundred species create swellings or galls of various distinctive sizes and shapes, usually as a result of their egg-laying in tissues of oak leaves and twigs. (It is actually the plant tissues that create the

*Small cynipid wasps cause oak galls in numerous shapes and sizes. The leaf galls at near right typically occur on pin oak. Also common on twigs and branches are horned oak galls (far right), the work of **Callirhytis cornigera**. Note how this gall causes branching at the twig tip.*

galls in response to chemical or other irritation caused by insect egg-laying and larval feeding.) The wasp larvae feed and mature inside the galls.

Several common galls can be found on pin oak leaves. Small leaf blisters are produced in spring by first generations of the gouty oak gall wasp *(Callirhytis punctata)*; the second generation creates round, woody galls encircling twigs and small branches in summer. Another common summer gall, similar but with projecting horns, is the work of the horned oak gall wasp *(C. cornigera)*. Occasional heavy infestations of the latter insects can form almost continuous masses of galls on twigs and branches. Most gall insects are in turn parasitized by other tiny insects, often ichneumons (Ichneumonidae).

Layered, bark-colored crusts on trunks and branches are probably masses of scale insects, sap-suckers that may damage the trees. A common species on pin oak is the obscure scale *(Melanaspis obscura)*.

Wrinkled yellowish or purplish blisters on upper surfaces of leaves and corresponding depressions on the lower surfaces indicate a leaf blister fungus *(Taphrina caerulescens)*. Usually it appears on leaves only during cool, wet springs.

The aforementioned insect irruptions may attract an influx of bird predators that are able to digest hairy caterpillars. Such predators may include yellow-billed and black-billed cuckoos, white-breasted nuthatches, and yellow warblers, among others.

SWAMP WHITE OAK. The most destructive disease of oaks, severely affecting this species at times, is oak wilt, caused by the fungus *Ceratocystis fagacearum*. It

is sometimes transmitted from diseased to healthy trees by natural root-grafting, also by squirrels and sap-feeding and bark-boring insects. Oak wilt is a tree killer, invading the tree's cambium vascular system. Infected red oaks may perish in a single season; white oaks die more slowly, a few branches at a time over a period of years. Symptoms include leaf wilt beginning in the crown, then progressing downward and inward, and consequent death of the tree. Mats of the fungus thrive beneath the bark of wilt-killed trees, providing sources of new infection.

Another common fungous disease is oak anthracnose, which appears on the leaves as brownish or blackened areas along the veins and also produces cankers on the twigs. The causative sac fungus is *Gnomonia quercina.*

Insect feeders are essentially the same as for white oak (*Q. alba*; see *The Book of Forest and Thicket*).

Prominent gall makers on swamp white oak include several *Neuroterus* gall wasp species. *N. escharensis* creates tiny galls on twigs just beneath the leaf scars; *N. distortus* causes bent twigs and distorted leaves. *N. noxiosus,* the noxious oak gall, makes swellings on leaf midribs and stalks, curling and dwarfing the leaf.

Fall, winter. Pin oak acorns are important foods for migrating waterfowl, especially mallards and wood ducks. Wild turkeys and woodpeckers are also prominent consumers. Blue jays sometimes cache the acorns; I have found them inserted into the ragged seed heads of cattails in the fall (see Cattails).

Mammal feeders include squirrels and white-tailed deer.

Acorns of swamp white oak are likewise consumed, especially by waterfowl and squirrels.

Fall and winter are the best seasons to observe the aforementioned insect galls on oak twigs. Most of them are dry and vacated by now, but some may still

host overwintering gall wasp pupae or other insects *(inquilines)* that invade the gall for shelter. The aforementioned noxious oak gall, in yet another seasonal incarnation, is a potato-shaped growth on swamp white oak twigs.

On warm winter days, watch for large, gray, hairy-bodied moths flying around pin oaks. These noctuids may be Grote's pinion moths *(Lithophane grotei)*. They lay eggs on pin oak, one of their larval food plants; the green caterpillars are often called green fruit-worms.

On oak trunks, the tannish, fuzzy patches of gypsy moth egg masses remain conspicuous all winter.

Brownish, furry patches on the bark are the first signs of gypsy moth, the most destructive insect pest of oaks. These egg masses, deposited in summer, remain on trees over winter and hatch in early spring.

Lore: Pin oak is a popular landscape planting in both America and Europe. Its tolerance of urban fumes and drought makes it a valued street tree (and a colorful one in the fall). Pin oak lumber, used selectively for construction material because of its characteristic pin knots, is generally sold as "red oak."

Swamp white oak, with its greater moisture needs, has limited landscaping value, but its wood (not separated commercially from "white oak") finds many uses in such items as flooring, interior trim and paneling, and wooden containers. Its decay resistance also makes it valuable for posts, piling, and railroad ties.

American natives apparently made no rigid distinctions between oak species in their use of them for food and medicines. White oak acorns, of course, were edible "off the tree," but bitter acorns of the red oak group were also made palatable by boiling out the water-soluble tannin. Astringent tannin teas and tonics made from oak bark treated a variety of skin and internal ailments.

Orchids, Lipped *(Platanthera, Pogonia, Arethusa, Calopogon, Spiranthes, Liparis* spp.). Orchid family. Herbs in a variety of bog, fen, and dry sites. Recognize lipped orchids (in contrast to the *pouched* lady-slipper orchids [see Lady-slippers]) by a protruding, tonguelike lower petal (the lip or *labellum*), which shows various colors, shapes, and sizes among species. Two smaller petals and three flaring, bractlike sepals, plus (in most genera) a protruding rear spur, complete the flower aspect. The flowers grow in spikelike terminal clusters. Leaves, usually sheathing the flower stalk, are parallel veined.

Common names for these orchid genera and species include fringed orchids *(Platanthera)*; rose pogonia *(Pogonia ophioglossoides)*; arethusa *(Arethusa bulbosa)*; grass-pink *(Calopogon tuberosus)*; ladies'-tresses *(Spiranthes)*; and bog twayblade *(Liparis loeselii)*. Other genera also exist, but these are the most commonly seen.

Other names: Rein-orchids *(Platanthera)*; sweet pogonia, adder's-mouth, snake-mouth, beard-flower, ettercap, sweet crest-orchid *(Pogonia ophioglossoides)*; dragon's-mouth, wild pink, Indian pink, bog-rose *(A. bulbosa)*; Loesel's twayblade, fen orchid, olive scutcheon *(L. loeselii)*.

Close relatives: Lady-slippers *(Cypripedium)*; rattlesnake-plantains *(Goodyera)*; coral-roots *(Corallorhiza)*; twayblades *(Listera)*; and all other orchid genera.

Lifestyle: All orchid flowers are bisexual and insect pollinated. The lipped orchids produce pollen in sticky masses or packages called *pollinia,* which adhere to insect bodies or heads. Both male and female parts are fused into a cen-

tral column, beneath which the insect passes to seek the nectar. Pollination and deposition on the insect of new pollen occurs when the insect backs out of the flower. The complex interior arrangement of sticky surfaces is positioned so precisely that an insect can hardly fail to pick up and deposit pollinia in exactly the right places. Despite this mechanism, most of these orchids regularly self-pollinate; grass-pink and hooded ladies'-tresses, however, require insect pollination.

Many *Platanthera* orchids have a conspicuously fringed lip. These include white-fringed orchid *(P. blephariglottis)*, yellow-fringed orchid *(P. ciliaris)*, large purple-fringed orchid *(P. grandiflora)*, and tall northern bog orchid *(P. hyperborea*; this is one of the most common orchids, bearing greenish, nonfringed flowers, also called Northern green orchis).

The red, spurless orchids, rose pogonia and arethusa, bear only a single flower at the stem tip. Pogonia's lip is pink-fringed and -crested; arethusa's is conspicuously yellow-crested and clawed or slightly lobed. "No orchid in our flora is lovelier," wrote orchid botanist Fred Case of arethusa. The only other *Arethusa* species is a native of Japan. Case likened the fragrance of rose pogonia to red raspberries—"a person familiar with the odor can sometimes detect the presence of the plants before seeing them." Thoreau, on the other hand, thought pogonias smelled like snakes.

Grass-pink, also red, reverses the usual orchid flower orientation; its lip protrudes from the top, making the flower appear upside down. In all other native orchids, the flower ovary turns 180 degrees so that the lip petal, which actually forms in an uppermost position, as in grass-pink, becomes the lowest in position. Grass-pink flowers grow in a loose cluster atop the plant.

Ladies'-tresses, by contrast, show relatively inconspicuous spikes of small, white, unspurred flowers and long, grasslike leaves. The most common wetland species include nodding

Northern bog orchid, a greenish-flowered, inconspicuous species, is a common resident of various wetland habitats. It stands two or more feet tall, with several long, narrow leaves rising from the base.

ladies'-tresses *(Spiranthes cernua)*; shining or wide-leaved ladies'-tresses *(S. lucida)*, which sometimes thrives on disturbed sites; and hooded ladies'-tresses *(S. romanzoffiana)*. A pollinating bee usually works the flower spikes systematically, landing on the lowest flower of a spike (always the oldest) and spiraling up the flower stalk. Indeed, the "spiral staircase" form of *Spiranthes* flowers may represent the coevolved outcome of a bee's typical path up a vertical stem.

Bog twayblade has paired, shiny leaves rising from the stem base and yellow-green flowers with narrow, flaring side petals and a broad lip. Adaptable to both bog and fen habitats, this little orchid often grows at the water's edge in damp, sterile soil, or in matted-down animal trails in bogs. Raindrops falling on flower parts at least sometimes cause self-pollination in this species.

Orchid seed, often produced asexually (by a process called *apomixis* or *parthenogenesis*) in some species, is extremely fine, dustlike. Notoriously difficult to germinate in the laboratory or greenhouse, seeds remain dormant until, by some yet-unknown process in nature, their dormancy is broken. Although researchers have managed to germinate a few species under controlled conditions, raising native orchids from seed to flowering remains nearly impossible. Orchids guard their secrets well; this is part of the ongoing mystery and fascination of these complex, often bizarre plants.

Once germinated, the young plant must nourish underground, usually for a period of years, before it can produce aboveground leaves and flower stalk. The rhizome produces a new bud each fall, from which a new aboveground plant will rise the next year—provided it remains uninjured by frost, trampling, or other circumstances.

The sudden appearance of orchids where nobody has seen them before and likewise their disappearance from sites where they have usually grown are fairly common occurrences. In the former case, long-dormant seeds may have germinated and finally produced aboveground plants. In the latter, physical injury to plants, natural succession, or subtle changes in soil chemistry may wipe them out. In some cases, the *lack* of slight but continuous habitat disturbances can eliminate them. So specialized are the microhabitat requirements of some native orchids that they have probably always been (and always will be) rare. Where habitat conditions remain stable, however, other species may form long-lived, if localized, thriving colonies.

Associates: Vital to almost all North American orchids is the root-fungus symbiosis known as *mycorrhiza*, whereby fungal threads (usually *Rhyzoctonia*, an algal fungus, as well as other soil fungi) invade orchid root cells and provide their means of nutrient uptake. The fungus receives food from the orchid. For orchids, this relationship (common in most land plants, but absent in most aquatics) is one of absolute dependence; without it, germination and growth cannot occur.

Summer. All of the mentioned orchid species flower in summer. *Arethusa* and *Spiranthes lucida* begin in early summer, while *S. cernua* and *S. romanzoffiana* flower from late summer into fall.

Bog orchids, whose chief plant associates are sphagnum mosses and bog heaths, include the white-fringed and yellow-fringed orchids, rose pogonia, arethusa, and grass-pink (the three latter orchids often occur together, arethusa blooming a bit earlier than the others).

Typical orchids of open sedge fens, shrub-carrs, or northern white cedar swamps are tall northern bog orchid, large purple-fringed orchid, hooded ladies'-tresses, and bog twayblade. Nodding ladies'-tresses favor neutral or slightly acid, grassy areas. Shining ladies'-tresses often associate with meadow spike-moss *(Selaginella apoda)*, a fern relative, in disturbed fen sites.

Orchid pollinators are long-tongued insects, typically the larger bees, moths, and butterflies. Moths and bees usually pollinate the white orchids, while pollinators of orange or red orchids are mainly butterflies. White-fringed orchids are often pollinated by white-lined sphinx moths *(Hyles lineata)*; yellow-fringed orchids by spicebush swallowtail butterflies *(Papilio troilus)*; and large purple-fringed orchids by tiger swallowtail butterflies *(P. glaucus)*. The sticky pollinia usually adhere to the compound eyes of these insects as they probe into the spur for nectar; these attached masses seen on the heads of large butterflies are good signs that orchids bloom in the vicinity. Look for small slits in the nectar spurs, often made by carpenter bees (Xylocopinae) or other bees tapping into the sweets.

Rose pogonia, arethusa, and grass-pink attract bumblebee *(Bombus)* pollinators (though grass-pink produces no nectar). Hinged anthers release pollinia on these insects when they back out of the flower. The bulblike corms of grass-pink and bog twayblade are eaten by mice, voles, and eastern chipmunks.

Pollinators of ladies'-tresses include bumblebees, leafcutting bees (Megachilidae), and halictid bees (Halictidae). Slugs sometimes feed on the leaves.

Lore: Orchids make up the world's largest plant family (some thirty thousand or more species). About 80 percent of them are natives of tropical latitudes (thus the term *weeds of the tropics*). The phenomenal evolutionary success of orchids is difficult for temperate-zone dwellers to comprehend. Our native orchids are relatively sparse, both in species and abundance. And, notwithstanding their legally protected status in most states, many uncommon species continue to dwindle—not primarily because of enthusiastic collectors of the past (like Grace Greylock Niles, who wrote the charming *Bog-Trotting for Orchids* in 1904), but because of America's ongoing zeal to drain and convert its wetlands into "productivity" (that is, deserts for biodiversity). Today the only orchids many Americans ever see are those gaudy greenhouse varieties commercially grown to help celebrate special occasions. The world of orchids is vaster than that, but the opportunity of viewing our unique native species in their own habitats is becoming an increasingly rare special occasion in itself.

Orchids probably owe their biological success to the billions upon billions of near-microscopic seeds they release each year—seeds that require exactly the right combination of circumstances to germinate, let alone thrive to become seed producers themselves. Since orchid seeds, unlike seeds of most plants, carry no stored food for the rudimentary embryos, the aforementioned mycorrhizal symbioses must be quickly established. How such a fragile-seeded plant family became dispersed worldwide has long mystified botanists. Some have suggested that high jet-stream winds may have quickly transported orchid seeds across oceans, or that birds carried the seeds in mud on their feet.

Native peoples found scant use for orchids. Arethusa is said to have once been used as a toothache remedy. The tropical orchid *Vanilla,* source of vanilla flavoring, is the only plant of the family that yields an edible food product in any quantity.

The cultivation, cloning, and hybrid creation of tropical orchid varieties form a large horticultural industry. Orchid hobbyists and gardeners publish their own journals and hone their expertise in several national organizations.

Pickerel-weed *(Pontederia cordata).* Pickerel-weed family. Emergent herb in marshes, shallow margins of ponds, lakes, streams. Identify pickerel-weed by its three-inch, violet-blue flower spike and its large, glossy, usually single arrowhead-shaped leaf with rounded bases.

Other name: Tuckahoe (also a name for arrow-arum, *Peltandra virginica*).

Close relatives: Water-hyacinth *(Eichhornia crassipes)*; water star-grass *(Zosterella dubia)*; mud-plantains *(Heteranthera)*.

Lifestyle: Beds of blue-spired pickerel-weed provide color to shallows and shorelines from June to October, when the plants are in continuous flower. Look closely at the bisexual, insect-pollinated flowers. They come in three distinct forms, each in separate colonies, based on the three varying lengths of the female reproductive parts. A pistil can only be fertilized by pollen from another flower's stamens of the corresponding length. This arrangement, virtually guaranteeing cross-fertilization, is called *tristyly;* the only other flowers in this book exhibiting a similar arrangement are loosestrifes (see diagram for Loosestrife, Purple).

The crowded flower spike is the work of an entire summer. Usually only a few flowers bloom at a time; blooming begins at the bottom of the spike and progresses upward as the season advances. Each nectar-rich flower lasts only about a day; after pollination, the upper petals close, and it develops a single seed called an *utricle.* When flowering is finished, the spike bends over and releases seeds into the water. Seeds require about two months of cold stratification in order to germinate. Most reproduction, however, occurs vegetatively by means of the creeping, mud-buried rhizome, from which arise numerous individual shoots producing the familiar colonial growth form. Thoreau noted the prevalence of pickerel-weed borders on the inside curves of stream meanders, where most sediment is deposited—"the river has its active and its passive side."

Pickerel-weed seldom grows in water over three feet deep. Like many aquatic leaf stalks, those of pickerel-weed have aerated chambers that function as interior flotation devices, holding the leaf upright in water. Leaves of pickerel-weeds stranded on summer mud banks lie prostrate, for they have no supporting tissue of their own.

Associates: *Summer, fall.* Other emergent aquatic plants with arrowhead-shaped leaves (arrowheads and arrow-arum) often occupy the same shoreline habitats as pickerel-weed, providing opportunity to compare differences between these intriguing leaves (see Arrowhead, Broad-leaved). Other common plant associates include bur-reeds, cattails, purple loosestrife, water-lilies, pondweeds, and smartweeds.

Pollinators are primarily bees, including bumblebees *(Bombus).* Thoreau noted pickerel-weed colonies

Air-filled stems of pickerel-weed, seen here in cross section, provide buoyancy in water. Small partitions divide the central column into chambers.

"alive with butterflies, yellow and others." Syrphid flies (Syrphidae) and ruby-throated hummingbirds are also occasional pollinators.

Insect feeders in the stems include larvae of waterlily leaf beetles (*Donacia*; see Water-lilies), plus several noctuid moth caterpillars that are stem borers: the white-tailed diver (*Bellura gortynoides*), which also mines in the leaves; the cattail borer moth (*B. obliqua*; see Cattails); and the pickerelweed borer moth (*B. densa*). Adult moths of this species are mostly brownish, hairy, and quite large.

Pickerel-weeds are frequent birth sites of adult dragonflies and damselflies; the aquatic nymphs climb this and other emergent plants when they are ready to shed their final nymphal exoskeletons and take to the air. The cast skins of these insects often remain attached to the plant for days. Some female adult Odonata, such as the green darner dragonfly (*Anax junius*) and black-winged damselfly (*Calopteryx maculata*), return to the plants and deposit their eggs in stem tissues just below the water surface.

Seeds are eaten by surface-feeding waterfowl, most notably American black ducks, gadwalls, mallards, common pintails, green-winged teal, and wood ducks.

Muskrats sometimes use the stems as lodge material; they consume the seeds and also eat the leaves, as do white-tailed deer. In its general value to wildlife, however, pickerel-weed ranks lower than many of its emergent plant associates. Although it does provide shade and shelter to aquatic organisms, the plant has no special associations with pickerel or other fishes.

Lore: Leaves and seeds of this common plant are edible and nutritious. The young, unfurled leaves can be used in salads or cooked for greens. Starchy pickerel-weed seeds can be eaten off the plant or dried, roasted, or ground into flour.

So rapidly do the rhizomes sprout colonies that dense beds of pickerel-weed sometimes become a nuisance to property owners on recreational lakes, especially those lakes developed by marsh dredging.

Pitcher-plant (*Sarracenia purpurea*). Pitcher-plant family. Low herb in bogs and fens. Its semiprostrate, purple-streaked leaves, forming keeled, pitcher-shaped water containers make this one of the easiest wetland plants to identify.

Other names: Northern or purple pitcher-plant, Indian dipper, huntsman's-cup, side-saddle flower, Adam's-pitcher, fever-cup, smallpox-plant, dumb-watch, whippoorwill-boots.

Close relatives: Trumpets (*S. flava*); California pitcher-plant (*Darlingtonia californica*).

Lifestyle: Pitcher-plant, along with sundews and bladderworts, ranks among the most common insect-trapping plants of North America. Its passive method is unique. The modified leaf that forms the pitcher has several easily seen interior zones. The topmost zone is a flared-out lip—a sort of landing platform—with nectar glands and conspicuous reddish veins. On the inside rim, a coating of fine, downward-pointing hairs and a numbing secretion make an insect's escape from the container almost impossible. Just below this zone is a slippery, smooth-walled, sticky constriction, a further impediment to escape.

Then comes the actual water container, where the prey dies by drowning. The water held in the pitcher is rain (though one observant naturalist has suggested that the hollow leafstalks may indicate water pressure from beneath). The liquid hosts bacteria (often the anaerobic *Rhodopseudomonas palustris*) and possibly plant enzymes, a "digestive fluid" that helps decompose trapped insects and converts their tissues into nitrogen and other nutrients absorbed by the plant. This absorption occurs by means of special cells at the bottom of the pitcher.

The lowest zone is the long, narrow stalk, where indigestible remnants of insects accumulate. Split open a dried pitcher leaf of a previous season (they often remain intact on the plant for months) to see the plant's scrap pile of insect parts. Plants that don't produce flowers in a given year, research has shown, actually don't do much insect digestion; the liquid remains relatively enzyme dilute.

Botanists once believed that nutrient-poor bog environments accounted for pitcher-plant's evolved reliance on trapping insects for nourishment. But pitcher-plants also grow in nutrient-rich fens where minerals are not in short supply (the plant's pH tolerance ranges from about 5 to 9). Yet some minerals—phosphorus, for example—may be rendered insoluble by chemical actions of other minerals (such as iron and aluminum), making even fens practically deficient at times in certain nutrients that plant carnivory can quickly supply.

The single flower rising a foot or two above the leaves is spectacular in itself, a large, maroon, nodding globe that is bisexual and insect pollinated. The pistil is large and umbrellalike, enfolded by the petals.

A five-parted seed capsule replaces the flower and frequently persists into the winter. The seeds require a period of freezing before germination can occur. Most of the plant's reproduction, however, occurs by continuous budding from the perennial rhizome.

At least a few dwarfed, evergreen, pitcher leaves usually remain on plants throughout the year; flowers and new pitcher leaves, radiating from the rhizome, appear only in spring and summer. New leaves are constantly replacing old ones, which die and detach from the plant. Living leaves often turn quite red in the fall. Usually fewer than eight pitcher leaves are present on a single plant at any given time. You can number the chronological sequencing of leaves by observing their stalks; the base of the newest stalk almost surrounds the plant stem, encompassing and overlapping all older leafstalks; and each next-youngest leafstalk does likewise. A new leaf develops almost opposite the position of the previous leaf in the radiating cluster. The younger leaves (those less than fifty days old) attract most of the insect prey; older leaves seem to lose their attractant nectar and (possibly) odor.

Light surface fires in bogs apparently have a rejuvenative effect on pitcher-plant growth. Observers have often noted increased abundance of the plant in years following such fires.

Associates: Probably the most common plant companions of pitcher-plant in both bog and fen habitats are mosses. In bogs, sphagnums and haircaps are the main moss associates; sphagnum and true moss calciphiles of various species predominate in fens. Shrub heath species in bogs and sedge species in fens are the typical groundcover plants.

Spring, summer. Flower pollinators are mainly bumblebees *(Bombus)* and honeybees *(Apis mellifera).*

"I never found a pitcher-plant without an insect in it," claimed Thoreau— remarkable if true, for in most pitcher-plant populations, most of the containers do not show recent captures at any given time. The true indicator, of course, lies in the bottom scrap pile, if any, of the pitcher.

Much research has been done on the number and types of insects that fall prey into the pitchers. In one Michigan study of 214 pitcher leaves, 504 individual insects from 13 orders and 49 families were recovered, most of

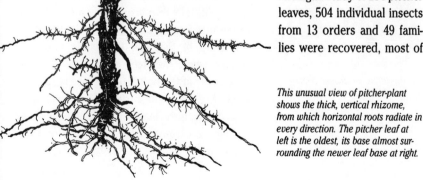

This unusual view of pitcher-plant shows the thick, vertical rhizome, from which horizontal roots radiate in every direction. The pitcher leaf at left is the oldest, its base almost surrounding the newer leaf base at right.

them fly species. Another study found that almost half of the pitcher victims consisted of large calyptrate flies (such as flesh flies [Sarcophagidae], which are often attracted to "raw meat coloring" and red veining in plants). Ants too (often *Crematogaster pilosa*) are frequent victims; they sometimes nest inside dried and dead pitcher leaves. Other ant victims include *Camponotus* and *Myrmica* species.

Even more interesting than its victims, however, are the pitchers' guests, or *inquilines* (including at least seventeen arthropod species). These not only resist the digestive brew of the leaves but thrive in it, feeding upon smaller residents: bacteria, diatoms, protozoa, rotifers, and nematode worms, plus fragments of drowned insect victims. They also contribute their own waste products to the mineral needs of the plant. Most of these residents operate in separate microhabitats of the pitcher.

Tiny aquatic mites swim in these rich microhabitats, scavenging organic materials; *Anoetus gibsoni, Kanoetus hughese, Macroseius biscutatus,* and *Histiostoma* are common species.

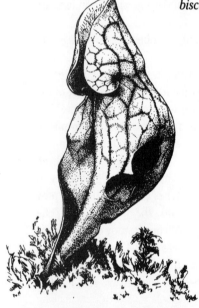

Various insect feeders and pitcher residents cut holes in the leaf, draining its liquid. This leaf's top lip, flared out when functional, now hoods the opening as the leaf declines and dies. Note the leaf's flattened keel at left and its purple veining.

Probably the most common inquilines are the larvae of three fly species. The large flesh fly maggot *Blaesoxipha fletcheri,* usually only one in a pitcher, feeds on freshly drowned prey at the pitcher's liquid surface. The pitcher-plant mosquito *(Wyeomyia smithii),* a filter-feeder, grazes on organic debris in the pitcher liquid. And the pitcher-plant midge *(Metriocnemus knabi)* burrows into the scrap pile of insect fragments to feed there. Each of these larvae consumes pitcher-plant prey in different stages of decomposition.

Another common fly inhabitant is the eastern flesh fly *(Sarraceniomyia sarraceniae);* young maggots hatch from eggs laid on the flaring lip of the leaf, then slide into the pitcher, where they feed on partially decomposed prey at the bottom. They rise occasionally to breathe at the surface. They finally cut holes through the leaf wall, often draining the pitcher, and transform to adult flies outside the plant.

Other resident fly larvae may include the pitcher-plant sciarid *(Bradysia mac-farnlanei)*, a dark-winged fungus gnat; and the pitcher-plant phorid *(Dohrniphora cornuta)*, a humpbacked fly.

A solitary thread-waisted wasp *(Sphex)* also cuts a hole low on the leaf, draining the pitcher and converting the cavity to a nest stuffed with pieces of grass. Here it lays eggs and stocks the nest with sting-paralyzed caterpillars as food for its young.

Occasional vertebrate residents include tiny tree frogs *(Hyla)*, which sit on the leaf tip or crawl in and out of the pitcher, feeding on passing or falling insects. One spider, a sheet-web weaver (Liniphiidae), catches prey before they fall into the pitcher by building a web across the pitcher mouth. Sometimes the spider itself falls victim to the plant.

Two leaf-mining moth caterpillars feed on the pitcher leaves. *Exyria rolandiana,* a noctuid, weaves a silken mesh across the mouth of the pitcher, thus protecting itself from predators, then feeds on the interior lining of the pitcher. Sometimes it girdles the topmost portion of the leaf; look for dried leaf tops fallen over and sheltering the opening. These reddish caterpillars, hatched from eggs on the plant, distribute themselves so that each pitcher holds only a single caterpillar. *E. semicroca,* a related species, tunnels between the outer leaf layers, creating a mine that extends toward the leaf base, where the insect pupates over winter. The small adult moths are yellowish.

Caterpillars of the pitcher-plant borer moth *(Papaipema appassionata)*, another noctuid, tunnel into stems and roots of the plant, emerging in late summer and fall. Another borer is *Endothenia daeckeana,* while *E. habesana* feeds on pitcher-plant seeds; both are tortricid moth caterpillars.

Pitcher-plant aphids *(Macrosiphum jeanae)* feed on buds and flowers.

"What wells for the birds!" suggested Thoreau, but even he, apparently, never actually observed birds drinking from the pitchers.

Probably the only mammal consumers of any significance are white-footed mice, meadow voles, cottontail rabbits, and snowshoe hares. Leaves in early spring sometimes show signs of extensive nibbling.

Fall, winter. When cold weather comes, larvae of the aforementioned pitcher-plant mosquito and midge undergo a period of dormancy *(diapause)* inside the pitchers; their activity and growth cease. They survive the freezing of the pitcher liquid into solid ice during this period and resume activity when spring thaws warm the bog or fen surface. In this way, these insects (neither of them biters) carry over their populations from fall to spring.

Lore: In native tribal practice, this plant became a kind of medical panacea for the prevention and cure of smallpox, brought by European settlers to this continent in the seventeenth century. Tribal elders and medicine men prescribed infusions of the root for this purpose. Modern pharmaceutical research, however, has failed to find any therapeutic substance in the plant. Indians also used the root for various other ailments and drank tea of dried leaves for fevers and chills.

Another claim is that water contained in the pitchers of this plant is safer to drink than bog water. After sampling both, my own judgment is that pitcher-plant water is generally less *untasty* than bog water, but that the likelihood of protozoan presence in the pitchers would give preference, for safety's sake (should the need arise), to relatively less plankton-populated bog waters. American natives used the pitchers for improvised cups, but there is no record that they drank their natural contents.

Pitcher-plant, legally protected in most areas, is the official flower of Newfoundland.

Pondweeds (*Potamogeton* spp.). Pondweed family. Submersed and floating-leaved herbs often forming dense growth in ponds, lakes, streams, along shorelines. Recognize pondweeds by their alternate, parallel-veined leaves and their numerous greenish-brown, pencil-like flower spikes in early summer. Some thirty highly variable species, divided into broad-leaved and narrow-leaved groups, occupy mostly shallow waters of east-central North America.

Three of the most common ones are sago pondweed (*P. pectinatus*), a bushy species with narrow, linear leaves tapering to sharp points; curly pondweed (*P. crispus*), bearing translucent, brownish, straplike leaves with crisped, ruffled edges; and floating-leaved pondweed (*P. natans*), with two kinds of leaves: submersed threadlike filaments and oval, surface-floating leaves on long stems. The latter two pondweeds are broad-leaved species.

Other names: Bushy or fennel-leaf pondweed, horsetail moss (*P. pectinatus*); brown-leaf, ruffle-leaf, curly-leafed, crimped-leafed, or crisp-leafed pondweed (*P. crispus*); floating brown-leaf (*P. natans*).

Close relatives: Wigeon-grass or ditch-grass (*Ruppia maritima*); horned pondweed (*Zannichellia palustris*); eel-grass (*Zostera marina*); naiads (*Najas*).

Lifestyle: Pondweeds are the dominant submersed aquatic plants in most North American lakes and ponds. Notoriously difficult to key down to precise species, many pondweeds also display variable characteristics within species depending on water depth, temperature, clarity, and velocity in their aquatic habitats. Species also hybridize widely. The three common pondweeds mentioned, however, are fairly easy to identify in the field because of their well-marked features.

Sago pondweed, though usually thriving in shallow waters, can grow at depths to fifteen feet. In deeper sites, the plant may grow eight feet long. Its flower spikes, floating at or near the surface, are pollinated by water movement. Sago is a prolific seed producer; one plant may produce many thousands of fruits annually as well as thousands of tubers from the slender rhizomes. This is the only pondweed with clearly visible teeth on its leaf margins.

Curly pondweed erects emergent (that is, above-water) flower spikes. Male and female parts of the bisexual flowers mature at different rates, thus preventing self-pollination. The pollen is dispersed by wind. This species, a European native, flowers and fruits earlier in spring than native pondweeds. It produces little seed, propagating mainly by dormant branch tips, which sink to the bottom in late fall and produce new shoots in spring. It also reproduces by fragmentation of short, woody branches. Curly pondweed thrives in overfertile, polluted, and brackish waters, sometimes to eight feet deep.

Floating-leaved pondweed shares with unrelated arrowheads, water-buttercups, water-milfoils, and a few other aquatics the double arrangement of leaves adapted to function in two environments *(heterophylly)*. Its submersed leaves are long, flexible, undulating streamers that reflect every movement of water current; the rigid, floating leaves lie on the water surface like small, oval-shaped lily pads. Its emergent, wind-pollinated flower spikes, projecting fingerlike above the surface, are common sights in almost any summer pond. After flowering, the spikes "lie down" in the water, sinking or floating horizontally at the surface. This plant normally grows in the quiet shallows, seldom over five feet deep.

Examine closely a pondweed flower, one of many on its spike. It lacks petals and

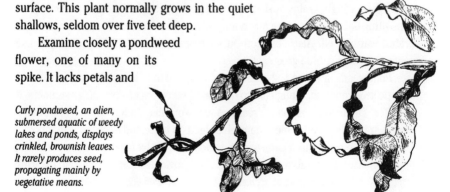

Curly pondweed, an alien, submersed aquatic of weedy lakes and ponds, displays crinkled, brownish leaves. It rarely produces seed, propagating mainly by vegetative means.

The native floating-leaved pondweed shows two kinds of leaves. Its lower, streaming, grasslike leaves are adapted for submersed aquatic existence. Its wider leaves float on the water surface. The flower spike emerges a few inches above the surface.

is shaped like a Maltese cross, with four central pistils surrounded by four stamens; the whole is bracketed by four green flaps. These flaps, initially closed over the stamens, open after the female portion has matured, permitting the outward release of pollen. When pondweeds are pollinating, the water surface may be thickly coated with the white, dustlike particles. Many pondweed species can also regenerate from fragmented stems. Pondweed achenes are commonly called nutlets.

Dense pondweed growth in a pond or lake usually reflects highly fertile, mineral-rich conditions. In overfertilized, algae-clouded waters, however, narrow-leaved species such as sago pondweed generally persist longer than the broad-leaved species, which require good light penetration into the water.

Associates: *Spring, summer, fall.* Look for pondweeds in dense beds among other submersed and floating-leaved plants such as waterweed, bladderworts, water-milfoils, water-lilies, water-shield, and smartweeds.

Often the submersed plants collect limy deposits on their stems and leaves, giving them rough, grainy surfaces. These precipitates indicate the work of lime-depositing bacteria and algae and temperature-chemical reactions in the lime-saturated water itself. Also common on submersed plants are brownish, jellylike coats of *Rivularia,* blue-green algae.

Pondweeds feed and shelter many zooplankton, insect larvae, and other aquatic invertebrates, though not to the abundant extent of some other submersed aquatics. Often the dominant creatures are wormlike midge larvae (Chironomidae), a staple fish food, which themselves feed on algae and decayed vegetation.

Several pyralid moth caterpillars, which breathe by means of gills, construct portable cases from submerged plant parts. Known generally as lily-leaf caterpillars, they include *Munroessa icciusalis, Synclita obliteralis,* and *Parapoynx obscu-*

ralis. Leaf mines may be the work of a shore fly larva *(Hydrellia).*

Aquatic snails on pondweeds include pond snail *(Lymnaea),* tadpole snail *(Physa),* and wheel snail *(Planorbis)* species.

For fishes, pondweeds provide food, shelter, and shade. Bluegills eat the leaves, and several fish species, including carp and goldfish, spawn in or near pondweed beds. Carp often uproot aquatic plants in their bottom-feeding activities; sago and curly pondweeds, however, are more resistant to such damage than most aquatics. Sago has an extensive rhizome system, and curly pondweed quickly reattaches its anchorage roots. Snapping turtles are known to feed on these plants as well.

Virtually all North American waterfowl species except fish eaters (such as loons and mergansers) relish pondweed nutlets and tubers. These birds include grebes, swans, geese, and both surface-feeding and

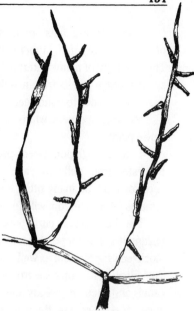

This narrow-leaved pondweed provides attachment to numerous case-building caddisfly larvae, only one of many larval insect types that feed and shelter in pondweed beds.

diving ducks. American coots and king, sora, and Virginia rails also consume pondweed parts. Shorebird pondweed consumers include plovers, common snipe, dowitchers, and sandpipers. Probably no food plants have more staple value and utility for water birds than pondweeds (though at least one waterfowl biologist has suggested that their heavy use may reflect plant abundance more than bird preference). Pondweed "presence or absence affects the use of areas by waterfowl during fall migration," assessed one research team. Sago pondweed has been called the single most important waterfowl

"Tailed" egg cases of water scavenger beetles (Hydrophilidae) can often be found attached to undersides of floating pondweed leaves.

food plant because of its prolific seed and tuber production. Shoreline windrows of this plant, torn up by tuber-eating diving ducks in the fall, are common sights. The tendency of many waterfowl (especially drakes and young ducks) to ingest spent shotgun pellets from marshes and pond bottoms may result from the pellets' resemblance to pondweed seeds.

Muskrats, beavers, white-tailed deer, and moose are major consumers of the entire plant.

Lore: Though pondweeds probably contain nothing toxic to humans (unless harvested from polluted waters), they have apparently never been frequently used for food. So many other edible, more tasty greens exist that *Potamogeton* remains fairly safe from wild-food gatherers.

But the foliage of curly pondweed, especially, contains high nitrogen levels, making it good composting material. It apparently has some potential as a livestock feed supplement as well. More often heard, however, are its negative traits: This plant's often profuse growth has a distressing tendency to choke irrigation canals and become a weedy nuisance in fish hatcheries and recreational lakes. In such cases, of course, the plant's presence is a useful indicator of overfertilized waters and possible pollution.

The great importance of pondweeds as waterfowl and fish habitat food plants outranks, on the whole, their less desirable traits. Wildlife refuge managers, especially in wetlands along the fall migration flyways, are well aware of pondweed's value in maintaining the food needs of mobile waterfowl populations at this season. The planting and establishment of sago pondweed has become an important management procedure in many of these areas.

Reed *(Phragmites australis)*. Grass family. Tall, canelike herb in swamps, marshes, ditches, along wet shorelines. Easily recognized, reed is the tallest nonwoody plant to be seen in wetlands, often towering ten or twelve feet in extensive colonial groups. Its large, stiff, pennantlike leaves and plumelike seed heads are also distinctive.

Other names: Marsh reed, reed grass.

Close relatives: Wild-rice *(Zizania aquatica)*; and all other grasses.

Lifestyle: In popular usage, the name *reed* has become a generic term designating any number of large grasslike or rushlike wetland plants. *Phragmites,* however, is the only plant that is correctly called a reed—and this tall, conspicuous grass can hardly be mistaken for anything else. Some marshes almost wholly consist of it; in others, reed forms dense, colonial, bamboolike thickets in localized areas or patches.

This rich-fen species dwells in both marine and freshwater wetlands worldwide. It is probably the most cosmopolitan plant in this book. Indeed, it may be the most widely distributed seed plant in the world.

Such abundance is startling when one realizes that reed often produces no fertile seed. Most of its reproduction occurs by means of long, underground rhizomes and stolons that may extend scores of feet. Thus a reed patch may consist of only a single plant with many separate aerial shoots rising from a rootlike rhizome or its extensions. Clonal colonies may be extremely long-lived (at least one researcher believes that they may have survived a thousand years in certain locales). Since reeds are land-formers, however, they are usually temporary residents of the plant succession, building soil levels until the increasingly drier ground encourages its replacement by other species.

In contrast to cattails, which thrive best where some water flowage occurs, reed cannot establish itself where there is much wave or current movement. Usually it grows on shore, but plants standing in several feet of still water are not uncommon.

Reed's distinctive tall growth and flower plumes can be found in most marshy areas of the globe. This grass is highly valued for many uses in countries outside North America.

As with all grasses, reed flowers, which occur in large, purple plumes, are bisexual and wind pollinated. Stalks without flowers are quite common, however, and even some florets that do develop remain sterile. Fertile maturing florets develop long, silky beards, giving the flower plume a feathery aspect. Noted for its vigor, persistence, and rejuvenation following cutting or fire, reed (like purple loosestrife) typically invades wetland sites that have been filled, dredged, diked, or otherwise disturbed. Thus its presence is often an indicator of such disturbances and a general symptom of increasingly urban and industrial land uses. The large leaves contain high amounts (almost 80 percent) of silica.

Associates: *Spring, summer.* Reed is usually the dominant plant where it occurs. According to one plant ecologist, it occupies "the very hinge of aquatic and palustrine ecosystems" (that is, zones between open water and marsh). Its typical habitat lies (sometimes quite narrowly) on the muddy fine line between true aquatic vegetation and emergent or shoreline marsh plants. Ordinarily, however, there is considerable overlap. Individual stands of cattails and purple loosestrife may be codominants in the same area, but usually the extensive colonial growth of these species does not permit close mixings.

Deformed flower heads may indicate the presence of gall midge larvae *(Asteromyia phragmites)*.

Beyond its utility as cover, reed has relatively little to offer birds and mammals. For that reason, wetland wildlife biologists hate to see it invade, especially since it often crowds out and replaces plants more valuable to wildlife. Once established, it becomes almost impossible to eradicate. Marshes completely covered by reed or cattails offer little variety of food and cover.

A few birds, including black-crowned night herons and yellow-headed blackbirds, sometimes nest in dense reed stands. The only mammal that feeds on the plant to any extent is muskrat.

Lore: Despite some of reed's negative traits in our wetlands, viewing this plant with an exclusively North American focus gives a false impression of its value and utility elsewhere. In England, especially, where reed has been grown and harvested for centuries as roof thatching, botanical research has been lavished on every aspect of its ecology and life cycle. A well-thatched reed roof will last up to eighty years, considerably longer and much better insulated than most shingle roofs. The technique of reed thatching, one of the world's oldest building crafts, remains little changed from the Middle Ages. It requires skilled cutting, binding, placing, and trimming as well as considerable knowledge of the plant's growth stages.

Also in Europe, reed is frequently used for stabilizing the banks of rivers and canals. The Dutch, long familiar with the plant's ability to lift and transpire copious quantities of water, have used it to aid reclamation of polder land from the sea. Young shoots are often harvested for livestock fodder. In Russia, among other places, the plant is a basic raw material in the cellulose industry. Reed has never been exploited for commercial or agricultural uses in America, however — a source of puzzlement to our European friends, who find it such a versatile and inexpensive natural resource.

Parts of the plant are humanly edible. The small, reddish seeds (when they can be found) make a fine oatmeal substitute ("reed porridge"), and the dried, ground rhizomes and young shoots have been used as a flour. American natives apparently made no large use of the plant; probably it wasn't nearly as abundant on this continent in presettlement times as it is now.

For constructing temporary (though hardly fireproof) shelters and buoyant reed boats, bundles of stems make durable, lightweight materials.

Rose, Swamp *(Rosa palustris)*. Rose family. Thorny shrub in swamps, on margins of ponds, lakes, streams. Recognize swamp rose by its wet habitat, its short, down-curved thorns, its evenly toothed leaflets, and its fragrant, pale pink flowers.

Other names: Late rose, river rose.

Close relatives: Meadowsweet *(Spiraea alba)*; cinquefoils *(Potentilla)*; water avens *(Geum rivale)*; raspberries and blackberries *(Rubus)*; cherries *(Prunus)*; apples *(Pyrus)*; chokeberries *(Aronia)*; hawthorns *(Crataegus)*; shadbushes *(Amelanchier)*.

Lifestyle: This high, bushy shrub, our only common wetland rose, flowers quite abundantly during summer in swampy lowlands. It shares many floral characteristics with the upland wild roses (see *The Book of Forest and Thicket*). Because of its unique habitat, however, it probably has less tendency to hybridize with other rose species, though it does hybridize occasionally with wild or smooth rose *(R. blanda)*, a dune and rocky shoreline species. This is often the latest native rose to flower, not blossoming until July in its northern range.

Rose flowers are conspicuously bisexual and insect pollinated. The central cluster of pollen-bearing stamens radiates outward from the hub of pistils, making self-pollination less likely. The scarlet, fleshy fruits (called hips), often showing glandular hairs in this species, contain the achenes. Hips often remain on the plant all winter.

Associates: Buttonbush, speckled alder, shrub willows, common elderberry, and red-osier dogwood are frequent shrub associates of swamp rose.

Summer. Numerous insects feed on rose leaves, stems, and flowers. Most swamp rose feeders are not exclusive to this species, being often found on upland roses as well.

On leaves, moth feeders include the stinging rose caterpillar *(Parasa indetermina)*, a sluglike, striped caterpillar whose large spines can sting. A tortricid moth caterpillar *(Argyrotoxa bergmanniana)* folds single rose leaves and pupates inside the fold. *Nepticula rosaefoliella*, a tiny moth caterpillar, makes serpentine mines in the leaves.

Massed sawfly larvae resemble caterpillars; some specialize in defoliating roses. The bristly roseslug *(Cladius isomerus)*, greenish-white with bristles, skeletonizes leaves, as does the curled rose sawfly *(Allantus cinctus)* and the roseslug *(Endelomyia aethiops)*.

Stippled and slightly curled leaves may indicate feeding of rose leafhoppers *(Edwardsiana rosae)*, creamy yellow in color.

Among beetle foragers are Japanese beetles *(Popillia japonica)*, metallic green and copper-colored; and rose leaf beetles *(Nodonota puncticollis)*, small and shiny green or blue.

Oval or circular sections cut from the margins of rose leaves mark the work of leafcutter bees *(Megachile)*, which carry away the leaf sections and line their nests with them in twig cavities or inner stems of various plants.

Rose stems and foliage are subject to the sap-sucking of many aphid species. A frequent associate of the aphids is the common black garden ant *(Lasius niger)*, which guards groups of aphids and feeds on the honeydew they exude.

On rose flowers, holes eaten in the petals are probably the work of rose curculios, also called rose snout beetles *(Rhynchites bicolor)*, bright red weevils that feed in the unopened buds, sometimes killing them.

Rose chafers *(Macrodactylus subspinosus)*, tan beetles with spiny legs, feed first on the flowers, then on the foliage. These insects contain a heart poison known to have killed birds that ate them.

European earwigs *(Forficula auricularia)*, small, beetlelike insects with forcep tails, feed on rose stamens and petal bases.

Tiny yellowish insects crawling around the base of petals may be flower thrips *(Frankliniella tritici)*, also called wheat thrips. They migrate daily to flowers from grasses and weeds and often cause distorted buds and blossoms.

Bumblebees *(Bombus)* are the primary pollinators. Other bees also collect pollen. A brown and greenish scarab beetle *(Tri-chiotinus piger)* feeds on the pollen as well.

Stem-boring insects include small carpenter bees *(Ceratina)*, also called pith borers, whose larvae hatch and develop in tunnels mined in the stem. Larvae of rose stem girdlers *(Agrilus aurichalceus)*, greenish buprestid beetles, make spiral mines around the canes, which swell and sometimes split at these points. Rose stem sawflies *(Hartigia trimaculata)*, wasplike horntails, puncture the canes in which they lay their eggs; the developing larvae cause shoots to wilt.

Rose thickets are favored nesting sites for gray catbirds, northern mockingbirds, brown thrashers, yellow warblers, and northern cardinals.

Fall, winter. Rose stems host more than fifty gall-making insects, most of which are tiny wasps of the genus *Diplolepsis*. Some of these galls are globular, others mossy, bristly, or tapering. Though formed in spring and summer, they become most visible after the leaves fall.

Birds' nests, now vacated by their builders, are often adapted as nest foundations or feeding platforms by white-footed mice. Piles of chewed-apart rose hips or seed remnants in these nests indicate mice have fed here.

*Wild roses exhibit numerous kinds of stem galls, each caused by different species of tiny **Diplolepsis** wasp larvae. This rose branch contains two: the smaller one at top and the large growth at center.*

Birds and small mammals consume rose hips and seeds as winter foods after more preferred foods are snow-covered or depleted; though high in vitamin nourishment, the hips are low in fat content. Common winter feeders include ring-necked pheasants, ruffed and sharp-tailed grouse, American robins, and northern mockingbirds. Meadow voles and cottontail rabbits frequently gnaw the stems.

Lore: Three rose hips, it is said, contain as much vitamin C as a single orange, up to sixty times as much as a lemon. The hips are also richer by weight than oranges in calcium, phosphorus, and iron. The only problem is in the eating; most hips contain very little flesh in proportion to seed and have only a slight citrus taste. They can be used in quantity, however, for making an excellent beverage and, when mixed with apples, a jam. Hips of swamp rose, however, must be carefully filtered to remove the glandular hairs, which can cause bowel irritation. The fresh petals are also edible raw, candied, or jellied. American natives found many medicinal uses—mainly as mildly astringent teas and tonics—for rose roots, bark, leaves, and petals.

Roses have adorned the history, religion, and mythology of Western cultures since earliest recorded times (see *The Book of Forests and Thicket*). Their juxtaposition of fragrant beauty with sharp thorns gives roses a richly ironic symbology. Probably no other flower has been such a constant companion of humanity's struggle to understand the universe—and itself.

Rushes (*Juncus* spp.). Rush family. Grasslike or sedgelike herbs, mostly in open marshes and wet ground, along shorelines. Recognize rushes by their smooth, round, spirelike stems; leaves that are round or grasslike when present; and three-parted flowers and fruit capsules. Almost fifty rush species inhabit our region. The

most common ones include soft rush (*J. effusus*), leafless with one-sided flower clusters (see illustration for Bulrushes); Canada rush (*J. canadensis*), with round, erect leaves and often branching flower clusters radiating from the stem top; and *J. balticus*, with leafless stems in rows rising from straight, subsurface rhizomes.

Close relatives: Wood rushes (*Luzula*).

Lifestyle: Most *Juncus* species are practically impossible to identify without the

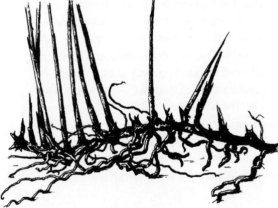

Juncus balticus often grows in straight lines, as shown at top. This growth form results from its long, straight, horizontal rhizome (bottom), which produces shoots along its length.

use of a pocket magnifier, which shows highly complex though distinctive characters of the flowers or seed clusters.

In form and general aspect, many rushes closely resemble bulrushes *(Scirpus)*, which belong to the sedge family. The flowers, small as they are, are the best and quickest way of separating the two: Bulrush flowers and seed heads are scaly and rather conelike, whereas rush flowers and seed capsules always divide into threes.

The often "splayed-out" flower clusters emerging from one side or the top of the stem (depending on species) are bisexual and wind pollinated. Underground rhizomes send up new stems each year, often resulting in large clonal colonies.

Rush leaves (when present) often display horizontal bands, somewhat like segments, more visible on the dried plants.

Most rushes are emergents, favoring shallow-water, mineral-rich habitats, though many species grow equally well in damp or wet soil marginal to the water. On land, soft rush may form large, sometimes geometrically patterned tussocks where frost-heaving occurs.

A comparison of rush (top) and bulrush (bottom) seed heads provides the best way of distinguishing these two unrelated but similar grasslike plants.

Associates: *Spring, summer.* Rushes usually occur in pure stands as a result of their colonial growth form. Soft rush and soft-stem bulrush, however, form frequent, near-neighbor colonies in the shallow margins. Other common plants in the rush community include bladderworts, stoneworts, duckweeds, pondweeds, smartweeds, pickerel-weed, and water-lilies.

On leafy rushes, midge larvae *(Procystiphora)* sometimes infest the sheath where leaf meets stem. Caterpillars of subflava sedge borers *(Archanara subflava)*, noctuid moths, bore into the stems, usually killing them.

Canada rush, especially, is often parasitized by a gall-forming insect. The "tassel galls" resemble, if not mimic, the bushy flower clusters at the stem tops. They are apparently caused by a sap-sucking, aphidlike psyllid, *Livia maculipennis*.

Nymphal dragonflies and other aquatic insects frequently climb and use rushes as launching stations for transforming into their winged adult forms.

Stands of rush in water are frequent spawning grounds for common bluegills, northern rock bass, and other sunfishes.

Though consumed by a few birds and mammals, rushes do not rank as important food plants. Common pintails, green-winged teal, king, sora, and Virginia rails, northern bobwhites, and sharp-tailed grouse have been observed eating seeds and other parts of the plant; a few songbirds may also eat the seeds. Probably rush's greatest wildlife value is as screening cover.

Muskrats and moose are the foremost (though infrequent) mammal consumers.

Lore: Few human uses are recorded for rushes. They supply no food and are generally too insubstantial to serve as building or craft materials.

In late summer and fall, as rush stems are dying from the top down, I often note the horizontal rainbow effect that is visible when stands are viewed from a distance. Though subdued in color, these bands of several varying hues run straight across the entire colony at the same levels, giving a pleasing autumnal aspect to lake borders. Thoreau noted "five distinct horizontal and parallel bars . . . like a level rainbow." The effect is much increased, he also observed, when seen reflected in the water. This is one of those natural phenomena that disappear when examined closely, for individual stems show no distinct banding.

Sedges *(Carex* spp.). Sedge family. Grasslike herbs mostly in wetlands; many species also grow in forests and dry upland areas. Recognize *Carex* sedges by their (usually) triangular stems, unisexual flower spikes, and a bulbous sac (perigynium) that encloses the female flower.

More than two hundred *Carex* species reside in east-central North America. A few of the most commonly seen ones include *C. flava,* with yellowish-green flower spikes, growing in mineral-rich fens; *C. lasiocarpa,* showing fuzzy perigynia, growing in bogs and poor fens; tussock sedge *(C. stricta)*, forming large, leafy clumps or tussocks in fens, marshes, and swamps; sawgrass *(C. lacustris)*, another fen species; and *C. oligosperma,* a mat-former growing in both fens and bogs.

Other names: Marsh hay, marsh grass *(C. stricta)*; hairy-fruited sedge *(C. lasiocarpa)*; few-seeded sedge *(C. oligosperma)*.

Close relatives: Nut-grasses *(Cyperus)*; spike-rushes *(Eleocharis)*; bulrushes *(Scirpus)*; cotton-grasses *(Eriophorum)*; beak-rushes *(Rhyncospora)*.

Lifestyle: "Grasses are round, sedges have edges" is a generally useful identification ditty referring to the stem shapes of these plants (though exceptions occur in both groups).

A better method, when the plants are in flower or seed, is to compare their altogether different flowering or fruiting spikes. Lacking one of these, most sedge plants are practically impossible to identify at species level. The shape of the perigynium is often the key element in precise identification. Without a pocket magnifier and the obsessive curiosity required by sedge and grass botany, however, one can still easily separate grasses from sedges by sight. Often, too, one can identify certain well-marked species of each by gross features or characteristic growth forms.

Most wetland sedges carry male and female flowers in separate places on the same plant, though some plants are totally unisexual. In such species as *C. flava* and tussock sedge, the male spikes are slim vertical clusters found at the top of the stem; the fatter, bushier female spikes emerge lower on the spike or stem. Others, such as *C. exilis* and *C. scoparia,* show numerous single spikes carrying bushy female flowers at the top, male flowers below. The flowers are wind pollinated.

"Sedges seem to reverse our notion that the roots of plants are merely aids supporting and watering the 'real' aboveground plant," wrote bog ecologist Charles W. Johnson. Sedge roots and rhizomes contain much more biomass (living material) than the visible stems and leaves.

Most wetland sedges are fen species, thriving best in sites nourished by stream or groundwater inflow. Some species, however, such as *C. oligosperma, C. trisperma,* and a few others, favor sphagnum bogs.

In the typical fen-to-bog successional sequence, sedges (usually *C. lasiocarpa*) are the pioneers. They

Sedges show various flowering forms. The species displayed here all show flowers of both sexes on the same spikes. Larger, bushier clusters (whether located at the top or bottom of the spike) are all female; the slimmer clusters are male flowers.

form thick, advancing, shoreline mats that gradually seal off water entry from beneath. Decomposition of the floating peat mat creates acidic conditions, thus bringing about the chemistry that favors the growth of sphagnum mosses and bog heaths. But sedge fens do not always develop into sphagnum bogs. Where peat decomposes rapidly and aerated groundwater with high calcium content continues to flow in, the successional outcome is often a swamp dominated by northern white cedar.

Invasive in ponds, tussock sedge forms thick, circular pedestals, or "stools," that stand two or more feet high. These bushy hillocks prove unstable as "stepping stones" for crossing a marshy area. Tussock sedge, which fruits infrequently, mainly relies on its creeping and ascending rhizomes for reproduction, producing numerous *tillers* (sprouts) from its subsurface parts (see Cottongrasses). The tussocks, complex meshes of roots, rhizomes, and dead leaves and stems, ultimately raise the marsh surface; they often form hummocky grass meadows as succession proceeds.

Sedge fens and heath-sphagnum bogs are the two classical extremes and expressions of wetland chemistry and ecology (see Mosses, Sphagnum). Transitional gradations between them, caused by disruptions and vagaries of water and nutrient flowage, result in overlapped plant mosaics of differing complexity. Sedge fens often show patchy areas of acidic concentration where sphagnum mosses have gained a foothold; and even in highly acidic bogs one may find occasional plants that indicate a slight groundwater influence.

Associates: *Spring, summer, fall.* Sedges are the characteristic dominant herbs of mineral-rich wetlands, almost ubiquitous associates of all other fen vegetation. But just as a few sphagnum mosses (notably *Sphagnum teres* and *S. subsecundum*) reside in sedge fens, so also several sedge species (such as *C. oligosperma, C.*

trisperma, C. disperma, and *C. canescens*) tolerate the acid environments of bogs. A plant frequently growing atop the pedestals of tussock sedge in summer and fall is beggarticks *(Bidens frondosa).* Blue

Tussock sedge, one of the most common marsh species, builds bushy, unstable hummocks that gradually fill in the marsh, forming dry land.

Sedge growth (left and center) in this boggy, poor-fen wetland indicates quite obviously the sources of nutrient inflow along pools and channels.

vervain often appears at a later stage atop old tussocks.

Many insects feed on sedges. Froghopper nymphs or spittlebugs *(Lempyronia angulifera* and *Philaenus parallelus,* among others), which suck plant juices, create frothy masses on the stems. A stem-boring beetle larva, the billbug *(Sphenophorus),* also feeds on the leaves as an adult. Underwater weevils feed on both submersed and aerial parts of the plants (see Arrowhead, Broadleaved). Smut beetles *(Phalacrus politus),* shiny black, oval-shaped insects, appear on sedge leaves in early spring.

A pale green, striped caterpillar with red-tipped horns is probably the eyed brown *(Lethe eurydice),* one of the satyr butterflies.

Numerous moth caterpillars feed on sedges. Mostly noctuid species, they include Henry's marsh moth *(Simyra henrici);* the ignorant apamea *(Apamea indocilis);* sedge borers *(Archanara);* American ear moth *(Amphipoea americana);* and looper moths *(Plusia).* The Virginia ctenucha *(Ctenucha virginica)* is a wasp moth; its caterpillars are hairy, and the adult insects are black-winged and wasplike. *Munroessa icciusalis,* a case-making pyralid moth, is an aquatic larva that feeds on submersed stems.

Around sedge pools, watch for North America's smallest dragonfly, the blue bell *(Nannothemis bella),* which favors this habitat. The adult insects are black with yellow striping; their bodies turn bluish-white with age (a common occurrence in dragonflies, called *pruinosity).* Their mosquito prey also reside abundantly here. One study found seventeen larval mosquito species (mostly *Aedes, Culex,* and *Anopheles;* not all of them are blood feeders as adult insects) regularly inhabiting sedge pools.

Open sedge mats are favored habitats of northern leopard frogs. Spring peepers, chorus frogs, and green frogs are also common. In fen pools, salamanders (including red-spotted newts) swim and crawl on the vegetation.

Spotted and bog turtles, both small and the latter an endangered species, favor fen habitats. Other reptiles found here include red-bellied snakes, small and

Sedge fens usually host many vertebrate as well as invertebrate species. At top, a snapping turtle lays its eggs in a depression it has scooped in the mud. Green frogs (bottom) are common fen voices, their calls twanging like loose banjo strings.

nonbiting; northern water snakes, large and sometimes aggressive; and (regionally) our only poisonous wetland reptile, the eastern massasauga rattlesnake, a shy, retiring species that more often flees than bites.

Sedge fens and meadows often support abundant bird life. Herons stalk aquatic organisms here, and northern harriers (marsh hawks) cruise and hover low over the open wetland as they hunt prey. Nesting waterfowl in the sedge cover may include blue-winged teal and ring-necked ducks. Other nesters may include northern harriers, sedge wrens (which use sedges for nesting material), common yellowthroats, and LeConte's, Lincoln's, and swamp sparrows.

Sedges rank relatively low as waterfowl food plants. Surface-feeding ducks consume the seeds in small amounts; probably American black ducks, mallards, blue-winged and green-winged teals, and wood ducks are the foremost feeders. Other water birds that eat the seeds in some quantity include sora and yellow rails and American coots.

Sedge seeds and insects are major food items for ruffed grouse chicks; sharp-tailed and spruce grouse also relish the seeds, as do ring-necked pheasants, wild turkeys, and American woodcock. Prominent songbird seedeaters include horned larks and finches: northern cardinals, redpolls, rufous-sided towhees, song, Lincoln's, swamp, and American tree sparrows, and longspurs.

Sedges are relatively insignificant in the diets of mammals such as muskrats, beavers, and white-tailed deer. Moose are probably the most regular sedge feeders. Bog lemmings, despite their name, are actually more prevalent in "sedge edges" of bogs among beak-rush and other fen vegetation. They feed on sedges and grasses, often leaving inch-long, clipped fragments of the plants and bright green droppings along their runways.

Sedge meadows often result from beaver dam-building activity. When beavers vacate a wetland area (usually because their aspen food supply runs out), their dams deteriorate and the flooding created by the dams subsides. Sedges invade the silt-rich land from which most woody plants have been drowned or cut by beavers, forming meadows that are usually invaded in turn by shrub-carr. Fire is also a frequent creator of sedge meadows.

Lore: Up until the last fifty years, sedge meadows provided ample gratuitous sources of livestock feed and bedding, especially for pioneer farmers. Tussock sedge, especially, was laboriously hand-harvested as "marsh hay"—not as nourishing as pasture grasses but a useful supplement to them. Marsh hay also provided efficient insulation for storing ice in the summer and to "keep Milwaukee beer cold until it reached Chicago," as one observer wrote. Though no longer used for such purposes, this sedge is still sold—in bags as garden mulch.

Beaver lodges, often built in areas flooded by their dams, are often vacated when this animal's food supply becomes depleted. As water levels diminish, sedges may grow on the former flooded land, producing "beaver meadows."

Skunk-cabbage *(Symplocarpus foetidus)*. Arum family. Low, colonial herb in mud of swamps, woods, stream borders. Its streaked, mottled purple, shell-like *spathe* that envelops the round, fleshy flower cluster *(spadix)*; its large, broad leaves; and its rank, unpleasant odor identify this common wetland plant.

Other names: Swamp cabbage, meadow cabbage, foetid hellebore, skunk-weed.

Close relatives: Jack-in-the-pulpit *(Arisaema triphyllum)*; arrow-arum *(Peltandra virginica)*; wild calla *(Calla palustris)*.

Lifestyle: Skunk-cabbage is probably the earliest flowering plant to emerge from the ground. Its rolled-up, spirelike spathe often pokes up through February snow. The plant is actually well advanced by then; emerging cone-shaped buds of next year's growth often begin to show in early fall. It is usually in flower by March or April, its bulging spathe enclosing the big, knoblike spadix like a monk's cowl. The spathe gaps open on one side, allowing entry to insects. Lavender, flesh-colored flowers on the surface of the spadix are bisexual and pollinated by some of the earliest flying insects of the year.

In late winter, as the flower buds enlarge, they increase in temperature, often melting snow around them. When the surrounding ground and air warm to above freezing, respiration of the spadix produces a quite constant warmth of about 72°F, which the surrounding, air-pocketed spathe helps maintain. The tiny flowers on the spadix have no petals. They are *protogynous* (that is, their female parts mature first); they begin to bloom at the spadix top and progress downward. By the time the lowermost flowers emerge, the upper ones have produced their male parts and are beginning to pollinate. Male flowering likewise descends on the spadix.

After pollination, the spadix bends toward the ground on its stalk, the spathe disintegrates, and the bright green leaves push up in vertical, rolled-up spires. Soon after opening, the cabbagelike leaves increase in size on their thick stalks, often becoming two feet long or longer by early summer. The smaller leaves are easily confused with marsh marigold leaves, but the latter leaves are slightly toothed, whereas skunk-cabbage leaves have smooth margins.

The spadix, turning black with age, now becomes a compound fruit; the heavy, marble-size seeds are released as the old spadix decomposes. Seeds usually germinate within a few feet of the parent plant. Five to seven years of growth are required before the rhizome becomes large enough to permit flowering. The thick, vertical rhizomes center a radiating mass of long, descending roots that resemble earthworms. These roots contract slightly each year, pulling the rhizome and the entire plant downward several millimeters, thus keeping the surface parts close to the ground. The rhizomes, which sometimes grow two feet long, may be quite long-lived, perhaps surviving indefinitely in stable habitats. Some skunk-cabbage rhizomes have apparently persisted for centuries.

Notice the spathe, its opening "lapped like tent doors," observed Thoreau; it's a marvel of aerodynamic geometry. Composed of tissue that one botanist likened to "fine styrofoam," it not only shelters and insulates the spadix, but also deflects incoming air currents into a cyclonic vortex around it. Such circulation keeps the temperature stable and possibly provides a means of "wind" pollination. Thoreau believed that most of the spathes open southward, thus orienting toward the spring sunlight, but subsequent research indicates that compass direction of the gap is random. The particular direction it faces seems to make little difference to the spathe's capacity to deflect airflow into the chamber. In such a way, wrote another observer, the spathes "create their own near-tropical microclimate in a north temperate spring."

Associates: Look for skunk-cabbage at just about any time of year—flowers in early spring, leaves and fruits in summer and fall, emerging shoots in fall and winter—in the muddiest areas of marshes, fens, and shorelines. Common plant associates include marsh fern, sedges, marsh marigold, and jewelweeds.

Spring. This plant (along with shrub willows) is probably the first pollen source in spring for honeybees *(Apis mellifera).* Honeybees do not fly well below 65°F, but they are sometimes seen inside skunk-cabbage plants when air temperature drops as low as 42°F. The warmth in successive spathes, it is theorized, serve as "heat stops" for the bee, allowing it to restore energy for flights between spathes and to and from the hive. Sometimes bees become trapped in narrow-gapped spathes.

The fruiting head of skunk-cabbage, formerly the spadix sheltered by the hoodlike spathe, turns black with age. A cross section (bottom) shows the pulpy, decomposing mass that releases seeds.

Other pollinators are chiefly flesh flies (Sarcophagidae) and carrion or blow flies (Calliphoridae), metallic bluish, green, and black insects resembling house flies. These early-season scavengers are attracted by the plant's liver-colored streaks and fetid odor; some botanists cite this as an example of dung mimicry, which may have evolved as an attractant for these pollinators. Stalk-eyed flies *(Sphyracephala brevicornis),* though quite rare, breed in decaying vegetation and are also attracted to this plant.

Another pollen feeder is the waterlily leaf beetle *(Donacia;* see Water-lilies). Smut beetles *(Phalacrus politus),* oval and shiny black, are often found on the new leaves, as are plant bugs *(Liocoris rufidorsus).*

Pollinator predators may include a thick-jawed spider *(Pachygnatha brevis),* a tetragnathid species that builds no web. It often sits on the spadix surface, probably awaiting mates in the warm chamber. Some eleven species of spiders, some of which construct webs across the gap in the spathe, have been found in skunk-cabbage. A common one often found at the spadix base, where it mimics a pollinating male flower, is *Enoplagnatha marmorata*, a theridiid spider. *Clubiona mixta* makes its web in a rolled leaf.

Oval holes eaten in the leaves are made by slugs *(Deroceras reticulatum)*, which also feed in the spathes. The amber snail *Oxyloma decampi* also grazes on the foliage.

Ring-necked pheasants consume the emerging, rolled-up leaves. Black bears may do the same and also dig and eat the rhizomes. Early Swedish settlers around Philadelphia named the plant "bear-weed," having noticed that bears apparently relished the new leaves (but black bears just out of winter hibernation relish almost anything).

Common yellowthroats sometimes nest in the central hollows of the large leaves.

Summer, fall. Rotting spathes in late spring or early summer attract tiny flies, mainly moth flies (Psychodidae), frit flies (Chloropidae), and pomace or fruit flies (Drosophilidae).

Hairy caterpillars of the ruby tiger moth *(Phragmatobia fuliginosa)* feed on skunk-cabbage leaves, among other plants. Larvae of the cattail borer *(Bellura obliqua)*, a noctuid moth, mine the leaves and later bore into the stalks. Look for drowned insects in the wells of rainwater sometimes held at the base of leaf-stalks.

Flattened, insectlike crustaceans called sowbugs or isopods *(Tracheoniscus rathkei)* frequent the decaying spathes, as do millipedes such as *Ophyiulus fallax* and *Cylindroiulus teutonicus.* Wood ducks, ruffed grouse, ring-necked pheasants, and northern bobwhites feed on the seeds. Skunk-cabbage is, however, a relatively unimportant wildlife food plant.

Lore: Skunk-cabbage is doubly misnamed; it is unrelated to cabbage and other mustards, and its odor only slightly resembles mammal musk. Various descriptions usually include the words *putrid* or *foul.* It "combines the skunk, putrid meat, and garlic," "mustard plaster and raw onions," "fresh cabbage with a slight suggestion of mustard." Thoreau noted its resemblance to the odor of certain currants (such as skunk currant, *Ribes glandulosum*). Whatever odor one associates with the plant, its volatile, odoriferous chemicals (including skatole and cadaverine) mimic putrescence successfully enough to attract insects that specialize in scavenging dead and fecal matter.

Like most arums, skunk-cabbage is full of calcium oxalate crystals that produce an intensely acrid, burning sensation if eaten raw. Grazing mammals usually let it alone. Only thorough drying, not boiling, removes this toxic property. After treatment, the leaves can be added to soups or stews and the rhizomes ground into a cocoalike flour.

American natives found many internal and external medicinal uses for the plant. Menomini tribes also used the rhizome in combination with other herbs as an ingredient for tattooing the skin as a talisman against disease.

Physicians once valued the dried rhizomes (under the drug name Dracontium) as an antispasmodic for treatment of epilepsy and asthma. They also used the leaves as poultices for skin irritations.

Thoreau claimed that the skunk-cabbage leaf "makes the best vessel to drink out of at a spring. . . . It does not flavor the water and is not perceived in drinking."

This same species occurs in Japan and other locales in eastern Asia, its probable origin. Paleobotanists believe that the plant migrated to North America via the Pleistocene land bridge that existed at several times between Siberia and Alaska. This makes skunk-cabbage—like humans—a relative newcomer to our continent.

Smartweeds (*Polygonum* spp.). Smartweed family. Emergent and shoreline herbs in marshes, shallow water, lake and pond margins. Recognize smartweeds by their swollen stem joints encased by sheaths and pink or white flower spikes at the top.

Some fifty species of *Polygonum* exist in our area, but only about ten of these favor wet habitats. The most common include water smartweed (*P. amphibium*), with short, stubby flower clusters and floating leaves, or erect stems on muddy shorelines; swamp smartweed (*P. coccineum*), equally variable in growth habit but with long flower spikes; mild water-pepper (*P. hydropiperoides*), with sparsely flowered spikes and fringed sheaths at joints; arrow-leaved tearthumb (*P. sagittatum*), with four-sided, prickly stems, narrow, arrow-shaped leaves, and small flower clusters; and common smartweed or water-pepper (*P. hydropiper*), with greenish, nodding spikes.

Other names: Jointweeds; water persicaria, amphibious bistort, willowweed, ground-willow, heartsease, red-shanks (*P. amphibium*); pepper-plant, biting persicaria, snake-weed, sickle-weed (*P. hydropiper*). The dryland species of this large genus are called knotweeds, showing flowers in the leaf angles. **Close relatives:** Rhubarb *(Rheum rhaponticum)*; docks *(Rumex)*; buckwheat *(Fagopyrum esculentum)*.

Lifestyle: Pink, emergent flower spikes of smartweeds, standing several inches above the water surface in large, colorful colonies, are familiar sights along shorelines in summer. Water and swamp smartweeds adapt well to changing water levels, appearing in aquatic forms with floating leaves or as erect, land-based plants in muddy habitats—true botanical amphibians.

Smartweeds display so many variants that botanists puzzle whether certain of them are true species or mere forms and varieties of other species. Almost every plant manual treats them differently—in itself a significant indicator of plants undergoing rapid evolutionary changes. Botanists are likewise uncertain as to what extent many smartweeds are natives or aliens introduced from Europe and Asia.

Smartweed flowers, usually pink but with white variants, are bisexual and insect pollinated. Lacking petals, the tiny flowers on the spike show colored sepals. Both annual and perennial species exist. Annuals, including arrow-leaved tearthumb, common smartweed, and nodding smartweed *(P. lapathifolium)*, must rely exclusively on seed production to reproduce (the seeds of common smartweed, at least, may remain viable for fifty years). Perennials such as water smartweed, swamp smartweed, and mild water-pepper reproduce chiefly by means of extensive rhizome systems.

In water smartweed, each new shoot from the rhizome is able to sprout new shoots if broken off. Water and swamp smartweeds display two kinds of flowers, each on separate plants: long styles with short stamens; or short styles and long stamens (these are usually sterile, producing no seeds). Common smartweed also produces two types of flowers, as in jewelweeds and violets: the regular insect-pollinated ones on the spike; and lower, *cleistogamous* flowers, which never open and are self-fertilized. Smartweed seeds are *achenes*.

Look for habitat preferences. Water smartweed is probably the most aquatic species, thriving in shallow water and rarely flowering on land. Mild water-pepper also grows in water but can tolerate situations where water levels are sporadic or seasonal (hydroperiods). Other species, like common smartweed, favor shoreline habitats.

Associates: *Summer, fall.* Smartweeds, especially water smartweeds, often occur as dominant colonial plants in almost pure stands. Two or more smartweed species—mixed annuals and perennials—may grow in close proximity, providing

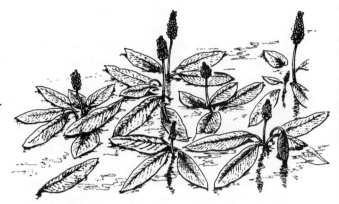

Water smartweed's floating leaves and erect, pink flower spikes add color to shallow waters in summer. These complex plants often occur in large, cloning colonies, which attract many insects but give them little in return for pollination.

opportunity to analyze and possibly identify slight differences in habitat preference. Other common plant associates include pondweeds, water-lilies, watershield, and emergent sedges, bulrushes, pickerel-weed, and other plants of the pond shallows and edges. On ephemeral mud flats, nodding smartweed and pinkweed or bigseed smartweed *(P. pensylvanicum)* often compete with beggarticks *(Bidens frondosa)*.

Insects gain little from smartweed flowers; both pollen and nectar quantities are sparse. Yet, in one seasonal study of mild water-pepper, sixty-nine insect species were recorded as visitors. Pollination is chiefly effected by small bees, such as andrenids, and flies.

Foliage feeders include several caterpillars. Yellowish-green, sluglike caterpillars are probably bronze copper butterflies *(Lycaena thoë)*. Others may include the smartweed caterpillar, larva of the smeared dagger moth *(Acronicta oblinita)*, a hairy, brownish noctuid; the black-dotted and pink-barred lithacodias *(Lithacodia synochitis, L. carneola)*, also noctuids; the chickweed geometer *(Haematopis grataria)*, an inchworm moth; and the bent-line carpet moth *(Orthonama centrostrigaria)*, another inchworm.

Waterlily leaf beetles *(Pyrrhalta nympheae)* feed on floating-leaved smartweeds (see Water-lilies).

Stem borers include underwater weevils (see Arrowhead, Broad-leaved) and caterpillars of the bidens borer *(Epiblema otiosana)*, a tortricid moth. At least one species of aquatic bug, a backswimmer *(Buenoa margaritacea)*, punctures smartweed stems with its egg-laying.

Mammal feeders on the plants include muskrats and white-tailed deer.

Fall, winter. "Any aquatic area bordered by extensive growth of smartweed is likely to be popular with ducks," reported one research team. Indeed, smartweeds are the wetland counterparts of ragweeds *(Ambrosia)* in their value and importance to many seed-eating birds, especially fall migrants and winter resident species. Only bulrushes rival them as a seed source for wildlife.

Tundra swans, Canada geese, American black ducks, mallards, common pintails, wood ducks, blue-winged and green-winged teals, redheads, ring-necked ducks, and scaups are major seed consumers. Sora and yellow rails, American coots, and common snipe also relish the seeds, as do northern bobwhites, ruffed grouse, and wild turkeys.

Prominent songbird feeders include horned larks, bobolinks, eastern meadowlarks, red-winged blackbirds, brown-headed cowbirds, northern cardinals, rose-breasted grosbeaks, common redpolls, rufous-sided towhees, dark-eyed juncos, and many sparrows: savannah, grasshopper, Henslow's, vesper, American tree, chipping, white-crowned, white-throated, fox, and swamp. Smartweed beds are always worth checking for the presence of winter finch feeding flocks. The most important smartweeds for waterfowl and other birds are water smartweed, mild water-pepper, common smartweed, nodding smartweed, pinkweed, dotted smartweed *(P. punctatum)*, and lady's-thumb *(P. persicaria)*.

Lore: Smartweed leaves have a peppery taste ranging from mild and pleasing to acrid and inedible, depending on the species. For cooked greens or eating raw in salads, mild water-pepper is one of the best—and common smartweed one of the worst. Juice from stems and leaves can cause skin irritation in allergic individuals.

These plants provided medicinal teas and tonics for generations of both Old and New World users, chiefly as astringents for external poultices and for internal bleeding, menstrual, and urinary disorders. Rutin, a glycoside ingredient found also in tobacco and buckwheat leaves, strengthens blood capillaries, acting as a coagulant to prevent or stop bleeding. *P. persicaria* was also used for producing a durable yellow dye for woolens and other cloth.

Spruce, Black *(Picea mariana).* Pine family. Needle-leaved tree in bogs, stagnant swamps, muskegs. Spruces are steeple-shaped conifers with squarish, sharp needles and cross-shaped branch ends. Recognize black spruce by its short needles, small, rounded seed cones, rusty-haired down on the twigs, and its habitat.

Other names: Bog spruce, swamp spruce, shortleaf black spruce.

Close relatives: All other spruces *(Picea)*; balsam fir *(Abies balsamea)*; hemlocks *(Tsuga)*; tamarack *(Larix laricina)*; pines *(Pinus)*.

Lifestyle: Black spruce is the characteristic, often dominant tree of the cold northern bogs and muskegs. Because of its layering growth habit (that is, sunken and buried branches taking root and giving rise to cloning stems around the parent trunk), black spruce frequently appears as "bog islands" or "candelabrum spruce," dense colonial thickets rising around the tall parent tree. Where the parent tree is dead or broken off, its surrounding circle of clones marks its former presence. The taller trees often appear scraggly with many short, dead branches and club-shaped, top-heavy crowns. Flat, shallow root systems make black spruce well adapted for growing in permafrost soils but also make it vulnerable to wind-throw.

But the tall, standing tree you see in a bog may well be only the top third or so of the entire trunk. As the tree grows, it slowly sinks into the soft, unstable peat from its increasing weight. Sets of progressively younger adventitious roots that emerge from the buried trunk stabilize it. Finally the sinking tree drowns, leaving its cloned surviving offspring to repeat the process.

In one study, a thirty-one-foot-tall black spruce held 7.8 million needles. Unlike pines, many of which cast their needles every two to three years, black spruce needles may remain on the branches for ten years or longer.

Pollen and seed cones develop high in the crowns of the same tree in spring, the pollen cones on outer branches just below the seed cone level. The cones are wind pollinated. Seed cones, ripening in the fall, persist on the tree for a year or longer and release their seeds intermittently. Seeds are dispersed by wind, birds, and mammals. Occasionally seeds remain sealed and viable in the cones for much longer periods—even one or two decades. Peak seed crops occur about every four years.

Black spruce is, to some extent, fire-dependent, even though the tree itself is easily killed by fire. Fire quickly opens the sealed cones, and the seeds germinate best on moist, fire-cleared soil. Postfire stands often contain uniform, even-aged trees. Seedlings also become established on moist but unsaturated hummocks of sphagnum moss.

The role of black spruce in bog plant succession remains controversial. Because of its unbalanced energy budget (that is, its rate of growth exceeds its rate of decomposition), its particular requirements for germination and freedom from competition, and its consequent limited capacity for self-perpetuation, black spruce may not qualify as a bog climax species. This is true even though it apparently terminates the plant succession in many of these habitats (one researcher calls this "climax by default").

Black spruce is moderately shade tolerant, less so than balsam fir and northern white cedar.

Associates: Sphagnum mosses and bog heaths are black spruce's chief plant associates. Such heaths as leatherleaf and blueberries may compete with—and even restrict growth of—the seedlings through crowding. On old, grounded bogs, black spruce frequently replaces tamarack as the dominant tree species, but the two occur together in many bogs. Black spruce also occurs in northern white cedar swamps, though cedar seldom grows in spruce bogs. Black spruce also thrives in the dry, acid-soil forests of the far north, occurring in almost pure stands and in mixtures with white spruce, balsam fir, and jack pine.

Spring, summer. Look beneath clumps of black spruce in a bog for certain kinds of mosses and liverworts that favor these wet, shady habitats. Feather mosses, with delicate fernlike leaves, may include mountain fern moss *(Hylocomium splendens)*, ostrich plume moss *(Ptilium crista-castrensis)*, and *Pleurozium schreberi.* In some black spruce stands, one or more of these mosses may form the dominant ground cover. Dark, wet holes may harbor such leafy liverworts as *Mylia anomela, Kurtzia setacea, Calypogeia sphagnicola,* and *Cladopodiella fluitans.*

The sedge *Carex trisperma* also favors the shade of spruce clumps, as do such wildflowers as clintonia, goldthread, pink lady-slipper or moccasin-flower, creeping snowberry, Canada mayflower, Indian-pipe, dwarf raspberry, and three-leaved false Solomon's seal.

In late summer look beneath black spruce for reddish or orange-buff mushrooms with depressed centers and toothed undersides. These are depressed hedgehog mushrooms *(Hydnum umbilicatum)*, tooth fungi. Also common are red-hot milkcaps *(Lactarius rufus)*, gill fungi with reddish-brown caps and white latex.

The parasitic eastern dwarf mistletoe *(Arceuthobium pusillum)*, displaying tiny, brownish shoots on spruce branches, flowers very early in spring, about the same time as red maple. The unisexual flowers are insect pollinated and small, though they make the inconspicuous plant itself most noticeable at this time. They produce small, dry berries, which are eaten and dispersed by several birds and mammals. Gray jays and red squirrels are probably the chief seed vectors.

A common disease on spruce and other conifers is diplodia tip blight caused by *Diplodia pinea,* one of the fungi imperfecti. Look for brown, drooping twig tips. Diplodia seldom kills trees but often stunts and deforms branch growth.

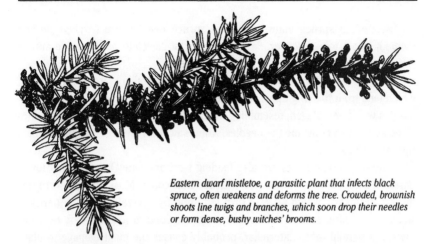

Eastern dwarf mistletoe, a parasitic plant that infects black spruce, often weakens and deforms the tree. Crowded, brownish shoots line twigs and branches, which soon drop their needles or form dense, bushy witches' brooms.

Several aphidlike adelgid species create conelike galls at twig ends of black and other spruces in early summer. These include *Chermes floccus, C. consolidatus, C. abietis* (the eastern spruce gall aphid, causing pineapple-shaped galls at twig bases), *C. similis,* and *Pineus pinifoliae.*

Spruce spider mites *(Oligonychus ununguis)*, speck-size, greenish sap-suckers, are pests of almost all conifers, feeding on the twigs in great abundance and creating fine webbing between needles.

Foliage feeders include several caterpillars. Bog elfin butterflies *(Incisalia lanoraieensis)* mine in the needles of young twig tips before growing large enough to feed on the exterior of needles in summer. The small, brownish adult butterflies fly in spring and early summer.

Look for hairy caterpillars of the bicolored moth *(Eilema bicolor)*, a lichen feeder often found among the lichens growing on black spruce.

Probably black spruce's worst insect defoliator is the spruce budworm *(Choristoneura fumiferana)*, a tortricid moth caterpillar that occurs in cyclic irruptions. It is a major pest of balsam fir and spruces. Usually when the reddish-brown, yellow-striped caterpillars appear on black spruce (often webbing the needles), they have first built up their populations on adjacent old-growth balsam fir stands. Although their infestations do not often kill the spruce, they weaken trees sufficiently to make them vulnerable to more efficient tree killers.

These are eastern spruce beetles *(Dendroctonus piceaperda*—the genus name means "tree killer"), crenulate bark beetles that bore into trunks and girdle them. Such beetle-killed spruce often indicate a previous outbreak of spruce budworm defoliation.

Related to spruce budworm is the spruce needleworm *(Archips packardianus)*, also a foliage feeder. Several species of gelechiid moth needle miners *(Coleotechnites)* devour needles from the inside.

Gregarious foliage feeders that resemble caterpillars are sawfly larvae, which feed from the twig tips down. The European spruce sawfly *(Diprion hercyniae)* is well camouflaged, resembling the needles in color; other spruce sawflies *(Pikonema)* also consume the needles. Adult sawflies resemble wasps, to which they are related.

The developing cones are also feeding territory. One Ontario study found nineteen insect species associated with the new cones. Most of these were tiny moth caterpillars, which were in turn fed upon by several species of parasitic wasp larvae. After spruce budworm, the spruce coneworm *(Dioryctria reniculelloides)*, a pyralid moth caterpillar, probably causes the most damage to black spruce.

Certain fly larvae are also destructive to cones. When flower scales on the female cone open for pollination in early spring, adult spruce cone axis midges *(Dasineura rachiphaga)* emerge from the previous year's cones and lay eggs on the scales. These gall gnat larvae feed inside the cone axis or central stalk. The spruce cone maggot *(Lasiomma anthracinum)*, an anthomyiid fly, destroys many cones by its feeding.

Probably the spruce grouse is the foremost bird associate of black spruce, often nesting on the ground in spruce areas adjacent to bogs. Tree nesters may include black-backed woodpeckers, olive-sided flycatchers, boreal chickadees, kinglets, Cape May warblers, and purple finches.

Fall, winter. The aforementioned spruce cone axis midges create feeding chambers inside the cone axis, where they stay all winter; a cone split lengthwise reveals them. Although they weaken the cone structure, they do not feed on the seeds. But another gall gnat, the spruce seed midge *(Mayetiola carpophaga)*, devours seeds inside the unopened cone.

Because a high proportion of black spruce cones remain sealed on the tree, seedeaters such as boreal chickadees, red-breasted nuthatches, pine grosbeaks, pine siskins, and white-winged crossbills are fairly restricted to feeding from partially opened cones. But the heavier-billed red crossbill, whose bill is adapted for extricating seeds from closed cones, needs not await their natural opening.

Red squirrels often gather the cones in large quantities. Because black spruce has apparently evolved tough, thick cone scales in partial defense against voracious squirrel foraging, however, red squirrels usually favor the cones of white spruce *(P. glauca)* if given a choice.

The winter diet of spruce grouse consists almost entirely of conifer needles, a high proportion of which are often black spruce; look for rows of clipped-off needles on twigs. Snowshoe hares gnaw the bark and also browse on the needles, sometimes causing extensive damage to seedlings and young trees. White-tailed deer and moose also browse spruce; but for them this forage is starvation food, generally indicating the lack of more nourishing browse in the vicinity.

All year. On dead branches, beard lichens *(Usnea)* are often common. Common too are visible signs of the aforementioned eastern dwarf mistletoe, which deforms branches and causes bunchy foliage growths called witches' brooms. Mistletoe parasitism reduces the tree's vigor, sometimes killing branches and entire trees. A mistletoe-infested tree can usually be recognized from a distance by its visible distortions in form and branching.

Lore: Because of black spruce's generally small size, its major commercial use is as pulpwood (it is Canada's most important pulpwood tree), harvested mainly from upland spruce forests of the far north. Millions of cubic feet annually go into the manufacture of high-grade papers (you may well be reading this print on black spruce fibers). Its lumber usage is minimal. Although many small black spruces are cut for Christmas trees, they prove generally undesirable for this purpose because they rapidly cast their needles after cutting.

Either black spruce or northern white cedar (nobody knows which for sure) provided an antiscurvy tea remedy for Jacques Cartier's sick and beleaguered French-Canadian explorers in 1535. The lesson was not immediately learned, how-

*Various sizes of beard lichen (**Usnea**) commonly adorn dead spruce branches. Lichens, symbiotic associations of an alga and a fungus, help decompose wood and other materials into their basic constituents.*

ever; two hundred years later, French colonists and even some Indian villages still suffered outbreaks of the vitamin C deficiency. The simple cure—drinking spruce tea—was rediscovered with astonishment time and again.

American natives found many other medicinal uses for black spruce. They used the inner bark and resin in poultices for sores and inflammations, and also drank a tea from the inner bark for numerous aches and pains. This inner bark provides a nourishing if not very tasty emergency food (as do pines and balsam fir) if one gets lost or marooned in the woods.

Amber pitch oozes from wounds on the tree. Dried and hardened, it is sold commercially as spruce gum, a fragrant if tough chew.

Stoneworts (*Chara, Nitella* spp.). Stonewort family. Submersed herbs in muddy shallows, calcium-rich ponds, lakes. Although they resemble seed plants in form and size, stoneworts (so-named because of their gritty, limy surfaces) are actually algae. Recognize them by their whorled branches at regular nodes, their gray-green color, and (especially *Chara*) their lime-encrusted stems and sulfurlike odor. *C. vulgaris* and *C. fragilis* are common stoneworts. *Nitella* is less abundant in most areas.

Other names: Muskgrass, candelabra plant, brittlewort.

Close relatives: *Tolypella; Nitellopsis.*

Lifestyle: *Chara* and *Nitella* look much alike, but the latter usually lacks the brittle, limy coating of *Chara* and is a smoother, more delicate plant. *Nitella* also favors deeper water (up to one hundred feet).

Chara grows in dense, wiry beds and is often the first underwater plant to appear and "take root" (attaching to the bottom by rhizoids) in new, nutrient-poor ponds or dredged shallows. Early in spring, as their new growth appears, they may look quite green; as the season progresses, they darken as they become encrusted with algae and limy coatings. Even so, their musky odor quickly identifies them.

This plant is one of the foremost marl formers. It precipitates large quantities of calcium carbonate as a photosynthetic by-product of its extraction of carbon dioxide from waters rich in calcium bicarbonate. Thick marl deposits often underlie *Chara* beds where the plants have been long present.

The plants' sexual reproduction resembles that of many other algae (see Algae, Green). Their simple round and oval reproductive organs (male *antheridia*, female *oogonia*), intricately patterned and visible with a hand lens, occur at the base of the cylindrical whorls along the branches. After fertilization, the egg falls from the plant and germinates. The plants also reproduce vegetatively by budding from rhizoids and stem nodes.

Another stonewort similarity to algae is the basically unicellular structure. The *Chara* internode (that is, the space on stem and branches between separate whorls) is a single core cell surrounded by a layer of fine cells. In *Nitella* this outer layer is absent, giving the plant a transparent appearance.

Stoneworts usually remain alive over winter, dying back mainly from the bottom as lower portions of the plant gradually become buried by dense growth. Growth of new rhizoids and branches begins higher and higher each year, supported by thick, oozy carpets of their own organic remains.

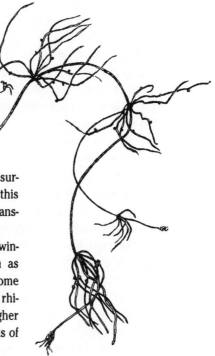

Associates: *Spring, summer, fall.* Stoneworts host vast numbers of other algae on their surfaces. Desmids, diatoms, and the brown, gelatinous blue-green alga *Rivularia* provide abundant food for protozoa and other zooplankton.

Chara, one of the most common submersed aquatics, resembles a seed plant in form but is actually an alga. It is easily recognized by its whorled branches and gritty, odorous surfaces.

As plant succession advances and water nutrients increase, *Chara* is often invaded and eventually replaced by other submersed plants, such as water-milfoil, coontail, bladderworts, and pondweeds. Cattails and bulrushes are also frequent associates.

Numerous invertebrate organisms feed and shelter in stonewort beds. *Hydra,* related to jellyfishes and resembling tiny pieces of frayed string, often attach and feed from *Nitella.* Small crustaceans, such as fairy shrimps (Branchiopoda), water fleas (Cladocera), copepods, ostracods, and amphipods, abound. Water bugs, including water boatmen (Corixidae) and spiderlike water striders (Gerridae), gather and spend the winter in *Chara* mats.

Many crawling water beetles (Haliplidae) feed on stoneworts; *Peltodytes* attaches its eggs to the plants; *Haliplus ruficollis* deposits eggs in dead, empty cells of *Nitella*. Other insect feeders include water scavenger beetles (Hydrophilidae), such as *Hydrophilus* and *Berosus*. Dragonfly nymphs crawl in the *Chara* ooze, snapping up and devouring insect larvae, crustaceans, and worms.

In early spring, the small salamanders called eastern or red-spotted newts lay eggs in beds of *Chara* and waterweed; the round, jellylike capsules are attached singly to the plants.

Fishes, feeding mainly on organisms found in *Chara* beds, are often numerous here. Young trout, northern redbelly dace, and largemouth and smallmouth bass are some of the more common ones. Carp devour large quantities of *Chara*.

All year. Almost all surface-feeding ducks and many divers, as well as swans and American coots, consume stoneworts, which rank among the most important waterfowl foods. Ducks especially relish the plants when they are bearing their tiny oogonia; more than 300,000 of these female reproductive structures have been found in the stomach of a single duck. At other times, waterfowl may consume the plants chiefly for their abundant animal populations. As one of the few aquatic plants that do not die back in winter, *Chara* remains available all year for duck feeding in ice-free waters.

Moose are probably the only regular mammal feeders.

Lore: Abundant *Chara* growth in a pond or lake can soften the water by removing dissolved calcium and precipitating it in solid form. The net result of such removal is a gradual change in water chemistry. This enables the establishment and growth of plants other than obligate calciphiles (that is, plants restricted to cal-

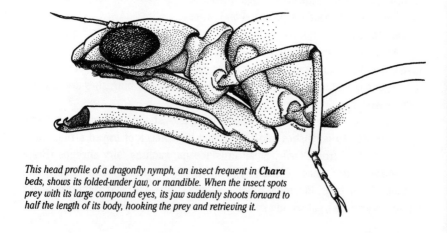

This head profile of a dragonfly nymph, an insect frequent in **Chara** *beds, shows its folded-under jaw, or mandible. When the insect spots prey with its large compound eyes, its jaw suddenly shoots forward to half the length of its body, hooking the prey and retrieving it.*

cium-rich environments). Thus begins the sequence of plant and animal succession that builds nutrients, abundance and variety of species, and habitat communities. *Chara* does not typically reside in overfertilized or polluted waters, where calcium removal and precipitation is largely accomplished by blue-green algae.

Sumac, Poison *(Rhus vernix)*. Cashew family. Scraggly shrub or small tree in swamps. Recognize poison sumac by its toothless, alternate compound leaves; its reddish leafstalks; its dangling, yellowish-green flower clusters in spring; and its waxy-white, drooping fruit clusters in the fall.

Other names: Poison-dogwood, poison-elder, poison-ash, swamp sumac, thunderwood.

Close relatives: Poison ivy *(R. radicans)*; all other sumacs *(Rhus)*; smoke-tree *(Cotinus coggygria)*; mango *(Mangifera indica)*; pistachio *(Pistacia vera)*; cashew *(Anacardium occidentale)*.

Lifestyle: Resembling the nonpoisonous upland shrub sumacs in form, this is the only sumac that grows in wetlands. To swamp walkers, it is a much more prevalent hazard than poisonous snakes or bottomless mires.

Its toxic substance, an oily phenol called *urushiol,* is the same as that found in poison ivy and causes the same inflammatory skin rash. Many of those who have experienced toxic reactions from both plants say that poison sumac is worse. Urushiol occurs in many parts of the plant. Merely touching the leaves or bark will not expose

Poison sumac, seen here in flower, resembles nonpoisonous upland sumacs in general form, but it is the only sumac that grows in wetlands. Its toxic juice (urushiol) is the same as that of poison ivy, a close relative.

you to urushiol unless a break or bruise in plant tissue has caused the sap to exude. But leaves are often punctured by insect feeders, and tiny secretions from such holes may be hardly visible. Therefore it's best to keep a healthy distance from this otherwise attractive shrub.

Poison sumac's greenish flowers are insect pollinated. Though sometimes bisexual, they are often unisexual on the same or different plants. The loosely clustered, berrylike fruits are *drupes* and contain significantly higher amounts of nitrogen and phosphorus than fruits of nontoxic sumacs.

In the fall, poison sumac leaves turn flaming red, making this shrub easily visible in the swamps. Such color probably provides the best wetland example of *foliar fruit flagging;* the red foliage attracts birds, which consume the fruits and disperse the seeds in their droppings.

Associates: Tamarack is a frequent tree associate of poison sumac. Common shrub companions include willows, highbush blueberry, chokeberry, common winterberry holly, mountain-holly, shrubby cinquefoil, and red-osier and gray dogwoods.

Spring, summer. Small bees (including honeybees, *Apis mellifera*) and flies pollinate poison sumac flowers.

Leaf blisters or tightly curled margins of new leaflets in spring indicate the presence of gall gnats *(Contarinia, Dasineura).*

Watch for an attractively patterned reddish-brown and white moth. This is the beautiful eutelia *(Eutelia pulcherrima),* a noctuid. Its caterpillars feed on poison sumac foliage.

Fall, winter. Like poison ivy, poison sumac attracts many bird feeders, which disperse the seeds. Gamebird consumers include wild turkeys, ruffed grouse, ring-necked pheasants, and northern bobwhites. Woodpeckers such as northern flickers and downy and hairy woodpeckers relish the fruits, as do black-capped chickadees, European starlings, yellow-rumped warblers, white-throated sparrows, and many others.

Cottontail rabbits gnaw the bark and also browse the twigs of small sumacs.

Lore: Thoreau admired poison sumac as "one of the chief ornaments of the swamps"; in another jotting, he called it "beautiful as Satan."

"Why didn't you warn me against it?" asked one white woman of Old Solomon, a Georgian Bay tribesman, in 1838. "He assured me that such warning would only have increased the danger, for when there is any knowledge or apprehension of it existing in the mind, the very air blowing from it sometimes infects the frame." Her friend Mr. Jarvis was not so lucky: "All I know is, I became one ulcer from head to foot; I could not stir for a fortnight."

Severe cases of "urushiol surprise" need a physician's attention. There is no sure antidote or cure, but any strongly astringent wash or poultice can reduce the discomfort. Crushed jewelweed rubbed on the rash reduces itching, and if used immediately following exposure, it may even dissolve the oil (as does alcohol) and prevent blistering. The tormenting skin rash usually runs its course, treated or untreated, in one or two weeks.

Despite its savage reputation, poison sumac was put to occasional medicinal use by Indians, mainly as skin poultices from the root for purposes of drawing blood to an infection or a wound. During sixteenth-century Indian wars, it is said, warriors used the plant to poison their arrowheads. They also burned it in defensive bonfires. The wafting smoke, carrying urushiol droplets, may have constituted the first (and only?) poison gas warfare on the continent.

The boiled juices make an indelible black dye, once used for coloring cloth and as a varnish ingredient. The closely related *R. vernicifluum,* an Asian species, produces various Oriental lacquers.

Sundews *(Drosera* spp.). Sundew family. Tiny, ground-level herbs in bogs and fens. Recognize sundews by their radiating rosettes (about three or less inches across) of small leaves covered with reddish, glandular hairs that exude a sticky juice. Of some seven species in east-central North America, the most common are round-leaved sundew *(D. rotundifolia)* and spatulate-leaved sundew *(D. intermedia),* differentiated by their leaf shapes.

Other names: Rosa solis, dew-plant, eyebright, youthwort, lustwort, red-rot, moor-grass; long-leaved or oblong-leaved sundew, love-nest sundew *(D. intermedia).*

Close relative: Venus flytrap *(Dionaea muscipula).*

Lifestyle: Together with the unrelated pitcher-plants and bladderworts, sundews make up the third common group of American insect-trapping plants. Their trapping method is different from those of the other two. Sundew's "flypaper trap" enmeshes insects in a sticky secretion, which glistens like morning dewdrops at the ends of the *tentacles* (the glandular hairs on the leaves). An insect, visually attracted by the crystal, gluelike droplets, alights on the leaf and becomes stuck. Its struggles trigger movement (actually an extremely rapid cell growth) in the tentacles, which begin folding over the insect body in about a minute, further securing it. Insect prey may be entirely enfolded in twenty minutes. The leaf itself also gradually rolls inward over the prey.

Sundew tentacles only move if they are touched several times in a few seconds; a falling leaf, dead insect, or inanimate particle will not trigger the mechanism or will trigger it only sluggishly. Charles Darwin, who thoroughly studied these plants, suggested that such a selective response was an energy-saving adaptation, preventing wasted movement of the tentacles.

Having captured the insect, the tentacles release an anesthetic that seems to stupefy the prey, along with digestive enzymes that dissolve the creature's internal organs. This dissolved nutrient is then absorbed by the tentacles and transported into the plant's vascular system. The entire digestive process, leaving only the insect's dried exoskeleton, may take a week or more. A single leaf may contain up to one hundred tentacles, though usually less.

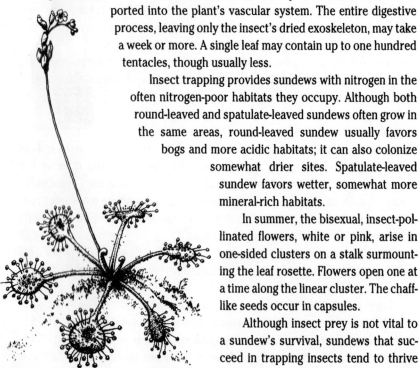

Insect trapping provides sundews with nitrogen in the often nitrogen-poor habitats they occupy. Although both round-leaved and spatulate-leaved sundews often grow in the same areas, round-leaved sundew usually favors bogs and more acidic habitats; it can also colonize somewhat drier sites. Spatulate-leaved sundew favors wetter, somewhat more mineral-rich habitats.

In summer, the bisexual, insect-pollinated flowers, white or pink, arise in one-sided clusters on a stalk surmounting the leaf rosette. Flowers open one at a time along the linear cluster. The chaff-like seeds occur in capsules.

Although insect prey is not vital to a sundew's survival, sundews that succeed in trapping insects tend to thrive and flower to a greater extent. The plants also reproduce vegetatively from buds on horizontal or subsurface stems. Often on spatulate-leaved sundew, the living leaf rosette crowns a series of pre-

Round-leaved sundew's flower stalk rises above the rosette of insect-trapping leaves. Scores of tentacles, each holding a drop of clear, gluelike liquid, project from each leaf, ready to ensnare the first insect attracted to the fake nectar.

vious rosettes, now dead, that remain on the stem. Sundew leaves are highly vulnerable to frost; they die back in the fall—and sometimes too after several false starts in cold spring weather.

Sundews favor open, unshaded sites.

Associates: *Spring, summer.* Probably sundew's foremost plant associates are sphagnum mosses. Sundews occur in acid bogs, where sphagnum and shrub heaths dominate, in sedge fens, and in northern white cedar swamps as well. Their reddish colonies, resembling the hue of some sphagnums, show conspicuously on flat, open sites that are usually water saturated.

The chief flower pollinators are small insects: flies, such as mosquitolike fungus gnats (Mycetophilidae), and gall wasps (Cynipidae).

Midges and other small flies such as *Oscinella* frit flies, also constitute the plants' main prey. But many other insects also fall victim to the sticky tentacles. Fairly common ones include marsh beetles (Helodidae) and crane flies (Tipulidae). Moths often escape capture because of the detachable scales on their wings, which also protect them from adhesion to spider webs. But even large butterflies frequently become trapped by their legs. Darwin once recorded thirteen insects trapped in a single leaf of *D. rotundifolia.*

As might be expected, sundews remain remarkably free from insect attack. One moth caterpillar, however, feeds with impunity on the tentacles from beneath, consuming the end droplet, the glandular bulb, and then the tentacle itself. This plume moth larva *(Trichoptilus parvulus),* active only at night, may denude leaves of all their tentacles, then eat the leaf itself. It also scavenges partially digested insect remains on the leaf. Its long bristles apparently function as "feelers," enabling it to avoid bodily contact with the sticky droplets. This caterpillar often attaches its cocoon lengthwise on the flower stalk.

A greenish noctuid moth caterpillar, *Epipsilia monochromatea,* feeds on the leaves in its early stages, then changes its diet to cranberry leaves in summer.

Although few if any vertebrates regularly feed on these minute plants, mammal activities may encourage their growth. Colonies often thrive in mammal trails of bogs, areas of disturbance where vegetation is matted down from animal runways or human footsteps.

Lore: More than ninety sundew species exist worldwide, some of them much larger than our native sundews. One five-foot-across species in Portugal *(Drosophyllum lusitanicum)* is gathered for use as a natural flypaper. In American wetlands, sundews are fragile species and do not tolerate much human encroachment. Most states legally protect them.

"At the moment, I care more about *Drosera* than the origin of all the species in the world," wrote Charles Darwin in an 1860 letter. Fascinated with these and other insect-trapping plants, Darwin made the most exhaustive studies on them that have ever been done, publishing the results in his small volume *Insectivorous Plants* (1875). His observations still remain the key source for most of what we know about sundews.

Folk remedies using these plants once abounded, though American natives apparently made little use of them. Sundew teas were especially recommended for respiratory and hypertensive ailments. They were also taken as an aphrodisiac. External applications are said to cure pimples, corns, and warts—a function of sundew's proteolytic enzymes. Plumbagin, another constituent, is an antibiotic. Many better medicines for these purposes now exist, however; sundews should not be collected for any purpose.

Sweet Gale *(Myrica gale)*. Bayberry family. Shrub in fens, swamps, along shorelines. Its thin, wedge-shaped leaves, showing resin dots on their undersurfaces and exuding a spicy, aromatic odor when crushed, identify this shrub.

Other names: Dutch, Burton, or bog myrtle or gale, scotch gale, bay-bush, sweet willow.

Close relatives: Common wax-myrtle *(M. cerifera)*; northern bayberry *(M. pensylvanica)*; sweetfern *(Comptonia peregrina)*.

Lifestyle: Sweet gale often grows in dense, colonial thickets consisting of clones from a single root system. It may grow six feet tall but can be easily overlooked in the marginal shrubcarr of wetland edges. Its distinctions appear only upon close inspection. Like all other species of its family, the plant is pleasantly aromatic. The source of that fragrance may be seen in the tiny resin specks covering leaf undersides (and sometimes upper sides too).

In early spring, the wind-pollinated, unisexual flowers are borne in catkins. Most

Sweet gale leaves bear numerous resin dots, the source of their fragrance. Note the leaf's characteristic shape—toothed above the middle, tapering at the base.

clones bear flowers of only one sex (which may change from year to year), but occasional shrubs produce flowers of both sexes on the same or separate stalks. Thus a given plant's sexual identity is not always a permanent characteristic. The female conelike catkins bear small nutlets in summer. New male catkins appear in the fall, remaining tightly closed on the plant over the winter. ("among the most interesting buds of the winter," wrote Thoreau).

Like speckled alder and legumes, sweet gale produces nitrogen-fixing nodules on its roots. Their capacity as soil enrichers may have made these shrubs important soil builders of glaciated areas following the retreat of Pleistocene ice.

Though moderately shade tolerant, sweet gale favors open fens and bog edges. It also favors moderation in soil type, seeming to prefer neither highly acid nor richly mineralized wetlands.

Sweet gale nutlets develop from catkins. Although wildlife feeders are relatively few, this shrub is an important nitrogen-building soil improver.

Associates: Speckled alder, shrub willows, sedges, leatherleaf, and sphagnum mosses are common plant associates of sweet gale.

Spring, summer. In the spring, look for the golden-orange heads of bog beacon mushrooms *(Mitrula elegans)*, cup fungi emerging from dead, submersed leaves along shorelines where sweet gale grows.

Sweet gale is an alternate host of sweetfern blister rust *(Cronartium comptoniae)*, which causes stem cankers in jack and red pines. In sweet gale, this actinomycete fungus produces spores on leaf undersides.

Sweet gale foliage hosts a variety of moth caterpillar feeders. Hairy caterpillars may be bella moths *(Utetheisa bella)* or ruby tiger moths *(Phragmatobia fuliginosa)*; both are tiger moth species. The old maid *(Catocala coelebs)*, a noctuid underwing, is quite rare and appears in late summer along with bella moths. The red-fronted emerald *(Nemoria rubrifrontaria)* is an inchworm caterpillar, as is the white-banded black *(Rheumaptera subhastata)* and *Itame sulphurea.* One of the most common caterpillars on sweet gale is the common eupithecia *(Eupithecia miserulata),* another inchworm. *Condylolomia participialis* and *Acrobasis comptoniella,* pyralid moths, often make webs in the terminal leaves.

Ring-necked ducks have been observed nesting in sweet gale thickets, but birds apparently favor this species less than its relative, northern bayberry (mainly an Atlantic seacoast species), for food. Sharp-tailed grouse consume the buds, catkins, and leaves; and probably such songbirds as eastern bluebirds, gray catbirds, and yellow-rumped warblers eat the nutlets.

Muskrats occasionally feed on the leaves and twigs, as do white-tailed deer.

Lore: The dried leaves make a pleasant tea. Leaves and nutlets can also be used for seasoning. The essential oil is toxic in large doses, producing narcotic effects and also inhibiting bacterial growth.

Both Europeans and American natives found many uses for sweet gale (the plant grows worldwide in the Northern Hemisphere). Fifteenth-century Icelandic settlers prescribed its fragrance for counteracting "shooting pains in the head [migraines?]." The oil, they claimed, "gives the hair strength to grow more." Bark tea made an astringent tonic for various internal ailments, as well as a diuretic given for gonorrhea and a treatment for worms. Bark washes and poultices were applied to sores and skin rashes.

In Europe the leaves were used as moth, flea, and louse repellents in closets and bedding and as substitutes for hops in brewing. The Ojibwa made yellow and reddish dyes from the boiled seeds and buds, using them to color porcupine quills and for other decorative purposes. Potawatomis lined their blueberry containers with the leaves and burned the green plant as a mosquito smudge repellent.

Tamarack *(Larix laricina).* Pine family. Tree in bogs, swamps, fens. Recognize tamarack, the only northern conifer that sheds all its needles in the fall, by its feathery clusters of many short, soft, light blue-green needles; its warty twigs; and its short cones (smaller than an inch).

Other names: American or eastern larch, black or red larch, larch tamarack, hackmatack, juniper cypress.

Close relatives: Pines *(Pinus);* hemlocks *(Tsuga);* spruces *(Picea);* balsam fir *(Abies balsamea).*

Lifestyle: This feathery tree of the northern wetlands becomes most conspicuous in the fall, when its needles turn golden yellow before they drop off.

Tamarack must have open sunlight. It grows rapidly for up to forty or fifty years, then slows considerably, and seldom reaches a height over seventy-five feet or an age beyond 150 years. Most of its annual linear growth is completed by midsummer; its annual stem increment (about one millimeter) is completed shortly after the new needles emerge. Needles on new branch growth are usually smaller than those farther back on the branch.

Tamarack flowers (cones) are unisexual on the same tree, emerging along with the leaves. Pollen cones are yellow, almost round. The wind-pollinated female cones show rose-red scales and usually appear on the two-to-four-year-old branchlets. The small, oval seed cones ripen in the fall and shed most of their seeds over a period of weeks or months. Trees begin producing seed at about age fifteen or less, and heavy seed crops occur every three to six years. In its northernmost range, however, tamarack reproduces mainly by layering (that is, by new shoots rising from lower buried branches).

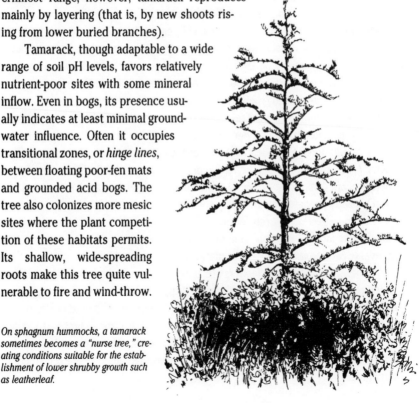

Tamarack, though adaptable to a wide range of soil pH levels, favors relatively nutrient-poor sites with some mineral inflow. Even in bogs, its presence usually indicates at least minimal groundwater influence. Often it occupies transitional zones, or *hinge lines*, between floating poor-fen mats and grounded acid bogs. The tree also colonizes more mesic sites where the plant competition of these habitats permits. Its shallow, wide-spreading roots make this tree quite vulnerable to fire and wind-throw.

On sphagnum hummocks, a tamarack sometimes becomes a "nurse tree," creating conditions suitable for the establishment of lower shrubby growth such as leatherleaf.

Associates: Tamarack seeds often germinate on compact hummocks of sphagnum moss, one of its frequent associates. True mosses, such as *Mnium, Drepanocladus,* and *Helodium,* also provide fine seedbeds. In some poor-fen habitats, I have observed tamarack trees centering islands or low aprons of leatherleaf shrubs; this "nurse tree" function seems to provide some sort of optimal conditions for leatherleaf establishment (see Leatherleaf). Common shrub associates in richer fens include poison sumac, shrubby cinquefoil, bog birch, and shrub willows. Tamarack also associates with, and is succeeded by, northern white cedar in mineral-rich swamps. Tamarack swamps are also good places to look for several orchid species.

In bog succession, black spruce tends to replace tamarack because of the latter's shade intolerance, but the two trees often grow together. Shrub heaths are also common bog associates of tamarack.

Spring, summer. Tamarack's most destructive insect pest is the larch sawfly *(Pristiphora erichsonii),* a needle defoliator that has virtually elimated most old-growth tamarack stands in eastern North America. Now it attacks second-growth stands in periodic irruptions. The greenish, caterpillarlike larvae forage on the trees in gregarious masses, working up from the lower branches. Wasplike adult females produce eggs by parthenogenesis (that is, without mating) and lay them in spring on the new terminal shoots. Where outbreaks of this insect occur, they leave stripped, weakened trees, increasing their vulnerability to invasion by bark beetles, which kill the trees. Trees with dead tops resulting from sawfly defoliation often produce bushy adventitious shoots, which may in turn support high sawfly populations. Parasites of larch sawflies include two inchneumons, *Olesicampe benefactor* and *Mesoleius tenthredeni;* and a tachinid fly *(Bessa harveyi).* A species of ant *(Formica whymperi),* which nests in drier tamarack swamps, is also a larch sawfly predator, as are many songbirds.

Several species of larch loopers *(Semiothisa),* inchworm caterpillars (also called angle moths), feed on tamarack foliage; their numbers often seem to exist in inverse ratio to larch sawfly populations.

Other moth caterpillar feeders are also numerous, though not as voraciously destructive as the aforementioned insects. Apple sphinx moths *(Sphinx gordius),* bright green, hairless caterpillars with a prominent rear horn, and northern pine or bombyx sphinxes *(Lapara bombycoides),* green with a triangular head and lacking the typical sphinx horn, are fairly common. The Columbia silkmoth *(Hyalophora columbia),* a spiny saturniid caterpillar, may feed exclusively on tamarack.

Noctuid moth caterpillars feeding here include the black zigzag *(Panthea acronyctoides)*, the eastern panthea *(P. furcilla)*, the major sallow *(Feralia major)*, and the brown-spotted zale *(Zale helata)*. The honest pero *(Pero honestaria)*, an inchworm moth, and the larch moth *(Paralobesia palliolana)*, a tortricid, also consume tamarack needles; in its early larval stages, the latter mines in the needles, then makes webbed nests at the tips and sides of the shoots. The spruce budworm *(Choristoneura fumiferana)*, another tortricid and a devastating pest of balsam fir and spruce, also feeds to a lesser extent on tamarack (see Spruce, Black). The larch shoot moth *(Argyresthia laricella)*, an argyresthiid species, is also a needle miner, as is the larch casebearer *(Coleophora laricella)*. The latter moth, a serious defoliator, is often attacked by the tiny parasitic wasp *Agathis pumilus.*

Eastern larch beetles *(Dendroctonus simplex)*, small and reddish-brown, often invade tamaracks weakened by larch sawfly or spruce budworm attacks, boring beneath the bark and girdling the trunk. Eastern larch borers *(Tetropium cinnamopterum)* are larger long-horned beetles. Where either beetle population is large, they sometimes spread to healthy tamarack stands as well.

Larch woolly aphids *(Chermes strobilobius)*, sap-suckers feeding in cottony masses on needles and twigs, are common on tamarack. Their alternate hosts are pines, to which they migrate; they move back to tamarack in late summer and hibernate in bark crevices over the winter.

Larvae of the seed chalcid wasp *Megastigmus laricis* feed on developing seeds in the cones.

Mound-building ants *(Lasius minutus)* are often numerous where tamarack and poison sumac are found together.

Many insects that feed on pines may also be found on tamarack (see *The Book of Forest and Thicket*).

Great gray owls favor tamarack trees in northern peatlands for nesting in early spring. Black-backed woodpeckers and olive-sided flycatchers are other recorded nesters. More common birds often seen in and around tamarack stands include common snipe, veeries, common yellowthroats, Nashville warblers, and song and white-throated sparrows. Infestation by larch sawflies usually attracts many birds to tamaracks; woodpeckers, blue jays, American robins, cedar waxwings, grosbeaks, several sparrows, and purple finches may become abundant feeders on both the larval and adult sawflies in areas of insect irruptions.

Fall, winter. Tamaracks often host a variety of fall mushrooms growing beneath the trees. In at least some cases, these are the fruiting bodies of *mycor-*

rhizae (symbiotic subsurface fungi enabling tamarack roots to absorb soil nutrients). A brown-capped pore mushroom or bolete that grows exclusively beneath tamarack is the hollow stalk *(Suillus cavipes)*; yellowish-red *S. grevillei* is a similar species. *Fuscoboletinus spectabilis,* another tamarack bolete, is reddish and sticky. Also exclusive to tamarack is the larch waxycap *(Hygrophorus speciosus)*, a gill fungus with a red, slimy cap.

The aforementioned larch casebearer caterpillars form cigar-shaped cases of cut-off needles in the fall and hibernate inside them over winter. Look for the cases attached to the bases of leaf buds.

Tamarack cones are havens and feeding places for spruce coneworms (see Spruce, Black).

In comparison to other cone-bearing trees, tamarack appears less frequently foraged by birds. Red crossbills, however, feed on them extensively. Spruce, ruffed, and sharp-tailed grouse consume the leaves and buds. Thoreau watched American tree sparrows "very adroitly picking the seeds out of the larch cones." Various observers have reported that eastern goldfinches feed in winter and early spring on the massed eggs of aphids deposited on tamaracks; flocks of the birds work the trees for insect eggs from the top down.

Studies indicate that up to half of the tamarack seed crop that falls to the ground is consumed or cached by rodents and shrews. These include white-footed mice, boreal redback voles, and masked and Arctic shrews. Red squirrels often nip off cone-bearing twigs before the cones are fully matured, carrying the cones to their middens. Bark feeders include snowshoe hares (which also devour many seedlings) and porcupines. Like spruces and balsam fir, tamarack is a "stuffing food" for white-tailed deer, eaten only when more nourishing browse is lacking.

All year. Heart rot fungi, identified by their shelflike fruiting bodies (conks) on the trunks, usually indicate weakened or dying trees. Tamarack's chief fungous diseases are brown heart rot *(Fomitopsis officinalis)* and red ring rot *(Phellinus pini)*. Both are polypores with woody, hoof-shaped brackets.

Lore: Tamarack, though not a favored pulpwood or building material, is valued for its hard, durable qualities, especially in contact with soil (gaunt skeletons of tamaracks often remain standing for decades in northern bogs). British colonial shipbuilders often imported tamarack timbers when English oak was lacking. Difficult to split, tamarack mostly goes for posts, poles, railroad ties, ladders, boxes, and crates. Transparent glassine used in window envelopes is often made from tamarack fibers. The skin of some people is sensitive to the sawdust where trees are being cut.

Native Americans used tamarack inner bark for wound poultices. Bark and leaf teas made astringent tonics for various intestinal ailments.

Tamarack wood makes a hot-burning fuel. Native peoples often used it for boiling maple sap. Indians also used tamarack rootlets for sewing birchbark canoes.

As with most conifers, this tree's inner bark provides a nutritious (if hardly delicious) survival food for emergencies. Tender shoots of the season may also be cooked and eaten.

Fast-growing yard and ornamental tamaracks, chiefly nonnative species, include European larch *(L. decidua)* and Japanese larch *(L. leptolepis).*

Thistle, Swamp *(Cirsium muticum).* Composite family. Spiny-leaved herb in swamps and wet meadows. Identify this thistle by its clustered rose-purple flower heads, its weakly spined leaves and spineless stem, and the sticky, cobwebby bracts beneath its flower heads. Marsh thistle *(C. palustre),* a less common alien species, is the only other thistle that habitually grows in wetlands (also in drier habitats).

Close relatives: Ironweeds *(Vernonia);* boneset, Joe-Pye-weeds *(Eupatorium);* asters *(Aster);* goldenrods *(Solidago);* bur-marigolds *(Bidens);* sunflowers *(Helianthus);* all other composites.

Lifestyle: The mark of the composite family is multiple florets in a single flowering head that superficially appears as one flower. In thistles, all the florets are disk flowers (corresponding to the central flower portions of such rayed composites as sunflowers, daisies, and asters). Hundreds of these bisexual, insect-pollinated florets occupy swamp thistle heads, which resemble shaving brushes in form.

Some sixteen thistle species range throughout east-central North America. All of them flower in summer and early fall, and almost all of them grow in upland and waste-ground habitats. Most are also shade intolerant. That swamp thistle is the only consistent wetland dweller among them is a great aid in identifying this species.

Like many other thistles, it is biennial (that is, its complete life cycle spans two years), producing only a ground-level rosette of spiny leaves during its first summer. This rosette lasts over winter; from it rises the second-year flowering stem, two to ten feet tall. The seeds (achenes), each attached to a ring of downy filaments that aid wind dispersal, form a compact, fluffy mass in the former flower head. "I know of no object more unsightly to a careless glance than an empty this-tle-head," wrote Thoreau. "Yet, if you examine it closely, it may remind you of the silk-lined cradle in which a prince was rocked."

The entire plant dies after producing its seed, so these plants—in contrast to most wetland herbs—depend exclusively on sexual reproduction for maintaining their populations.

Associates: *Summer, fall.* Not a colonial plant, swamp thistle rises singly among such associates as sedges, bog goldenrod, cattails, purple loosestrife, and other rich-fen dwellers.

The nectar-rich flowers attract many insects. Bumblebees *(Bombus)* and smaller bees are probably the chief pollinators. Many butterflies also feed on the nectar. Watch for several orange fritillaries, including the regal fritillary *(Speyeria idalia)*, the great spangled fritillary *(S. cybele)*, and the aphrodite *(S. aphrodite)*. The so-called thistle butterflies—the red admiral *(Vanessa atalanta)* and painted lady *(V. cardui)*—seem especially fond of thistle flowers. As a greenish yellow, bristly caterpillar, the painted lady also feeds on thistle leaves, constructing pro-gressively larger silken shelters on the plant. Another butterfly caterpillar feeder, green with long white hairs, is the swamp metalmark *(Lephelisca muticum)*; it suspends its hairy cocoon by a saddle from the thistle stem.

Ruby-throated hummingbirds visit these flowers for nectar. Probably this-tle's chief bird associates, however, are eastern goldfinches, late-season nesters that collect the seed-down in summer for nest construction. Thistledown scat-tered on the ground around the plant bases usually indicates that goldfinches have been raiding. Goldfinches also relish the nutritious seeds, as anyone who maintains a backyard thistle-seed bird feeder knows, and often nest close to an abundant source of thistle seed. Few other birds, apparently, feed on thistle seed to any extent in the wild.

Mammal herbivores generally avoid these plants, presumably because of their spiny foliage.

Lore: Despined leaves (carefully, with gloves) and peeled stems of young thistles make edible greens, raw or cooked. The roots of first-year plants can also be eaten. American natives used thistle root teas for intestinal complaints and "diseases of women." Both root and leaf were applied to skin irritations.

In yards or pastures, Scotland's national flower is often regarded as an unpleasant plant pest. But swamp thistle, not as aggressively spiny as many of its relatives, is a rather modest member of its tribe, providing color, interest, and wildlife value in wetland communities.

Turtlehead *(Chelone glabra)*. Snapdragon family. Herb in wet ground, along streambanks, rarely in water. Its large, two-lipped, tubular, white or pinkish flowers crowded at the top of the stem and its narrow, opposite leaves identify this summer wildflower.

Other names: Balmony, snake-head, cod-head, cod-mouth, fish-mouth, shell-flower, salt-rheum weed, bitter-herb.

Close relatives: Mulleins *(Verbascum)*; snapdragons *(Antirrhinum)*; monkey-flowers *(Mimulus)*; beard-tongues *(Penstemon)*; speedwells *(Veronica)*; gerardias *(Gerardia)*.

Lifestyle: Superficially resembling the unrelated bottle gentians *(Gentiana)* in form, this plant wins no awards for visual subtlety or grace. Its spectacular, inch-long flowers, densely bunched like a tight, dirty white bouquet at the stem tops, give it an almost coarse appearance.

The bisexual, insect-pollinated flowers are hooded by a long, arching upper lip that overlaps the lower lip like a turtle's beak (hence the name). They exhibit *protandry* (that is, the male parts mature and decline before the female parts mature). This flower produces plentiful nectar at its base, but even large insects (usually bumblebees) must struggle to enter the stiff-lipped tube during its male phase. The flower tube entirely swallows the entering insect body. Watch the flower "chew" as the insect's interior movements cause the lower lip to move up and down. Then the insect emerges as if disgorged, with pollen dusted all over its velvety back. Later, when the pistil matures, the lips relax somewhat and insect entry is less difficult. Inside the flower now, a sterile fifth stamen obstructs nectary access to all but the larger, long-tongued insects, which can reach over the bar. The flower's sexual organs all project from the inner roof of the tube.

A turtlehead flower spike shows typical age sequencing. The opened flowers exhibit their final, female phase; higher, unopened ones are pollinating in their male stage. Unopened flower buds top the spike.

The oldest flowers are at the base of the cluster. They often become ragged and unkempt as new flowers above them open through late summer and early fall. The winged fruits, produced in capsules, are dispersed by wind.

Turtlehead usually grows isolated or in small clumps from perennial rhizomes.

Associates: Frequent plant companions include sedges, boneset, purple loosestrife, and meadowsweet. I often find swamp lousewort *(Pedicularis lanceolata)*, a yellow-flowered close relative of turtlehead, in the latter's near vicinity.

Spring. Turtlehead is the foremost larval food plant of the Baltimore butterfly *(Euphydryas phaeton)*. The spiny, orange, black-banded caterpillars emerge from hibernation in spring and feed singly on the leaves, where they also pupate in suspended, whitish cocoons. Then they transform into the black, orange-spotted adult butterflies, which seldom visit the flowers. They lay crimson masses of one hundred to seven hundred eggs on leaf undersides.

Summer, fall. Turtlehead's chief pollinators are bumblebees *(Bombus).* Sometimes they partially destroy the flower tube by biting their way in from the side.

Summer broods of the aforementioned Baltimore butterfly caterpillar feed gregariously in a communal web on the plant until autumn, then hibernate on the dead stems over winter. They sometimes defoliate entire plants.

Other occasional defoliators include two caterpillarlike sawflies *(Macrophya nigra* and *Tenthredo grandis)*, which feed gregariously on the plant. Recognize sawfly larvae by their often coiled positions on the leaves.

Larvae of a leaf-mining flea beetle *(Dibolia borealis)* feed between epidermal layers of the leaves.

A pollinator predator that frequents the flowers, capturing smaller bees as they alight, is a ground-nesting sphecid wasp, *Philanthus solivagus.*

Two larval seed feeders are common in turtlehead seed capsules: *Endothenia hebesana,* a tiny tortricid moth caterpillar; and *Phytomyza cheloniae,* a leafminer fly. Watch for certain winged ichneumons and chalcid wasps probing the capsules; these are parasites of the seed feeders, searching them out and depositing eggs in their bodies. *Macrocentrus* and *Agathis* species, small wasplike ichneumons, parasitize the moth caterpillars; another ichneumon *(Chorebus)* and the chalcid wasp *Pteromalus* seek out the fly larvae.

The tiny caterpillar of a borer moth *(Papaipema nepheloptera)* feeds inside stems of turtlehead; dead or dying plants in summer indicate their presence.

Turtlehead apparently provides no important food for birds and mammals.

Its spotty distribution and solitary occurrence in wetlands tend to make such usage incidental.

Lore: Leaf teas of turtlehead, exceedingly bitter, were staples of folk medicine introduced by similar native usage. Healers of various stripe often prescribed them for jaundice and liver ailments, as well as for worms and as an appetite stimulant and laxative. Decoctions of the plant were applied externally to tumors, herpes, and hemorrhoids.

Vervain, Blue *(Verbena hastata).* Vervain family. Herb in swamps, low spots, along water margins, as well as in less moist habitats. Blue vervain displays several erect, pencillike spikes of blue flowers like candelabra atop a four-angled stem; its narrow leaves are toothed and opposite. This is the most common of some dozen blue-flowered and white-flowered vervains in east-central North America.

Other names: False or American vervain, wild hyssop, purvain, iron-weed, simpler's-joy.

Close relatives: Garden verbena *(V. hybrida)*; moss verbena *(V. laciniata)*; lemon verbena *(Aloysia triphylla)*; frog-fruits *(Phyla)*; beautyberry *(Callicarpa americana)*; teak *(Tectona grandis)*; chaste tree *(Vitex agnus-castus).*

Lifestyle: Blue vervain begins flowering in midsummer and continues through early fall. Like many plants with flowers on spikes, the flowers come into bloom from the bottom up. On any given spike, you can usually see seeds on the lowermost portion, a circular fringe of flowers midway up, and unopened flower buds at the top. The nectar-rich flowers are bisexual and insect pollinated, producing linear nutlets. The flowers often self-fertilize as well.

Vervain's stalk dies in the fall but often remains standing throughout winter, dispersing seeds. In late summer, the thick, spreading rhizome produces small reddish buds just beneath the soil surface; from these, new stalks arise the following spring.

Although blue vervain adapts to almost any fairly moist, open, acid-neutral or alkaline habitat, it usually favors wetter sites than its close relatives, white and European vervains *(V. urticifolia, V. officinalis)*, which generally prefer drier ground.

Associates: *Summer, fall.* Plant companions of blue vervain include boneset, Joe-Pye-weeds, meadowsweet, reed canary grass, great lobelia, and jewelweeds, among others. It frequently grows atop hummocks of tussock sedge. On drier

Parasitic dodder, shown here in flower, climbs a stem of blue vervain, one of its many plant victims. This vervain is already showing dire effects of the parasitism.

sites, blue vervain sometimes associates with the two aforementioned vervains as well.

The twining, threadlike, parasitic dodder *(Cuscuta)* often enmeshes blue vervain in its yellowish, matted strands, tapping into the stem and not infrequently killing it (see Jewelweeds).

Bumblebees *(Bombus)*, honeybees *(Apis mellifera)*, and other bees are the chief pollinators.

At least two broods of a noctuid moth caterpillar, the verbena moth *(Crambodes talidiformis)*, feed on the leaves beginning in spring.

The verbena leaf miner *(Agromyza platyptera)*, a midge larva, produces large blotch mines near the leaf margins.

Despite their abundant presence and seed production, vervains have only slight value as wildlife food plants. Several songbird species eat the seeds; probably the foremost consumers are swamp sparrows. Others include northern cardinals, dark-eyed juncos, and song, American tree, and white-crowned sparrows.

Cottontail rabbits eat the plants to some extent.

Lore: American natives used blue vervain leaves and roots for making various medicinal teas and tonics that were emetic in large doses. The Mohawks had a further use: "For refreshment, cut the root into pieces, place on top of the head with a little cold water, and sit in a current of air" (the beneficial effect was said to result with or without the root topping!).

The only humanly edible part of the plant is said to be the seeds, which can be soaked, roasted, and ground for flour.

Related European vervain, also common in North America, has a long Old World history associated with the occult: Druid rites, Roman sacrifices and love potions, and witches' incantations (the Latin word *verbena* means "sacred herb"). Virgil and Pliny referred to the plant in their writings, and the ancient Greeks also considered it a holy herb and aphrodisiac, a general cure-all for sicknesses of soul and body. One source marvels that the plant has survived extinction, so abundantly was it once collected by herbalists and folk practitioners.

Watercress *(Nasturtium officinale)*. Mustard family. Low, submersed, partially floating or prostrate herb in shallow brooks, cold springs, along river margins. Recognize watercress by its darkish green, matlike growth in dense beds, its compound leaves with three to nine oval leaflets, and its four-petaled white flowers in spring.

Less common cresses favoring wet habitats include several bitter cresses *(Cardamine)*, lake cress *(Armoracia aquatica)*, and yellow cresses *(Rorippa)*.

Close relatives: Radish *(Raphanus sativus)*; horseradish *(Armoracia rusticana)*; toothworts *(Dentaria)*; winter cresses *(Barbarea)*; mustards *(Brassica)*.

Lifestyle: Sometimes level with the water surface or several

Watercress, conspicuous both in flower (top) and in seed (bottom), is a commonly seen plant in spring-fed brooks. Its erect seedpods characterize most mustard family plants.

inches above it, watercress's horizontal leaves and stems form wet, tangled masses along margins of cold streams.

Its small flower clusters surmount leafy branches that rise a few inches above the plant bed. The bisexual flowers may self-pollinate as often as insects pollinate them, producing the slender, erect seedpods *(siliques)* characteristic of many mustards. Watercress chiefly reproduces by vegetative means, however, rooting at intervals from its creeping, prostrate stems.

This plant favors fast currents and seepages of muddy springs. It seldom grows where mineral-rich waters do not flow to some extent. Often it becomes established in pockets of fine silt or mud deposited by stream eddies. In deeper waters, it sometimes grows entirely submersed.

Its foliage dies back in the fall, but the plants persist over winter as bright green, bushy rosettes, which begin expanding rapidly in early spring.

Associates: *Spring, summer.* Watercress frequents the same habitats as certain green algae, aquatic mosses, pondweeds, bur-reeds, marsh marigold, and forget-me-nots. Thick beds of it have a tendency to crowd out other emergents.

Bees and flies are the chief pollinators.

Several insect larvae feed on watercress foliage. The caddisfly *Limnephilus lunatus,* an aquatic case-making larva, is the only reported pest of the plant. Like watercress itself, this caddisfly is indigenous to Europe.

Resident feeders above the water line often include bean aphids *(Aphis rumicis),* blackish sap-suckers that cluster thickly on leaf undersides. Watercress leaf beetles *(Phaedon aeruginosus),* small, oval, bronze-black chrysomelids, feed on the foliage.

Smooth green caterpillars with a line extending along the back are probably larvae of the butterflies called whites *(Pieris).* Whites feed on many mustard family plants in addition to watercress. The mustard white *(P. napi),* a native species, has suffered severe competition from the imported European cabbage butterfly *(P. rapae),* now one of the most common butterflies in America. Adult first-brood butterflies of both species emerge in early spring after hibernating as pupae overwinter.

Another introduced mustard feeder is the diamondback moth caterpillar *(Plutella xylostella),* which eats holes in leaf undersides and pupates in meshlike cocoons attached to the leaves.

Beds of watercress are frequent subsurface havens for scavenging crustaceans such as water sowbugs *(Asellus)* and amphipods *(Gammarus).* Amphipods feed mainly on the yellowing older leaves; one recent study found that the plant's green leaves were toxic to them, an apparent chemical defense system evolved by the plant.

All year. Watercress is an excellent food producer for trout, which consume its young foliage and resident animals.

Though watercress ranks relatively low in preference as a waterfowl food, many surface-feeding ducks consume the foliage. It provides one of the few green foods available for waterfowl during winter in northern areas.

Muskrats and white-tailed deer also eat the plant.

Lore: Watercress came into this country from Europe, presumably in herb gardens as a source for homegrown salad greens, in the eighteenth century. Botanists argue over the plant's classification. Some unite it with the genus of marsh or yellow cresses *(Rorippa)*; its diploid and triploid chromosomal varieties hybridize and are sometimes split into separate species.

The succulent, pungent-tasting leaves, high in vitamins A and C and iodine, have long provided one of the best-known wild salad greens; they are also used in vegetable juices, sandwiches, soups, and casseroles. This plant's abundance precludes any danger of its extinction by food collectors, but a caution should be noted: Watercress has a high tolerance for certain kinds of water pollution and readily absorbs toxic heavy metals into its plant tissue. Thus today almost no collection sources in east-central North America are completely safe.

Leaf extracts of watercress are used in some countries to correct vitamin deficiency. The plant has a long history in folk medicine as a diuretic and remedy for various ailments.

Water-hemlock *(Cicuta maculata).* Parsley family. Tall herb in wet meadows, fens, swamps. Features of water hemlock include its smooth, purple-streaked stem; its compound, reddish-tinged leaves; and its white, umbrella-shaped flower clusters. The bulb-bearing water hemlock *(C. bulbifera)* is a smaller plant, has much thinner leaves, and bears small bulblets in the upper leaf angles.

Other names: Spotted cowbane, spotted water-hemlock, beaver-poison, musquash-root, poison parsnip, wild parsnip (actually the related *Pastinaca sativa).*

Close relatives: Angelicas *(Angelica)*; poison-hemlock *(Conium maculatum)*; dill *(Anethum graveolens)*; celery *(Apium graveolens)*; golden alexanders *(Zizia)*; Queen Anne's lace *(Daucus carota).* Water-hemlock is unrelated to the coniferous tree hemlocks *(Tsuga).*

Lifestyle: Many plants of the parsley family look much alike. Water-hemlock grows up to six feet tall, its flower head much resembling that of the common Queen Anne's lace, except it is looser and the clusters are more widely spaced ("like so many constellations or separate systems in the firmament," wrote Thoreau). The plant even more closely resembles water-parsnip *(Sium suave),* which (unlike Queen Anne's lace) grows in the same habitats. Flowers can be unisexual or bisexual. Water-hemlock also reproduces vegetatively from its tuberous roots.

Some authorities believe this to be the most violently toxic green plant in North America; eating even small amounts is usually fatal to humans and other mammals. The deadly poison is the alkaloid cicutoxin, a yellowish, oily liquid contained in all parts of the plant (except, probably, the flowers).

Associates: *Summer.* Water-hemlock associates with typical fen plants including sedges, shrubby cinquefoil, boneset, and many others.

Flowers and nectar attract bees, wasps, and butterflies—many more of these insects, according to some accounts, than visit most parsley family flowers.

Almost all parsleys are favored food plants of black or parsnip swallowtail butterfly caterpillars *(Papilio polyxenes).*

A tiny epermeniid moth caterpillar *(Epermenia cicutaella)* feeds in the flowers and seeds and may also mine the leaves.

Mallards have been recorded as eating the seeds. American natives, well acquainted with this plant, knew that it killed beavers that fed on it.

A black swallowtail butterfly caterpillar crawls on water-hemlock, one of its food plants. Few plant families contain so many edible and poisonous members both as the parsley tribe.

Lore: Indians generally avoided this plant except when seeking it deliberately for suicide (a not uncommon practice even among presettlement tribes), which the plant accomplished swiftly, if painfully; violent spasms and convulsions usually precede death by water hemlock poisoning. Use of the root for poultices—and mixing the seeds with tobacco for smoking as a charm—are also recorded.

This is not the same plant that Socrates took in a deadly potion; that was probably the closely related poison-hemlock *(Conium maculatum)*, which has somewhat less violent toxic effects. Many parsley family plants are edible and tasty, but unless you are completely familiar with the wild-growing members of this group, it is wisest to sample none. Accidental deaths (many of them children) have resulted from only casual tasting of this plant, usually when it was mistaken for a similar-appearing parsnip or carrot. Without immediate, aggressive treatment, fatality is almost certain.

Water-lilies *(Nymphaea odorata, Nuphar* spp.). Water-lily family. Floating-leaved and emergent herbs in ponds, slow streams. Recognize water-lilies by their broad, platterlike, surface-floating or (in spatterdock) emergent leaves and their large, floating, bright white or yellow flower heads.

The most common species include white or fragrant water-lily *(Nymphaea odorata)*, with large, fragrant, white flowers and purplish leaf undersides; yellow or bullhead lily *(Nuphar variegata)*, with large, yellow flowers; and spatterdock *(Nuphar advena)*, yellow-flowered with leaves held *above* the water surface.

Other names: Pond-lilies, lily-pads; American water-lily, sweet-scented white water-lily, water-nymph, water-cabbage, alligator-bonnet *(Nymphaea odorata)*; large yellow pond-lily or water-lily, beaver-root, cow-lily *(Nuphar variegata, N. advena)*.

Close relatives: American lotus *(Nelumbo lutea)*; water-shield *(Brasenia schreberi)*; fanwort *(Cabomba caroliniana)*. Water-lilies are unrelated to true lilies *(Lilium)*.

Lifestyle: A pond seems hardly a pond without water-lilies in spectacular spring and summer bloom and covering the water surface with their broad, flat, dry-on-top leaves from spring to fall. Leaves of white water-lily are usually rounder and broader-notched where the leafstalk connects than the more oval, narrow-notched yellow water-lily leaves. Nonfloating, wide-notched spatterdock leaves stand erect like broad funnels several inches above the water surface. Thus, even without flowers present, these water-lilies are all fairly simple to differentiate.

Some aquatic ecologists believe that all floating leaves have tended to evolve toward circular, untoothed shapes. Such shapes (manifested most obviously in water-lilies) provide maximum protection against tearing from wind and wave action. Water-lily leaves, leathery in texture, also resist penetration by heavy rains and hail. The upper leaf surface bears a heavy, waxy, water-repellent *cuticle* (surface cell layer). Also, in contrast to aerial plant leaves, the *stomata* (air pores) are located on the upper, air-exposed surface rather than the underside. Leaf undersides and stems bear a thick, slippery, mucous coating, which probably protects against some aquatic herbivores and also against mechanical abrasion when plants rub together in waves or currents. The red pigment on leaf undersides of white water-lily is believed to raise leaf temperature slightly above the water temperature, thus speeding transpiration.

Water-lily stems, rising from thick rhizomes in the bottom mud, are intriguing marvels of plant engineering. Several air-filled, tubular passages called *lacunae* run throughout the stems, giving them buoyancy. But the enclosed air is not static; studies of yellow water-lily have shown that the stems conduct gases both to and from the leaves. These "internal winds" flow under considerable pressure. Down in the sediment, gases (mainly carbon dioxide and methane) diffuse into the lacunae and travel upward to older leaves, "spraying" into the air from the leaf stomata. In younger leaves, the stomata draw air *into* the leaf lacunae, whence it travels down to the buried rhizome and roots. The process works like a pump; pressure generated in the young leaves is vented finally through the less-pressurized older leaves, which serve as the transport system's exhaust. The lacunae, writes one botanist, "represent an extension of the atmosphere into the sediment water." One study measured twenty-two liters of air passing through a single water-lily leafstalk in one day. At most hours and seasons, all parts of a water-lily plant contain considerable amounts of methane in passage (this "sewer gas," which can often be smelled around ponds, is the product of anaerobic decomposition in the bottom muds). The pressurized internal winds of water-lilies proceed in addition to the regular photosynthetic and respiratory processes that occur in all green plants. Many other emergent aquatic plants also have stem lacunae, which presumably transport gases in similar fashion.

Bisexual water-lily flowers are functionally unisexual, operating in the sexual timing sequence called *protogyny* (that is, the female parts mature before the male parts, thus preventing self-fertilization).

White and yellow water-lily flowers vary somewhat in anatomy and form. White water-lily displays numerous white petals surrounding the central, golden-yellow sexual parts. The large, fragrant flower, sometimes five inches across, opens in the morning, closes in afternoon.

In yellow water-lily, six large, yellow, overlapping sepals surround the small, yellow, stamenlike petals, which themselves surround the central barrel-shaped, yellow-green "brandy bottle" of sexual parts. This flower is often odorless.

Spatterdock's six sepals are green outside, yellow or purplish inside, and form a barely open spherical cup when it first blooms; the triangular aperture over the disklike stigma is just wide enough to admit a pollen-bearing insect. Next day, after it has been fertilized, the flower widely expands, exposing the now-mature anthers with their pollen ready to shed on insect visitors.

After fertilization and pollen release, the flower closes and its stem begins to coil, pulling the flower head underwater. There the seeds (some six or seven hundred of them) mature in about a month inside the fleshy *aril,* which breaks off, floats to the surface, and after a time releases the seeds. The seeds sink, germinating the following spring. In white water-lily, the new plant requires three years to flower; it remains submersed the first year and produces only floating leaves the second year.

Vegetative reproduction proceeds from the buried rhizome, which branches and buds from one tip as the older end decomposes. Flower and leaf stems die back to the rhizome in the fall.

Water-lilies can grow in very shallow water, as long as water levels remain stable, and in clear depths down to fifteen feet.

Associates: *Spring, summer, fall.* White water-lily favors slow-moving, somewhat more aerated waters than the yellow water-lily, which thrives best in quieter, more stagnant pond habitats. Despite their preferences, colonies of two or all three species may occur close together or intermixed in the same pond or backwater. Frequent other plant associates include bladderworts, coontail, pondweeds, duckweeds, water-shield, and smartweeds, among others.

Few flowers attract as many insects as the sweetly fragrant white water-lily. Chief pollinators include honeybees *(Apis mellifera)* and small halictid bees, such as *Lasioglossum versatum, Halictus nelumbonis, H. pastoralis,* and *Prosopis nelumbonis;* and syrphid flies, such as *Helophilus divisus.* During first-day blooming, you may find halictid bees drowned in the small bowl of liquid that pools atop the concave stigma. Insects land on the surrounding palisade wall of flexible stamens, which bend inward under the insects' weight, causing them to fall into the stigmatic fluid. Most of them escape, however.

Other common pollinators are long-horned leaf beetles *(Donacia)* that spend their entire life cycles on water-lily plants. The adult beetles (of about five species) can often be seen mating on the flowers or leaves. One study suggests that these nectar- and pollen-feeding beetles, which invade water-lily flowers during their earliest female phase, may actually cause self-fertilization of the flower by crawling over and amid the still-unexposed, pollen-bearing anthers and the stigma. In this view, the timed sequencing of flower opening is seen not as a means of ensuring cross-pollination but as an evolved, symbiotic coaction between beetle and flower: The beetle gets exclusive food and protection, and the flower receives prompt pollination. According to this theory, full expansion and cross-pollination of the flower becomes a backup procedure in case self-fertilization via the beetles fails.

Tiny blackish, almost microscopic insects crawling inside the flower are probably thrips (Thysanoptera). Other common insects found on and in the flowers include dance flies (Empidae) and shore flies (Ephydridae).

Water-lily leaves (lily pads) are one of the most populous microhabitats of any pond environment. They host numerous feeders, egg-layers, shelterers, and resters. One need only glance at the often ragged, riddled condition of many of the leaves in midsummer to note how heavily they have been used. Each leaf provides a detailed record of its uses and users, a historical census of its residents and consumers.

Topside, the leaves provide resting platforms and territorial perches for dragonflies and damselflies. Much tinier insects, abounding wherever lily pads exist, are flealike jumping plant lice (collambolans or springtails), mere specks leaping en masse from the leaf surfaces when disturbed; they also coat the water surface. Collambolans scavenge dead plant material. The water springtail *(Podura aquatica)* is a common species. Crowds of similar larger jumpers are delphacid plant hopper nymphs *(Megamelus davisi)*, sap-suckers that often appear in the fall. Pond lily aphids *(Rhopalosiphum nymphaeae)* are also sometimes numerous; their winter alternate hosts are fruit trees.

Waterlily leaf beetles *(Pyrrhalta nympheae)*, black and yellow feeders, channel irregular trenches, usually in the upper third of the leaf. These grazed areas quickly degenerate into holes, leaving wandering perforated trails in the leaf. Their life cycle begins with small rows of bright yellow eggs on the leaf. The many-legged larvae feed and also pupate on the leaf before transforming into adult beetles. Recent research on these beetles suggests that their feeding may speed up the water-lily "plant pump," increasing the rate of nutrient cycling from bottom sediments by raising the rate of leaf destruction, decomposition, and turnover.

The plant's consequent response, putting forth new leaves, thus "revs up" the entire nutrient transport system.

The lady beetles *Hippodamia 13-punctata* and *Coleomegilla maculata* often seek aphids on the leaves.

Several moth caterpillars also eat lines and holes in the leaves. White-tailed divers *(Bellura gortynoides)* mine the leaves as young larvae, then bore into the stems, finally swimming to shore where they overwinter and pupate in ground litter. The waterlily moth *(Homophoberia cristata)* feeds mainly on yellow water-lily leaves. Both of these caterpillars are noctuid moths.

Case-making caterpillars cut out two oval pieces of leaf and fasten them by silk above and beneath their bodies. Then they attach to the leaf undersides, where they feed upon their cases. These pyralid moth larvae are aquatic gill breathers. *Synclita obliteralis,* the lily-leaf caterpillar, and *Munroessa gyralis* are common case-bearers, as is *Parapoynx obscuralis.*

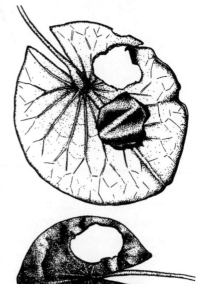

Leaves riddled with quarter-inch holes often indicate the presence of the aforementioned *Donacia* leaf beetles. The female adult beetle cuts a hole, then inserts and curls her ovipositor to the leaf underside, where she lays a double row of eggs in a concentric half-circle (or less) bordering the hole.

False leaf-mining midge larvae *(Cricotopus ornatus)* create serpentine mines in the leaves.

At least as much feeding and other activity occur on the leaves' submersed undersides as on their dry tops. Examination of the bottom surface almost always reveals something about organisms of the water-lily community. *Donacia* eggs often rim holes in the leaf. Other egg masses may include those of water mites (Hydrachnellae); narrow-winged damselflies such as *Enallagma;* long-horned caddisflies such as

Synclita, *a case-making moth caterpillar, cuts out pieces of water-lily leaf for top and bottom protection, then attaches its case to the leaf underside (top). Leaves thus utilized show characteristic oval-shaped holes (bottom).*

Triaenodes, Limnephilus, Leptocella, and *Oecetis;* whirligig beetles (Gyrinidae); water scavenger beetles (Hydrophilidae); and (in sausage-shaped jelly masses) snails *(Physa* and others). Water-lilies are literally floating hatcheries.

Look for attached or crawling animals on the leaf undersides, too. Fluffy, whitish patches may be colonies of *Vorticella* protozoans. Case-making rotifers *(Melicerta, Floscularia)* attach their tiny tubes here, and jellyfishlike *Hydra* hang suspended. Furry, creeping colonies of bryozoa *(Cristatella)* and freshwater sponges *(Spongilla)* attach here, as well as on the stems. Red water mites and snails such as *Physa, Gyraulus,* and *Ferrissia* species also graze on leaf undersides and stems; the small holes eaten in the leaf by snails often run in lines perpendicular to the leaf axis.

*On water-lily leaf undersides, crescent-shaped egg masses rimming holes cut in the leaf mark the presence of **Donacia** long-horned beetles.*

In addition to some of the aforementioned organisms, others reside more exclusively in the stem (actually leaf petiole) microhabitat. Snails and pill-clams *(Pisidium)* graze on the filamentous green or blue-green algae that coat most subsurface stems. Aquatic bugs, including water scorpions (Nepidae) and backswimmers (Notonectidae), insert their eggs into the air-filled stems, as do certain dragonflies such as green darners *(Anax junius)* and biddies (Cordulegastridae). Larvae of the aforementioned *Donacia* leaf beetle tap into the stems head foremost; their bodies hang out, surrounded by a constant stream of escaping bubbles (a mark of their presence). Other stem borers include *Hydromyza confluens,* an anthomyiid larva that transforms into an adult fly before it leaves the stem and floats to the surface, and the aforementioned diver moths. Certain underwater weevils, such as *Bagous longirostris* and *Onychylis nigrirostris,* feed on both petioles and leaves, as do midge larvae (Chironomidae).

Northern fathead minnows frequently spawn in water-lily beds, and common or chain pickerel, fish predators, lurk there. These are favorite habitats also for green and mink frogs.

Water-lily fruits rank as relatively unimportant bird foods except in the Gulf coast region, where many waterfowl eat white water-lily seeds. Gadwalls, wood ducks, ring-necked ducks, greater and lesser scaups, and rails are probably the foremost northern bird consumers.

For certain mammal herbivores, these plants are much more important. Muskrats consume the rhizomes and other plant parts. Beavers relish them, sometimes storing the rhizomes. (In summer, beavers in some areas feed almost exclusively on aquatic vegetation rather than woody growth). Their damming activities create water-lily habitat, and they widely disperse the plants by dropping rhizome fragments hither and yon. Porcupines also relish the plants, as do white-tailed deer. For moose, water-lilies are principal foods.

Lore: "It reminds me of a young country maiden," waxed Thoreau about the fragrance of white water-lily, elaborating that it is "wholesome as the odor of the cow." Elsewhere in his journal, he recalled that young men used to carry or wear water-lilies to church in Concord, "so that the flower is to some extent associated with bathing in Sabbath mornings and going to church, its odor contrasting and atoning for that of the sermon." He also confessed that, as a lad, he used to enjoy smoking the dried stems ("I have never smoked anything more noxious").

American natives made extensive use of the extremely astringent rhizomes. Medicinal teas treated bowel disorders, and skin poultices helped stop bleeding and heal cuts, sores, and swellings. For food, they cooked the young leaves and unopened flower buds and fried or parched the oil-rich seeds. The rhizomes of yellow water-lilies can also be eaten after plenty of boiling. Water-lily pollen grains bear sharp, microscopic spikes, sometimes causing irritation to human nasal passages.

Related Old World water-lily and lotus species have carried much religious and symbolic significance throughout history. Water-lily petals decorated the funeral wreaths of Egyptian pharaohs, and various white water-lilies became emblems of purity, virtue, and innocence—the more so because they arise from the slime and mud.

Horticulturists love these plants because the tropical species, especially, hybridize easily, leading to all sorts of color forms and variations for ornamental water gardens. Even native white water-lily has become a popular ornamental, easily transplanted and cultivated in backyard pools.

Water-milfoils *(Myriophyllum* spp.). Water-milfoil family. Submersed herbs in ponds, quiet waters. Recognize water-milfoils by their once-divided, featherlike leaves in flat-planed whorls of four and their dense, weedy growth. Two common species are water-milfoil *(M. exalbescens)* and Eurasian water-milfoil *(M. spicatum)*. Only the slender, reddish flower spike emerges above the water in these two species; some other species, such as *M. heterophyllum,* have small leafy bracts crowding the emergent spike.

Close relatives: Mermaid-weeds *(Proserpinaca).*

Lifestyle: These delicate-appearing plants often form dense, underwater beds. Native water-milfoil usually grows no deeper than three to six feet in marly bottoms of ponds or lakes. Eurasian water-milfoil often roots at depths of eleven to thirteen feet, branching at the water surface in profuse tangles.

The small, four-petaled, wind-pollinated flowers are *protogynous* (that is, the female parts mature before the male parts). Typically the upper flowers on a spike will be in their female earliest phase, the lower ones in their male later phase. After flowering, the spikes fall prostrate on the water. The released nutlets float for a few hours before sinking and may remain dormant in the bottom mud for years. As in most aquatic plants, however, seed reproduction and germination are erratic. The plants reproduce chiefly by vegetative means: from winter buds (native water-milfoil) or stem fragmentation (Eurasian water-milfoil). The very aggressive Eurasian species tends to dominate the underwater flora of any pond or lake within two or three years once it becomes established. All North American populations may be clones of a single plant introduced into Chesapeake Bay (possibly in ship's ballast) late in the last

Water-milfoil grows in dense underwater beds, providing food and shelter for numerous invertebrates. Water birds feed frequently but not heavily upon these plants.

century. Fragments of the plant often develop roots at the stem nodes and quickly crowd out native water plants. Eurasian water-milfoil, in short, is the submersed equivalent of purple loosestrife on land.

In the fall, native water-milfoil produces dense, compact shoots called *turions* at the tips of stems and branches. These leafy, cylindrical winter buds remain attached until the plant decays, then sink to the bottom. Before the ice melts in early spring, they begin elongating and sending out roots. A full-grown, pulled-up plant that has developed from a turion shows a bent, U-shaped base with the old turion leaves still attached. Eurasian water-milfoil produces no turions; it dies back each fall to its root crown.

In high-calcium waters, water-milfoils sometimes precipitate marl.

Associates: *Spring, summer.* Typical plant associates include pondweeds, waterweed, coontail, wild-celery, and naiads. But Eurasian milfoil tends to overwhelm and replace these plants, choking and shading both surface and subsurface areas with dense growth. It also competes with algae for water nutrients. Where this plant occurs, plant diversity suffers.

Rivularia blue-green algae, brownish and slimy, often coat the stems of water-milfoils.

Water-milfoil beds usually harbor abundant invertebrate populations, many of them herbivores and scavengers. These include attached rotifers such as *Melicerta,* threadworms (Nematoda), bristleworms (Oligochaeta) such as *Nais,* crustaceans such as the amphipod *Hyalella,* and numerous insect larvae: burrowing mayflies (Ephemeridae), damselflies (Zygoptera), long-horned caddisflies *(Leptocella),* and midges (Chironomidae), among others. Pond snails such as *Lymnaea* and wheel snails *(Planorbis)* are also frequent feeders.

Bass favor water-milfoil beds for spawning; these are often prime fishing locales.

Virtually all surface-feeding and diving ducks feed to some extent on water-milfoil

Many submersed aquatics produce turions, shown here on water-milfoil. These compact winter buds drop off the plant in late fall, overwinter on the pond bottom, and produce new shoots in spring.

nutlets and foliage, though the presence of even large beds of the plant does not guarantee ample seed production. Water-milfoils are generally taken in small quantities, and the nutlets rank as quite low-grade waterfowl foods. Shorebirds such as dowitchers and some sandpiper species also eat the seeds. Birds probably disperse the plants by their droppings.

Muskrats consume the plant sparingly, as do moose.

Lore: Milfoil means "thousand leaves." Although this foliage hosts few recorded insect pests or parasites, Eurasian water-milfoil is subject to a viruslike disease that, during the 1960s, dramatically reduced the abundance of this invader in Chesapeake Bay, its original North American home. Thus there is hope that self-regulating natural mechanisms, which sooner or later exert controls on all invasive species, are already operating.

Aquatic and irrigation engineers hate Eurasian water-milfoil. It clogs canals and recreational lakes and slows water flow, thus increasing its temperature and consequently altering its chemical balances; it becomes both a symptom and contributing cause of overfertilized waters. Its first appearance in many lakes occurs around marinas and boat landings, indicating that fragments of the plant are dispersed on boats, motors, boat trailers, ropes, anchors, and other equipment. Water-milfoils are popular aquarium plants and have probably been introduced in some areas by dumped aquarium water.

Eurasian water-milfoil has been harvested for experimental use as a soil fertilizer and conditioner and as animal feed, but with limited success.

Water-plantain *(Alisma plantago-aquatica)*. Water-plantain family. Emergent and shoreline herbs of ponds, marshes, ditches, and stream margins. Recognize water-plantain by its long-stalked, broadly oval, parallel-veined leaves and taller flower stalk with whorled branches bearing tiny, white, three-petaled flowers.

Other names: Mad-dog weed, devil's spoons.

Close relatives: Arrowheads *(Sagittaria)*; burheads *(Echinodorus)*. The unrelated true plantains *(Plantago)* occupy their own family.

Lifestyle: Like the related arrowheads, water-plantain adapts its growth form to its aquatic circumstances. In shallow-water habitats, it may develop lax, narrow, ribbonlike leaves and broader floating leaves; in its muddy shoreline habitats, the leaves stand erect.

The inconspicuous flowers, resembling miniature arrowhead flowers, are bisexual and insect pollinated. The male stamens ringing the central stigma point outward, thus minimizing chances of self-fertilization. To obtain nectar droplets at the stamen bases, insects landing on the stigma must subsequently brush against the pollen-bearing anthers. Nutlets are produced in a ringlike head.

The plant rises from perennial tuberlike corms.

Associates: *Summer, fall.* Common plant companions of water-plantain include sedges, arrowheads, pickerel-weed, bur-reeds, and swamp milkweed, among others.

Syrphid flies (Syrphidae) are probably the major pollinators.

Foliage and stem invertebrate feeders are generally the same as for arrowheads (see Arrowhead, Broad-leaved). Water scorpions *(Ranatra)*—brownish, elongated, predatory bugs that resemble walkingsticks—lay eggs in submersed water-plantain stems (and elsewhere). Waterlily leaf beetles *(Donacia)* feed on the subsurface stems (see Water-lilies).

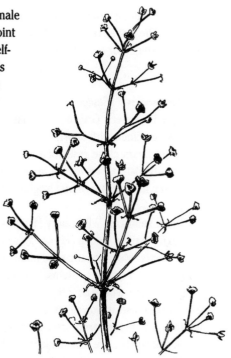

Water-plantain shows a whorled arrangement of branches on its tall flower stalk. This branching pattern repeats as the stems subdivide. The entire flower stalk often resembles an airy pyramid in shape.

Surface-feeding ducks such as mallards, common pintails, blue-winged and green-winged teals, and the diving scaups feed on the seeds to some extent, as do ring-necked pheasants. This plant is not, however, a major food source for wildlife.

Lore: Modern medical research has verified the therapeutic properties and diuretic effects of water-plantain root in kidney and other ailments. American natives knew about these benefits and drank root teas of the plant for urinary disorders and lung ailments. They also used external poultices of the root for bruises and wounds.

Animal experiments with this plant indicate that its medical usages may extend to lowering blood pressure and glucose levels and inhibiting fat storage in the liver. The leaves redden and irritate the skin when rubbed on, sometimes a useful treatment for certain sores or swellings.

Waterweed *(Elodea canadensis).* Frog's-bit family. Submersed herb in ponds, quiet waters. Growing in dense, underwater beds, waterweed has thick, brittle stems lined with short, dark green, translucent leaves in whorls of three. This plant bears close resemblance to the unrelated naiads *(Najas)* in general form, but the latter's leaves are broadened at the base.

Other names: *Anacharis,* frogbit, Canadian pondweed, water-thyme, ditch-moss.

Close relatives: Wild-celery *(Vallisneria americana)*; frog's-bit *(Limnolobium spongia)*; Brazilian elodea *(Egeria densa).*

Lifestyle: Most aquatic seed-plants conduct their sexual processes, at least, above water on emergent stems, but like its close relative wild-celery, waterweed is one of the few whose aquatic habit extends even to waterborne pollination. The flowers are unisexual on separate plants (another rare arrangement in aquatics), and male plants are rarely seen. Fruiting, consequently, is also rare; most water-weeds you will see are female plants that reproduce vegetatively.

Staminate plants, where they occur, produce leaf whorls further apart than those of the female plants, which usually appear quite bushy, especially toward the stem tips. The inconspicuous flowers of both sexes are sheathed by an enfold-ing *spathe.* From the flower spathe rises a long, threadlike tube with the surface-

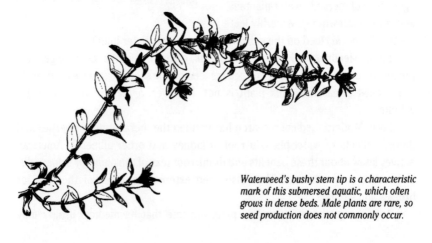

Waterweed's bushy stem tip is a characteristic mark of this submersed aquatic, which often grows in dense beds. Male plants are rare, so seed production does not commonly occur.

floating flower (male or female) at its tip. Pollen released from the male flowers is waterborne by drift to the female flower.

Most waterweed reproduction, however, occurs by fragmentation of the stem, pieces of which give rise to new plants. Rooted plants grow more vigorously, but waterweed does not require rooting to survive. Frequently plants that develop from fragmented stems become floaters, hanging just beneath the surface. Reproduction also occurs from buds *(turions)*. These break off the branch ends, lie on the bottom over winter, and produce new plants in spring. In places where water temperature remains above freezing, however, the entire plant may remain green and thriving (though reproductively dormant) over winter; it is one of the few green water plants to be seen when most other aquatics have died back.

Because of its low fiber content, this plant decomposes more rapidly when dead than most other aquatics. Favoring acid-neutral and mineral-rich waters, it especially thrives where iron sediments are prevalent. This plant's well-known function as a nutrient sink for phosphorus, mercury, and trace metals makes its occurrence a useful indicator of water-enrichment or pollution levels. Usually its presence in human populated areas signifies overfertilized waters. Instances of its rapid, spreading growth followed by sudden declines in abundance are fairly common.

Associates: *Spring, summer, fall.* Where present, waterweed usually dominates or codominates the subsurface plant community. Associates may include coontail, water-milfoils, bladderworts, and pondweeds.

Waterweed typically hosts and supports large numbers of invertebrate organisms; one study ranked it second of twelve submersed plant species in diversity and fourth in abundance of animal life that shelters and feeds here. Especially numerous are rotifers and various crustaceans including water fleas *(Cyclops)* and other copepods, ostracods such as *Cypris,* and amphipods *(Hyalella, Gammarus).* Water mites, insect larvae, and snails *(Physa, Planorbis, Graulus* spp.) are also common.

In some lake and stream areas choked by excessive waterweed growth, the triploid grass carp *(Ctenopharyngoden idella)* has been introduced as a biological control measure. Waterweed is the preferred food of this fish.

The small salamanders called red-spotted newts often lay eggs in the leaf angles (see Stoneworts).

Because of its rare seed production, waterweed ranks relatively low as a waterfowl food plant. Some surface-feeding and diving ducks, however, consume the leafy stems (probably aiding the plant's spread by fragmentation). These include gadwalls, mallards, American wigeons, wood ducks, blue-winged teal, redheads, lesser scaups, and American goldeneyes. Geese and American coots also eat the plant.

Muskrats and beavers feed sparingly on waterweed.

Lore: This plant's high nutrient levels (when harvested from unpolluted waters) and crude protein content (about 30 percent) make it a potential source of livestock and poultry feed. It has been experimentally used as a "salad course" for captive, grain-fed ducks and laying hens.

In a reversal of typical plant movements across the sea, waterweed was imported to Europe from North America about 1850. There it soon became an aggressive nuisance weed, clogging rivers and canals, even though no male plants became established. Here in its native waters, it usually becomes a severe problem only when human-caused physical or chemical disturbances disrupt aquatic environments.

Little record exists of this plant's use by American natives or pioneers. Probably it grew much less abundantly in our lakes and rivers before we began "improving" them for navigation and commerce and using them for sewage disposals.

Waterweed is a favorite aquarium and teaching plant and has been widely used for years in plant physiology and experimental biology classrooms.

Wild-celery *(Vallisneria americana).* Frog's-bit family. Submersed herb. Recognize wild-celery by its long, streaming, tapelike leaves showing a linear, three-zoned appearance; the central zone is greener and more heavily veined than the more transparent edge zones.

Other names: Tape-grass, eelgrass (also a name for the marine pondweed *Zostera marina,* which occupies seacoast areas).

Close relatives: Waterweed *(Elodea canadensis);* frog's-bit *(Limnolobium spongia);* Brazilian elodea *(Egeria densa).* Wild-celery is unrelated to celery *(Apium graveolens),* a member of the parsley family.

Lifestyle: Other submersed plants with flowing, ribbonlike leaves are bur-reeds *(Sparganium)* and the underwater leaves of arrowheads *(Sagittaria),* but the leaf vein patterns in these plants are different. Ordinarily, wild-celery grows rooted in the shallows (one to five feet) of lakes and creeks, but it can occupy depths of twenty feet or more. It favors sluggish currents and sandy or coarse-silt bottoms.

Plant leaves adapt, in both structure and form, to the medium (air or water) in which they function as energy producers and converters. Submersed plants display some typical forms; long, flexible wild-celery exemplifies one of them. The high surface-to-volume ratio of its leaf permits a greater exchange of gases between water and plant tissue than would be true if the proportions were reversed, as in many aerial leaves.

In aerial plants, the plant "skin," or epidermis, is mainly protective tissue; in submersed aquatics, however, the epidermis is very thin, allowing the absorption of gases directly through the cell walls. Some botanists believe that finely divided aquatic leaves (as in water-milfoils) are best adapted to quiet waters, and broader, flat leaves (as in wild-celery) are better adapted to running water. Experiments have demonstrated that both types are about equally efficient in gaseous exchange. Submersed leaves have no need of strong supporting tissues; removed from the water, the plants collapse. Since the plant's water medium is also its nutrient solution, the root system that serves in land plants to absorb and conduct nutrients is, in this case, mainly an anchorage to hold the plant in place.

Wild-celery flowers are unisexual on separate, cloning plants. Greenish female flowers, borne singly, float on the water surface at the tips of long, corkscrew stems. On male plants, flower clusters develop at the submersed base of the plant, then detach and rise to the surface. There they open, sometimes forming a thick surface "scum." Writes botanist Edward G. Voss, "The staminate [male] flowers drift upon the surface . . . and when one reaches the dimple formed by a pistillate [female] flower at the surface, it slides quickly to it and pollination occurs—barely above the surface of the water." Once pollinated in this fashion, the female stem coils and contracts, pulling the maturing fruit down into the water (as in water-lilies).

Wild-celery's most effective reproduction, however, occurs vegetatively from tuberous tips of the spreading rhizomes.

Associates: *Spring, summer.* Other plants of the submersed vegetation zone where wild-celery grows often include pondweeds, water-milfoils, waterweed, naiads, and stoneworts *(Chara)*.

One investigator found that, of seven submersed plant species, *Vallisneria* was the one least populated by aquatic animals such as rotifers, crustaceans, and mollusks—presumably because its flat leaf surfaces provide little protection.

The female wild-celery flower forms a dimple in the water surface, to which gravity brings the detached, floating male flowers. This pollination system is unique among American aquatic plants.

Caddisfly larvae *(Leptocerus, Triaenodes)* are sometimes numerous on this plant.

Several species of case-bearing pyralid moth caterpillars feed on wild-celery and other aquatic plants. These larvae construct protective cases from plant parts. Genera include *Monroessa, Synclita,* and *Parapoynx.*

Wild-celery is one of the major food plants for waterfowl, both diving ducks and surface feeders. They relish all parts of the plant, especially the tuberous growing tips of the rhizome. Foremost feeders include swans, scoters, redheads, ring-necked ducks, scaups, common goldeneyes, buffleheads, ruddy ducks, and American coots (a rail). The canvasback duck is so associated with this food plant that its Latin specific name *(Aythya valisineria)* refers to wild-celery. Surface feeders such as American black ducks, mallards, common pintails, American wigeons, wood ducks, and green-winged teal often feed on fragments of the plant uprooted by their diving-duck cousins.

Lore: In *Natural Theology* (1802), William Paley cited *Vallisneria*'s elaborate pollination mechanism as sure evidence of God's creative handiwork. Paley was unaware that seed reproduction in this plant ranks distinctly second to vegetative reproduction, its foremost means.

For some reason, not many guidebooks to wild foods bother to list *Vallisneria*. Leaves and rhizomes are, in fact, edible either raw or cooked. These days, however, even many of our so-called clean lakes and streams harbor unseen chemical or residual pollution in their soils and muds (much of it deposited by air). Use caution in collecting any aquatic plant to eat.

Vallisneria makes an excellent aquarium plant, providing abundant oxygen for fishes and other organisms.

Wild-rice *(Zizania aquatica).* Grass family. Tall herb in shallow margins of streams, lakes, ponds. Recognize this grass by its height (up to ten feet); its wide, lance-shaped leaves; and its sexually divided, yellow-green flower clusters. Female flowers hug erect, broomlike *panicles* atop the stem; male flowers dangle from spreading side branches beneath the female cluster.

Other names: Water-oats, Indian-rice, Canadian rice.

Close relatives: All other grasses. The related cereal grass *Oryza sativa* is commercial white rice.

Lifestyle: This beautiful grass, tall yet delicate, is a lingering remnant of America's wilderness wetlands, an unmistakable sight along isolated watercourses or backcountry lakes. It does not tolerate the disturbances of dredging, bank "improvement," or shifting water levels.

Unisexual, wind-pollinated flowers appear on vertically zoned sections of the upper stem. The subordinate position of male flowers on the stem probably reduces the chances of self-pollination. Male flowers last only a few hours; opening in the morning, they shed an abundance of yellow pollen, then drop. The pollinated female flowers atop the plant produce long, rodlike seeds that ripen from the top of the stalk downward. Only about 10 percent of the fruiting head matures at a time, and ripened grains immediately fall off the plant. Fruiting occurs in late August and early September. Because this grass is an annual, it depends exclusively on its yearly seed crop for its persistence in any area.

Wild-rice requires some degree of water movement, even a slight current; it does not grow where water is stagnant. It favors soft, muddy shallows with water from a few inches to five feet deep where competition from other plants is mini-

mal. The plants seldom emerge above water before mid-June, then increase rapidly in height.

Associates: *Summer, fall.* In habitats where it thrives, wild-rice usually occurs in dense "water meadows" of uniform stands. Cattails, bulrushes, rushes, pondweeds, and other aquatics may border these areas.

Wild-rice colonies occasionally become infected with ergot *(Claviceps)*, a dangerously toxic sac fungus. This pink or purplish parasite grows in the flower ovaries, eventually replacing and mimicking, to some extent, the seed.

Insect feeders on wild-rice are relatively few. Rice water weevils *(Lissorhoptrus oryzophilus)* feed as larvae on the roots of young plants; as adult marsh weevils, these beetles feed on the leaves.

Feeders on submersed leaves and stems may include larvae of large caddisflies *(Banksiola salina)* and trumpet-net caddisflies *(Nyctiophylax vestitus)*.

Although insects do not pollinate this plant, pollen collectors may forage in the male flowers. Bumblebees *(Bombus)* have been so observed.

Carp sometimes uproot and consume the seedling plants.

Wild-rice is a major wildlife food plant, primarily for waterfowl and songbird seedeaters. Probably its importance has been somewhat overrated, however, in view of the plant's relatively local occurrence and the brief seasonal availability of its seeds.

Despite appearances, the lower branches of this wild-rice plant are loaded not with rice grains but with male flowers. Female flowers in the erect, topmost cluster produce the rice, which birds relish and gourmets prize.

Almost every North American duck species as well as Canada and snow geese relish the highly nutritious grains. American coots; common moorhens; black, sora, Virginia, and yellow rails; and northern bobwhites are also heavy consumers. Among songbirds, a major feeder is the bobolink. Flocks of these, plus red-winged and rusty blackbirds, bring the wild-rice marshes alive with noisy activity in late summer and early fall. Song sparrows also feed here in abundance.

Ducks and coots frequently use wild-rice stands for autumn cover as well.

Mammal feeders relish the whole plant. Indeed, overpopulations of muskrat sometimes destroy entire small stands of wild-rice in spring and early summer. White-tailed deer and moose also feed on the plant.

Lore: Wild-rice provided a major food source for Indians (particularly the Chippewas and Menominees) of the Great Lakes region—about one-quarter of their total caloric diet. (The name Menominee means *wild-rice people*). Tribal wars between Chippewa and Sioux disputed possession of the northern rice lakes before European settlement. Wild-rice remains an important food and income source for the Chippewas, who often farm it in diked and flooded paddies.

The traditional harvesting method was a canoe poled through the wild-rice beds. The "ricer" in the canoe flailed grains from the seed heads by bending the stalks inward and tapping ripened grains into the bottom of the boat. A two-person team of skilled harvesters could collect 350 pounds of wild-rice per day. (Native wild-rice stands produce about 40 pounds of rice per acre; cultivated paddies may yield 300 pounds per acre.) After collection, the grains were spread and dried, then parched in kettles, pounded to loosen the hulls, and finally winnowed and stored. The rice was eaten parched or boiled, usually mixed with vegetables, meat, or maple sugar.

Today commercial processing for wild-rice uses essentially the same methods, albeit with modern harvesting machinery, conveyors, gas burners, screening and grading devices, and threshers. Despite numerous experimental efforts, wild-rice cultivation still produces notoriously unreliable harvests. The processed rice is expensively sold as a gourmet food. Traditional methods of wild-rice harvesting on public lands are stiffly regulated; in some areas, only local Indian communities are permitted to "rice."

Because wild-rice produces a *shattering* type of grain (that is, it falls off the stalk when ripe) and because the grains on a plant only mature at successive intervals, both traditional and commercial harvesting involves repeated visits to the rice marshes in order to glean the standing crop.

Minnesota produces most of the commercial crop, but Manitoba, Ontario, and Wisconsin also rank high in wild-rice production. Without genetic tinkering to increase yields, wild-rice will never become a common supermarket item. To many of us, that's just fine. A stand of tall, native wild-rice in its wetland habitat bears a wilderness mystique that no amount of gourmet cereal can replace.

Willow, Black *(Salix nigra).* Willow family. Tree or shrub in lowland borders of streams, lakes, swamps. Recognize tree-size black willow by its often massive, slanting or forked trunk; its heavy, black, deeply fissured, sometimes shaggy bark; its disheveled, bushy crown; its long, narrow, fine-toothed leaves with rounded bases and often curved tips; and its catkin flowers.

Other names: Swamp willow, Goodding willow, Dudley willow, southwestern black willow.

Close relatives: Shrub willows *(Salix)*; poplars *(Populus)*.

Lifestyle: A huge, black-barked tree slanting out over the water from a shoreline bank is most likely North America's largest native willow, the black. The trunk and branches are usually crowded with erect shoots and suckers, giving the tree a messy, tangled appearance, especially after its leaves drop in the fall. Its trunk may measure three or more feet across, though the tree commonly reaches only forty to fifty feet in height. It grows quickly, maturing in about fifty years and usually dying in less than eighty-five. Young branches are brittle at the base, easily broken off by wind and ice. These fragments sprout prolifically if deposited by water on a muddy bank; this accounts for much of the tree's wide dispersion along watercourses. Black willow thrives just at or slightly above water level. Flooding and silting do not disturb it.

Black willow is shade intolerant and does not compete well in the shadow of other plants or even of other black willows. Unless new sediment is deposited, the tree rarely succeeds itself. Thus most black willows are solitary or even-aged trees that began as pioneers in fresh silt. Seed crops begin when the tree is about ten years old and are abundant almost every year, but the seed dries out quickly. Unless floating on water, it must reach a moist, exposed seedbed within twenty-four hours in order to germinate. Thoreau observed that along rivers, black willows usually occupy the concave or inner-meander shoreline.

This is one of the first trees to flower in spring, usually at the same time its new leaves emerge. The unisexual catkins appear on separate trees and are pollinated by both insects and wind. Willow flowers are of the "brush-pollination" type, whereby insects receive and deposit pollen by means of direct bodily contact with the flower's sex organs (in contrast to explosive or other pollination mechanisms). Cone-shaped seed capsules, ripe by early summer, release thousands of silky-plumed seeds that ride the winds. Most of them dry out and die— even those that eventually reach suitable germination habitats. So the tree's abundant seeding is probably a much less efficient means of reproduction, on the whole, than its prolific sprouting from cast-off twigs and branches.

Associates: Black willow and sandbar willow, a shrub species, often become established together in the same locales, but the shrub is usually shaded out as the tree enlarges. The related eastern cottonwood, similar in its habitat needs, typically associates with black willow along river bottomlands. Other associates may include silver maple, red-osier dogwood, buttonbush, and various shrub willows.

Spring, summer. A yellowish, coral-like fungus on dead or decaying willow is probably the crown coral mushroom *(Clavicorona pyxidata)*.

Insect pollinators are usually pollen-collecting bees, including bumblebees *(Bombus)*, honeybees *(Apis mellifera)*, and various solitary ground-nesting bees (Andrenidae, Halictidae).

Pollen-eating beetles often found in the flowers include false darkling beetles *(Asclera)*, black and orange with long antennae, and punctate leaf beetles *(Orsodacne atra)*, variably black or brown.

A huge number of insects forage on black and shrub willow leaves. Relatively few, however, are totally exclusive to willows; many of them feed also on the related poplars (see *The Book of Forest and Thicket*) and other trees. What follows is a highly selective focus on some of the most common, readily seen willow foliage feeders.

Willow lacebugs *(Corythucha salicis)*, whitish with brown spots, suck sap from leaf undersides.

Beetle feeders include the willow leaf beetle *(Chrysomela interrupta)*, yellow with black markings; the spotted willow leaf beetle *(Lina interrupta)*, reddish with black spots; and the imported willow or shining leaf beetle *(Plagiodera versicolora)*, metallic blue or green in color. Adult beetles eat holes in the leaves; the more voracious larvae skeletonize them. Cottonwood leaf beetles *(Chrysomela scripta)*, flea beetles (Alticinae), and flea weevils *(Rhynchaenus)* likewise feed on the leaves. Flea beetles chew "shot holes" in the leaves, and flea weevils also mine in the leaves; both are flealike jumpers. Japanese beetles *(Popillia japonica)*, feeding en masse, ravenously skeletonize the leaves.

Common butterfly caterpillars on willows include the tortoise shells: Compton tortoise shell *(Nymphalis j-album)*, Milbert's tortoise shell *(N. milberti)*, and

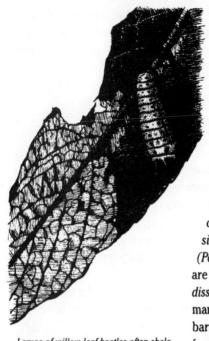

the mourning cloak *(N. antiopa)*. All feed in massed colonies, and all show bristly spines. Viceroy *(Limenitis archippus)*, white admiral or banded purple *(L. arthemis)*, and red-spotted purple (a subspecies of the latter) are solitary feeders, curiously humped and grotesque in form.

Moth caterpillars are legion on willows. They include several sphinx moths, identified by a projecting rear horn; one-eyed sphinx *(Smerinthus cerisyi)*, twin-spotted sphinx *(S. jamaicensis)*, and big poplar or modest sphinx *(Pachysphinx modesta)* are fairly common, as are forest tent moth caterpillars *(Malacosoma disstria)*. Noctuid caterpillar feeders include many dagger moths *(Acronicta)*; the pink-barred sallow *(Xanthia togata)*, which also feeds on the catkins; the herald *(Scoliopteryx libatrix)*; and many underwings *(Catocala)*.

Larvae of willow leaf beetles often skeletonize willow foliage, which hosts an abundance of voracious insect feeders.

Several tussock moths *(Dasychira, Orgyia)* and a notorious pest of many trees, the gypsy moth *(Lymantria dispar;* see Oaks), are also common feeders, as are many inchworm caterpillars (Geometridae). A leaf blotch miner caterpillar *(Micrurapteryx salicifoliella)* forms characteristic blotch mines in the leaves.

Leaf galls, created by midges and sawflies, are extremely common on willow leaves (see Willows, Shrub).

Willow sawfly larvae *(Nematus ventralis)*, which resemble black and yellow-spotted caterpillars, feed in masses; where abundant, they may defoliate willows.

Willow twigs and branches also host specialized feeders. In summer, giant willow aphids *(Clavigerus smithiae)* are common gregarious sap-suckers. Two of the many common scale insects on willows include the oystershell scale *(Lepidosaphes ulmi)* and the willow scale *(Chionaspis salicis-nigrae)*.

Several long-horned beetles bore into unhealthy or damaged trees. These insects include the willow-branch borer *(Oberea ferruginea)* and the cottonwood borer *(Plectrodera scalator)*; the latter may girdle tree bases. Willow scab or blight *(Pollaccia saliciperda)*, a fungus transmitted by these borers, causes leaves to turn black and die and often kills trees (if borers are present, however, the tree is probably dying anyway).

Black willow is a favored tree of beavers, often cut down by these animals where it is present.

Most birds and mammals that feed on the sometimes more accessible buds, twigs, and foliage of smaller willows also feed on black willow (see Willows, Shrub). Yellow-bellied sapsuckers create horizontal rows of pitted holes in the bark of this tree (among others), where they return at intervals to feed on exuding sap.

Fall, winter. A host of gall insects signify their presence by variously shaped growths on willow twigs and young stems (see Willows, Shrub). Galls are easiest to observe after the foliage drops in the fall.

All year. Though more resistant to cytospora canker than other tree willows, black willow shows occasional evidence of this fungous infection. *Cytospora chrysosperma* causes elongate cankers on branches and trunks. Another canker fungus, *Phytophthora cactorum,* causes slimy, "bleeding" lesions on the lower trunk.

Lore: The glucoside salicin, first isolated from willow bark in 1829, long provided the basic pain-killing ingredient of aspirin (it still does, but is now synthesized by chemical technology). American natives knew the beneficial properties of willow bark. Extremely bitter and astringent, it was brewed as teas and tonics for a variety of internal ailments—and, as washes and poultices, for almost any external sore or rash as well. Many tribes used the shaved bark as a tobacco substitute and the wood fibers for making cordage, fish nets, and bags.

One prescription of frontier doctors was a decoction of willow twigs and buds "to suppress sexual desire"; and its general use as an antiaphrodisiac was an apparently popular early form of birth control.

Because of its size, black willow is the only commercially useful willow. Its light, weak, split-resistant wood usually goes into crating and box construction. At one time it was the wood of choice for artificial limbs, and it is said to make the best polo balls. It is also harvested in some areas for pulpwood. One of black willow's most valuable uses, however, is for erosion control. Its shallow, fibrous roots help stabilize the banks of streams and ditches, especially those subject to flooding.

Weeping willow *(S. babylonica)*, native to western China, has become a popular yard and shade tree. Its gracefully drooping branchlets shed profusely, however, and the tree often suffers ice damage. Female trees are rare in North America, but male trees sprout prolific clones.

Willow-herbs *(Epilobium* spp.). Evening-primrose family. Herbs in various wet and dry habitats. Recognize willow-herbs by their four-petaled, magenta or lilac-colored flowers blooming from midsummer to fall and their long, erect seedpods.

Common wetland species include downy willow-herb *(E. strictum)*, with white-downy, opposite, linear leaves and tiny flowers; great hairy willow-herb *(E. hirsutum)*, with hairy stem, bushy aspect, opposite or alternate toothed leaves, and large flowers; northern willow-herb *(E. ciliatum)*, with slightly toothed, mostly opposite leaves and small flowers; and purple-leaved willow-herb *(E. coloratum)*, with narrow, toothed, opposite leaves often marked with purple, a purple stem, and tiny flowers.

Other names: Fireweed, rosebay, purple rocket, Indian wickup, herb wickopy, pigweed, blooming sally, French willow-herb, firetop.

Close relatives: Fireweed *(E. angustifolium)*; false loosestrifes *(Ludwigia)*; primrose-willows *(Jussiaea)*; evening-primroses *(Oenothera)*; gauras *(Gaura)*; enchanter's-nightshades *(Circaea)*. Willow-herbs are unrelated to willows *(Salix)*.

Lifestyle: Long pods ending with four-petaled pink or purplish flowers blooming along watercourses in summer and fall are sure to be willow-herbs. The seedpods eventually split, spilling masses of silk that carry the seeds far and wide. Some ten species of willow-herbs, most of them wetland dwellers, reside in east-central North America. Great hairy willow-herb is a Eurasian species that often spreads in disturbed wetland sites, but the other common species are native.

The bisexual, insect-pollinated flowers have a central, stalked, cross-shaped stigma, which projects beyond the circle of pollen-bearing anthers, thus aiding cross-fertilization. Failing insect pollination, however, the stigma lobes curl backward, touching the anthers, and the flower self-pollinates.

These plants also reproduce from slender rhizomes that creep underground, thus creating clonal colonies. Willow-herbs require lots of sunlight and do not thrive in shade.

Associates: *Summer, fall.* Willow-herbs adorn streambanks and wet soils with late-season color. Look for them in association with sedges, swamp thistle, turtlehead, purple loosestrife, northern white cedar, and tamarack, among others.

Pollinators are chiefly bees.

Several moth caterpillars forage on willow-herbs. Large, green, rear-horned caterpillars are sphinx moths, probably the white-lined sphinx *(Hyles lineata)* or galium sphinx *(H. galli)*. The pearly wood-nymph *(Eudryas unio)*, a noctuid forester moth, is also common; brightly patterned adult moths at rest resemble bird droppings. Inchworm moth caterpillars include the black-banded carpet *(Eustroma semiatrata)*, the small phoenix *(Ecliptopera silaceata)*, the double-banded carpet *(Spargania magnoliata)*, and the many-lined carpet *(Anticlea multiferata)*.

Willow-herbs have little importance as wildlife food plants. White-tailed deer and moose probably eat them to some extent.

Lore: Young shoots of willow-herbs are edible (cooked) if not choice; the plants are bitter tasting, though the leaves make a suitable tea. American natives used the plants medicinally—mainly externally as leaf and root poultices for sores and skin abrasions. Some tribes considered the tea an effective remedy for intestinal ailments as well.

Feathery masses of silk are familiar sights along watercourses in autumn as willow-herb pods split open (left). At the same time, new rosettes sprouting at stem bases herald renewed growth from the rhizome the following spring.

Willows, Shrub *(Salix* spp.). Willow family. Shrubs in various wet and dry habitats. Most shrub willows occur in cloning thickets and have long, narrow, toothed leaves. Willow flowers, emerging in early spring, are catkins.

About thirty shrub willow species occur in east-central North America. Most of them reside in, or marginal to, wetlands, but a few favor upland habitats. Because of individual variation, obscure identity marks, and considerable hybridizing between them, identifying species of shrub willow is often difficult, even for professional botanists. ("The more I study willows, the more I am confused," confessed Thoreau.) Some of the more common species (or variations thereof) include the following:

Sandbar or long-leaved willow *(S. exigua)* frequently occurs on river sandbars, sandy banks, and along roadside ditches and pond margins. Bog willow *(S. pedicellaris)*, seldom growing more than three feet tall, mainly inhabits sphagnum bogs. Basket or purple-osier willow *(S. purpurea)*, appearing on shorelines and streambanks, shows a distinctive purplish cast to the foliage; its almost opposite leaves are toothed only near the tip. Sage or hoary willow *(S. candida)*, growing in swamps and fens, bears untoothed leaves with white-woolly undersides—an easily recognized species. Beaked or Bebb's willow *(S. bebbiana)*, showing wider leaves than most willows, frequents almost any nonacidic wetland habitat. Pussy or glaucous willow *(S. discolor)*, also wide-leaved, favors damp or wet sites, as does peach-leaved or almond-leaved willow *(S. amygdaloides)*, which has leathery, long-pointed leaves.

These seven common species are among many other, generally less common wetland shrub willows. Consult shrub identification manuals for detailed keys describing the particular features of each species.

Other names: Osiers, sallows.

Close relatives: Tree willows *(Salix)*; poplars *(Populus)*.

Lifestyle: Shrub willow thickets screen almost every ditch and lowland pool and clothe sandy river deposits and shorelines with flexible, withelike stems. Most shrub willows branch upward. Multistemmed clones usually arise in clumps from roots or branch fragments that have rooted. Often where water levels fluctuate, stems sprout adventitious roots below the high-water mark, and these roots remain after the level drops.

The catkin flowers of many species emerge before or along with the leaves in early spring. Catkins are unisexual on different clones and are pollinated mainly by insects but also by wind. The familiar felted tufts of pussy willow, one of spring's best-known harbingers, are the catkins of this shrub (which, after it flowers, few people notice). Catkins of all species, however, are more or less fuzzy, at least in their early stages. The silky-haired seeds are produced in capsules, which split and release their contents to be dispersed by the wind. Willow seeds are extremely short-lived and must germinate quickly if at all (see Willow, Black).

Shrub willows are shallow rooted, grow quickly (up to seven feet in a single year), and are shade intolerant. They easily withstand flooding and silting. Having stabilized the marginal banks and shorelines of a watercourse, enabling other plants to become established, they quickly die out, unable to compete for sunlight and space. Shrub willows are thus frontline plants, setting the stage, as it were, for subsequent plant succession.

Associates: Common tree and shrub associates of shrub willows include black willow, eastern cottonwood, speckled alder, buttonbush, and red-osier and silky dogwoods.

Spring, summer. In some wetlands, up to six different shrub willow species may grow in close proximity, a situation that accounts for much of the hybridizing that occurs among shrub willows. Some of these species, however, flower earlier than others, thus reducing the total chances for hybridizing. Beaked and pussy willows, for example, flower early in spring; sandbar and peach-leaved willows flower some weeks later.

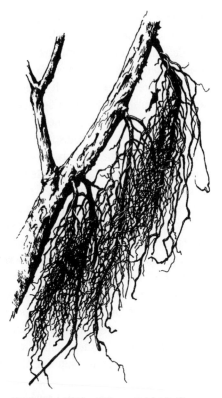

The presence of adventitious roots along willow stems indicates fluctuating water levels. Such "stem rooting" is often seen on alder and buttonbush stems, as well.

Plant associates may include sensitive fern, meadowsweet, blue-joint grass, and bugleweeds, among others.

Pollen-collecting insects forage on the male catkins, occasionally alighting on and pollinating the female catkins. Chief among them are andrenid bees (Andrenidae), bumblebees *(Bombus)*, honeybees *(Apis mellifera)*, and syrphid flies (Syrphidae). Pussy willow, for one, produces abundant pollen and nectar, and foraging ants often climb to the flowers.

Numerous foliage- and catkin-feeding insects are generally the same as for black willow (see Willow, Black). Like the closely related poplars, willows produce phenolic glycosides in their leaves, apparently in direct response to insect attack. These toxins do not stop all leaf-eaters (indeed, they seem to attract some), but they reduce their variety and abundance and probably influence distribution of the insects themselves.

Caterpillars of two hairstreak butterflies seem to favor shrub willow foliage. Acadian hairstreak *(Strymon acadica)* and the less common striped hairstreak *(S. liparops)* caterpillars are both green with yellowish markings. Watch for the small, brownish adult butterflies, showing hairlike tails on their hindwings, around shrub willows in summer.

Green, yellow, and reddish blisters or round swellings on the leaves are produced by several species of larval gall gnats and sawflies. The gall gnat *Oligotropus salicifolius* creates red-spotted willow blister galls on leaf undersides; *Trishormomyia verruca* produces the similar willow-lipped gall. Some sixteen species of tiny sawfly larvae *(Pontania, Euura)* cause most of the round, flat, and conical leaf galls on willows. Willow pea galls on leaf undersides, created by *P. pisum,* and willow apple galls *(P. pomum)* are two of the most frequent. *Eriophyes* mites produce small capsules or "pocket galls" on the leaves. The willow pod midge *(Dasyneura salicifolia)* makes podlike swellings. Tightly rolled end-leaves indicate the work of another midge larva, *Rhabdophaga plicta.*

A few birds favor willow thickets for nesting. Northern harriers, willow and alder flycatchers, gray catbirds, Wilson's warblers, yellow warblers, and American goldfinches build their distinctive nests in these shrubs, often using more than a single stem for nest support. Many waterfowl and marsh birds also use willow thickets for cover.

Mammal foliage and twig browsers include white-tailed deer, elk, and moose.

Fall, winter. Willows rank with goldenrods, roses, and oaks for abundance and variety of insect galls on twigs and stems. Galls are plants' responses to larval insect feeding in plant tissues. Rare is the shrub willow that doesn't show at least one or two galls, whose forms distinctively identify their makers. Though galls are mainly produced during spring and summer, when insects are active, they become easier to observe after the leaves drop. They usually persist on the shrub over winter and longer.

Most willow stem and twig galls are caused by only two genera of gall gnat larvae *(Phytophaga, Rhabdophaga).* Tip deformities result from bud infestation. Inch-long beaked willow galls, resembling black, sharp-pointed beaks at branch tips, indicate *P. rigidae.* Rosette galls on stem tips include the familiar pine-cone gall; its conelike shape and smooth, overlapping scales suggest a seed-cone mimicry. Its maker is *R. strobiloides.* Gall gnats *(R. brassicoides)* also produce willow-cabbage galls, leafy bunches that resemble woody flowers atop stems. Large,

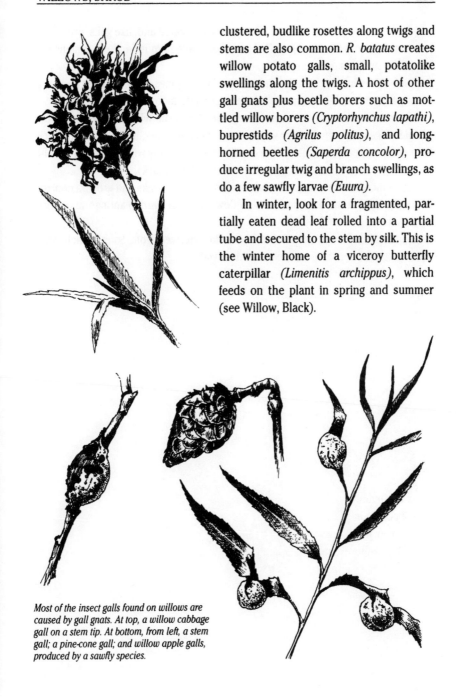

clustered, budlike rosettes along twigs and stems are also common. *R. batatus* creates willow potato galls, small, potatolike swellings along the twigs. A host of other gall gnats plus beetle borers such as mottled willow borers *(Cryptorhynchus lapathi)*, buprestids *(Agrilus politus)*, and longhorned beetles *(Saperda concolor)*, produce irregular twig and branch swellings, as do a few sawfly larvae *(Euura)*.

In winter, look for a fragmented, partially eaten dead leaf rolled into a partial tube and secured to the stem by silk. This is the winter home of a viceroy butterfly caterpillar *(Limenitis archippus)*, which feeds on the plant in spring and summer (see Willow, Black).

Most of the insect galls found on willows are caused by gall gnats. At top, a willow cabbage gall on a stem tip. At bottom, from left, a stem gall; a pine-cone gall; and willow apple galls, produced by a sawfly species.

Nests of the aforementioned birds are now vacated and, like galls, are easier seen on the shrubs in winter. Ruffed and sharp-tailed grouse and ptarmigans relish willow buds, as do squirrels.

Snowshoe hares, cottontail rabbits, and porcupines gnaw the bark and crop off twigs in winter. Muskrats, white-tailed deer, and moose also nip off twigs.

Lore: American natives found many uses for shrub willows. They wove the pliable twigs and branches for wicker items such as mats, baskets, and cradles. For medicinal teas and tonics, they apparently used many willow species with little attempt to distinguish between them (see Willow, Black).

All willows make good soil binders for stabilizing banks and erosion control. Probably the foremost ornamental willow, used in yard plantings and floral arrangements, is pussy willow.

The old-fashioned common name *sallow* derived from *Salix,* which originated from the Celtic *sal-lis,* meaning "near water."

Glossary

Achene. A one-seeded, dry fruit that does not split open along suture lines; the typical seed form of many wetland plants.

Adaptation. An evolved process, structure, or activity by which an organism becomes apparently better suited to its habitat or environment, or for particular functions.

Adaptive. Refers to any feature or characteristic of an organism that aids its ability to survive in its environment.

Adventitious roots. Roots occurring in unusual locations on the plant, usually from the stem in shrubs exposed to flooding, as in alders and willows.

Allelopathy. One organism's inhibition of another by secreted chemicals.

Alternation of generations. The reproductive scheme of nonflowering plants (mosses, ferns), whereby the sexual generation alternates with an asexual generation.

Anther. The pollen-bearing part of a stamen.

Aposematic coloration. Warning or threatening colors or patterns associated with poisonous organisms, as in the monarch butterfly.

Berry. A pulpy or fleshy fruit with seeds embedded in the pulp, as in blueberries.

Bisexual flower. A flower having both male and female sex organs; also called a perfect flower.

Bog. A wetland ecosystem characterized by high acidity and accumulation of peat. Some authors more broadly define it as any wet peatland.

Calciphile. A plant favoring soil or water high in calcium, as northern white cedar and most sedges and fen vegetation.

Catkin. A spikelike cluster of unisexual flowers that falls as a whole, as in alders and willows.

Cleistogamy. The process of self-pollination in certain subordinate or inconspicuous flowers that remain closed, as in jewelweeds.

Clone. A plant or group of plants produced by vegetative reproduction and carrying the same genetic makeup as its parent.

Coaction. An interaction between two or more organisms.

Commensalism. A form of symbiosis in which one partner benefits and neither is harmed.

Conjugation. In algae reproduction, the sexual union of two cells.

Drupe. A fleshy fruit with a hard or stony pit, as in dogwoods, hollies, and poison sumac.

Emergent. An aquatic plant with parts emerging above the water surface, as bulrushes, pickerel-weed, and smartweeds.

Epicormic branching. Small, stunted branches arising on a stem or trunk, often occurring as a compensatory result of unusual stress on the plant.

Epiphyte. A plant growing on another plant, using it as support but deriving no nourishment from it, as algae on submersed aquatics.

Eutrophic. Refers to waters rich in minerals and nutrients but low in dissolved oxygen, a condition resulting from high rates of organic decomposition; overfertilized.

Fen. A wetland ecosystem characterized by abundant nutrient inflow, low acidity, and the accumulation of peat; an alkaline bog.

Fission. In algae reproduction, the asexual division of a cell into two or more parts.

Follicle. A dry fruit that splits open by valves or slits along one side, as in meadowsweet.

Fragmentation. A method of vegetative reproduction in which a broken-off plant part produces a new plant, as in many submersed aquatics and willows.

Gall. A localized growth on a plant induced by a fungus or by egg-laying or feeding of certain mites and insect larvae, especially aphids, gall gnats, and gall wasps.

Gametophyte. In plants exhibiting alternation of generations, the plant produced by a spore and giving rise to male and female sex cells, which produce an asexual spore-bearing plant.

Habitat. The total set of environmental conditions in which an organism exists.

Herb. Any nonwoody plant (excluding fungi) whose aboveground parts die back each year.

Herbivore. Any animal that feeds on plants.

Hybrid. The offspring of a cross between two different though closely related species; usually this offspring cannot itself reproduce.

Hydroperiod. In wetlands, the portion of the year that soils are flooded or saturated.

Inquiline. An organism of one species that inhabits the nest or abode of another, such as nongallmaking insects that occupy galls.

Irruption. A sudden, temporary increase in population abundance and size, as in outbreaks of gypsy moths.

Layering. A method of vegetative reproduction in which an attached, buried branch develops its own roots and shoots, as in black spruce.

Marl. A soil deposit consisting chiefly of calcium carbonate precipitated in water by stoneworts, certain other algae, and some plankton.

Marsh. A wetland ecosystem dominated by grasslike vegetation.

Mesic. Refers to a habitat or environment of medium moisture, one that is not extremely dry or wet.

Microhabitat. A subdivision of a habitat, such as a stump, small pool, or moss bed, to which certain organisms may become specifically adapted.

Mimicry. The evolved adaptive resemblance of one species to an unrelated species or to inorganic material (as in certain moth resemblances to bird droppings).

Mycorrhiza. The symbiotic relationship of a subsurface fungus with vascular plant roots. The fungus aids, and in many cases is vital to, nutrient absorption by the roots.

Nectar guides. Colored lines or markings on flower petals or sepals, believed to aid alighting insects in finding the flower nectaries.

Parasite. Any organism living on or in another living organism from which it derives nourishment, as dodder on jewelweed and eastern mistletoe on black spruce.

Peat. Accumulations of partially decomposed vegetation, mainly sphagnum mosses in bogs, sedges in fens.

Photosynthesis. The process by which green plants manufacture sugars from carbon dioxide, water, and light energy.

Phytoplankton. Microscopic, free-floating plants in water.

Pistil. The female seed-bearing flower organ, consisting of ovary, style, and stigma.

Pome. A fleshy fruit with a papery core, as in chokeberries.

Protandry. Sex sequencing in a bisexual flower in which the male parts mature and decline before the female parts mature.

Protogyny. Sex sequencing in a bisexual flower in which the female parts mature and decline before the male parts mature.

Rhizome. An underground, rootlike stem that produces roots and aerial stems.

Samara. A dry, winged fruit that does not split open along suture lines, as in ashes and maples.

Saprophyte. A plant that obtains its nourishment from dead or decaying organic matter, as most fungi.

Shrub-carr. A wetland thicket dominated by tall shrub vegetation.

Spore. A one-celled, asexual, reproductive organ borne on sporophytes; spores produce sexual gametophytes.

Sporophyte. In plants exhibiting alternation of generations, the spore-producing plant that grows from a gametophyte.

Stamen. The male pollen-bearing organ of a flower, consisting of anther and filament.

Stigma. The pollen-receiving part of the female flower pistil.

Stolon. A horizontal stem on the ground surface, giving rise to roots and shoots along its length, as in many grasses.

Swamp. A wetland containing woody growth.

Symbiosis. Any intimate coaction between different organisms; includes parasitism, commensalism, and mutualism.

Turion. On many submersed plants, a winter bud that detaches, overwinters, and produces a new plant in spring.

Tussock. A compact, densely tufted growth form bearing many stems from a matlike crown, as in cotton-grasses and tussock sedge.

Umbel. An umbrellalike flower cluster with flower stalks radiating from the same point, as in most parsley family plants.

Unisexual flower. A flower having either male or female sex organs, but not both. Dioecious plants bear each sex on different individuals; monoecious plants bear each sex separately on the same individual.

Vegetative reproduction. Any replication of a plant not directly resulting from seed or spore germination, as in fragmentation, cloning, or sprouting from stumps, rhizomes, or turions.

Witches' broom. An abnormal growth of numerous weak shoots toward the branch tip of a tree or shrub, symptomatic of parasitism, fungous or viral infection, mite infestation, or combinations of these.

Zooplankton. Swimming or free-floating protozoa or other microscopic animals in water.